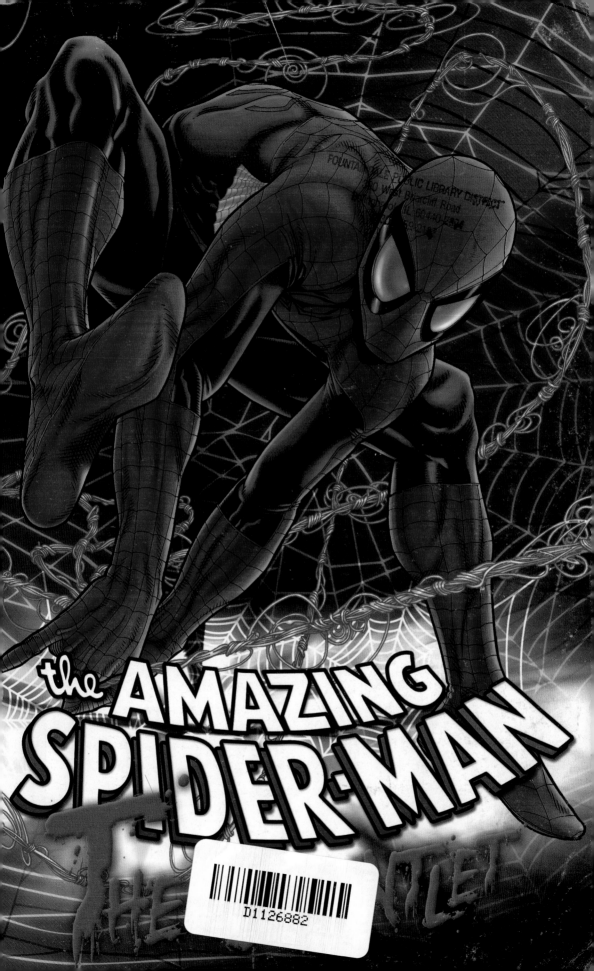

the AMAZING SPIDER-MAN

the AMAZING SPIDER-MAN
THE GAUNTLET
LIZARD

GAUNTLET ORIGINS: LIZARD
Writer: **FRED VAN LENTE**
Artist: **JEFTE PALO**
Colorist: **JAVIER RODRIGUEZ**
Letterer: **VC'S JOE CARAMAGNA**

SHED: PRELUDE
Writer: **ROGER STERN**
Artist: **XURXO PENALTA**
Colorist: **MATT HOLLINGSWORTH**
Letterer: **JARED K. FLETCHER**

SHED PROLOGUE
Writer: **ZEB WELLS**
Artist: **CHRIS BACHALO**
Letterer: **VC'S JOE CARAMAGNA**

ISSUES #630-633
Writer: **ZEB WELLS**
Pencilers: **CHRIS BACHALO & EMMA RIOS**
Inkers: **TIM TOWNSEND, JAIME MENDOZA, VICTOR OLAZABA, MARK IRWIN, CHRIS BACHALO & EMMA RIOS**
Colorist: **ANTONIO FABELA**
Letterer: **VC'S JOE CARAMAGNA**

Web-Heads: **BOB GALE, JOE KELLY, DAN SLOTT, FRED VAN LENTE, MARK WAID** & **ZEB WELLS**
Assistant Editor: **THOMAS BRENNAN** • Editor: **STEPHEN WACKER** • Executive Editor: **TOM BREVOORT**

Collection Editor: **JENNIFER GRÜNWALD** • Editorial Assistants: **JAMES EMMETT** & **JOE HOCHSTEIN**
Assistant Editors: **ALEX STARBUCK** & **NELSON RIBEIRO** • Editor, Special Projects: **MARK D. BEAZLEY**
Senior Editor, Special Projects: **JEFF YOUNGQUIST** • Senior Vice President of Sales: **DAVID GABRIEL**

Editor in Chief: **JOE QUESADA** • Publisher: **DAN BUCKLEY** • Executive Producer: **ALAN FINE**

SPIDER-MAN: THE GAUNTLET VOL. 5 — LIZARD. Contains material originally published in magazine form as WEB OF SPIDER-MAN #6 and AMAZING SPIDER-MAN #629-633. First printing 2010. Hardcover ISBN# 978-0-7851-4615-5. Softcover ISBN# 978-0-7851-4616-2. Published by MARVEL WORLDWIDE, INC., a subsidiary of MARVEL ENTERTAINMENT, LLC. OFFICE OF PUBLICATION: 417 5th Avenue, New York, NY 10016. Copyright © 2010 and 2011 Marvel Characters, Inc. All rights reserved. Hardcover: $19.99 per copy in the U.S. and $22.50 in Canada (GST #R127032852). Softcover: $14.99 per copy in the U.S. and $16.99 in Canada (GST #R127032852). Canadian Agreement #40668537. All characters featured in this issue and the distinctive names and likenesses thereof, and all related indicia are trademarks of Marvel Characters, Inc. No similarity between any of the names, characters, persons, and/or institutions in this magazine with those of any living or dead person or institution is intended, and any such similarity which may exist is purely coincidental. **Printed in the U.S.A.** ALAN FINE, EVP - Office of the President, Marvel Worldwide, Inc. and EVP & CMO Marvel Characters B.V.; DAN BUCKLEY, Chief Executive Officer and Publisher - Print, Animation & Digital Media; JIM SOKOLOWSKI, Chief Operating Officer; DAVID GABRIEL, SVP of Publishing Sales & Circulation; DAVID BOGART, SVP of Business Affairs & Talent Management; MICHAEL PASCIULLO, VP Merchandising & Communications; JIM O'KEEFE, VP of Operations & Logistics; DAN CARR, Executive Director of Publishing Technology; JUSTIN F. GABRIE, Director of Publishing & Editorial Operations; SUSAN CRESPI, Editorial Operations Manager; ALEX MORALES, Publishing Operations Manager; STAN LEE, Chairman Emeritus. For information regarding advertising in Marvel Comics or on Marvel.com, please contact Ron Stern, VP of Business Development, at rstern@marvel.com. For Marvel subscription inquiries, please call 800-217-9158. **Manufactured between 8/2/10 and 9/1/10 (hardcover), and 8/2/10 and 1/26/11 (softcover), by R.R. DONNELLEY, INC., SALEM, VA, USA.**

10 9 8 7 6 5 4 3 2 1

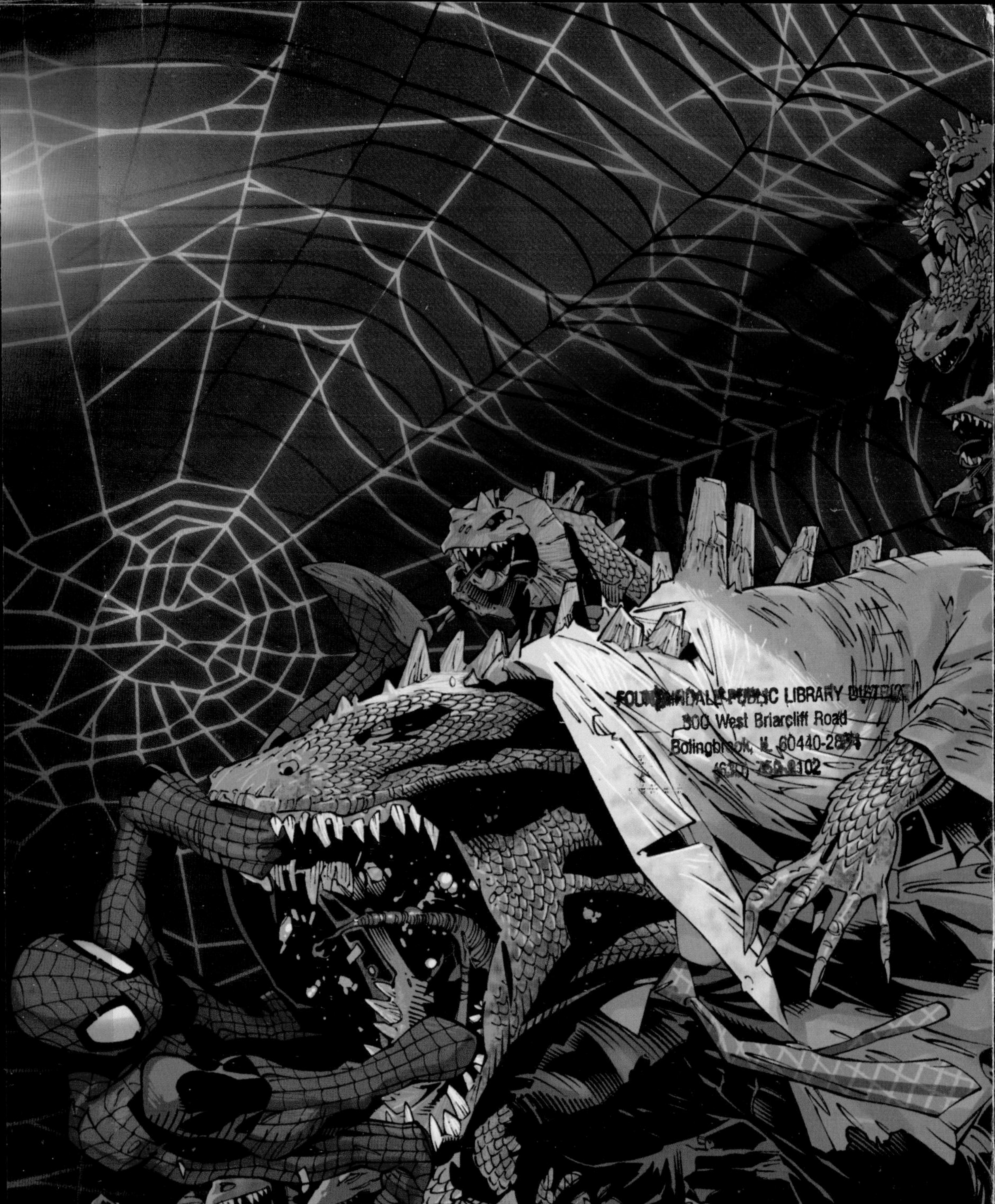

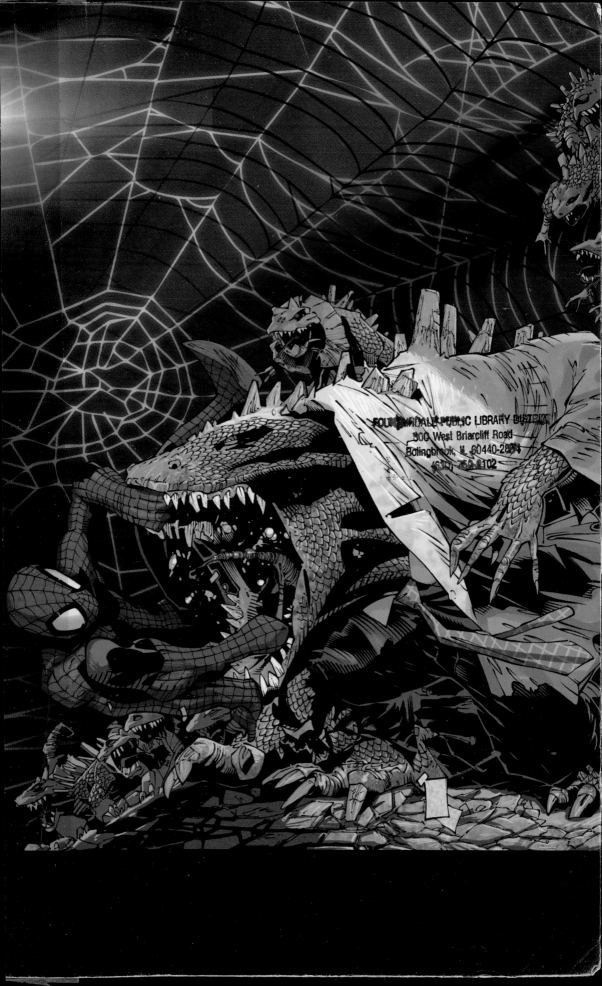

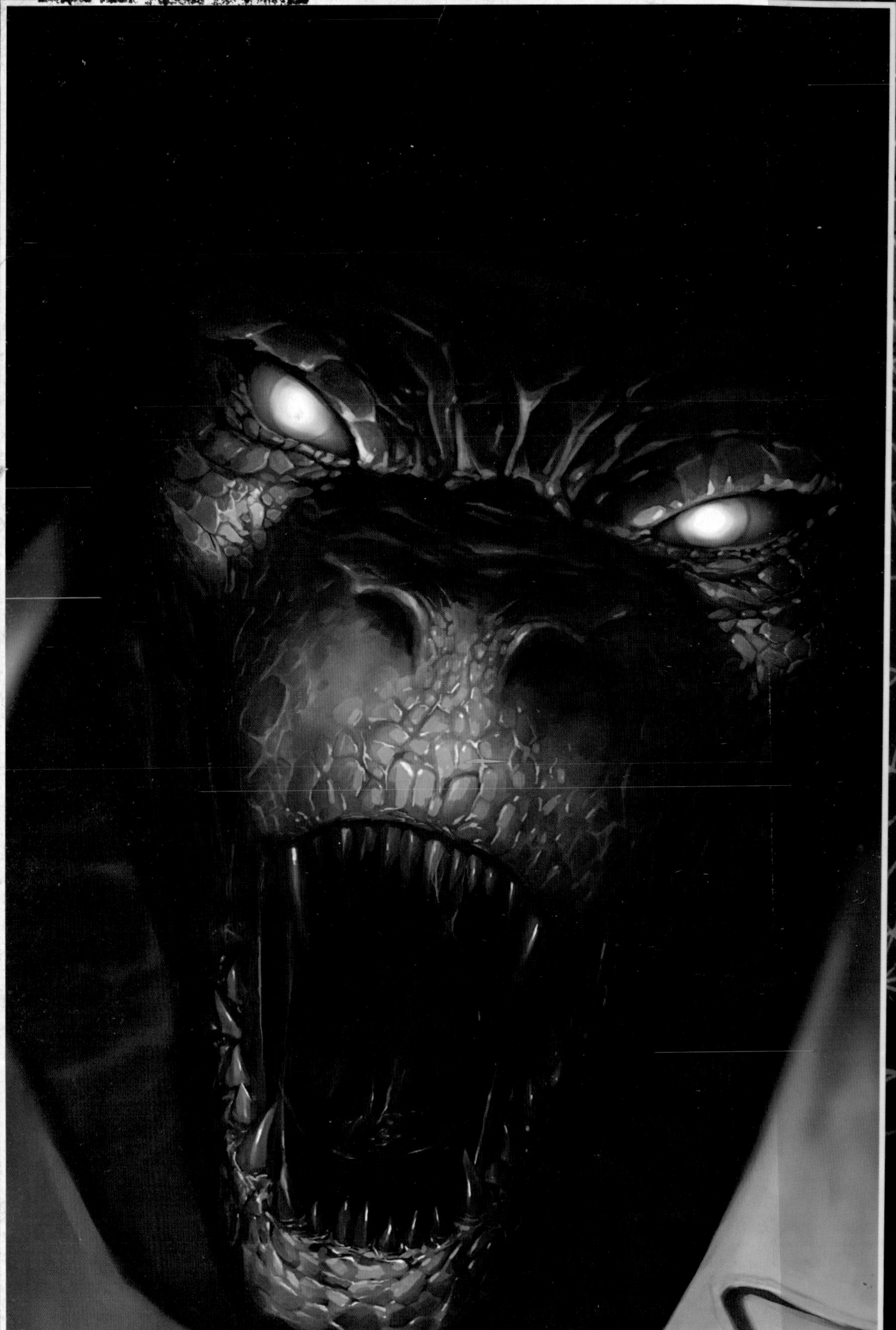

WEB OF SPIDER-MAN #6 – "GAUNTLET ORIGINS: LIZARD" & "SHED PRELUDE" COVER BY JELENA KEVIC DJURDJEVIC

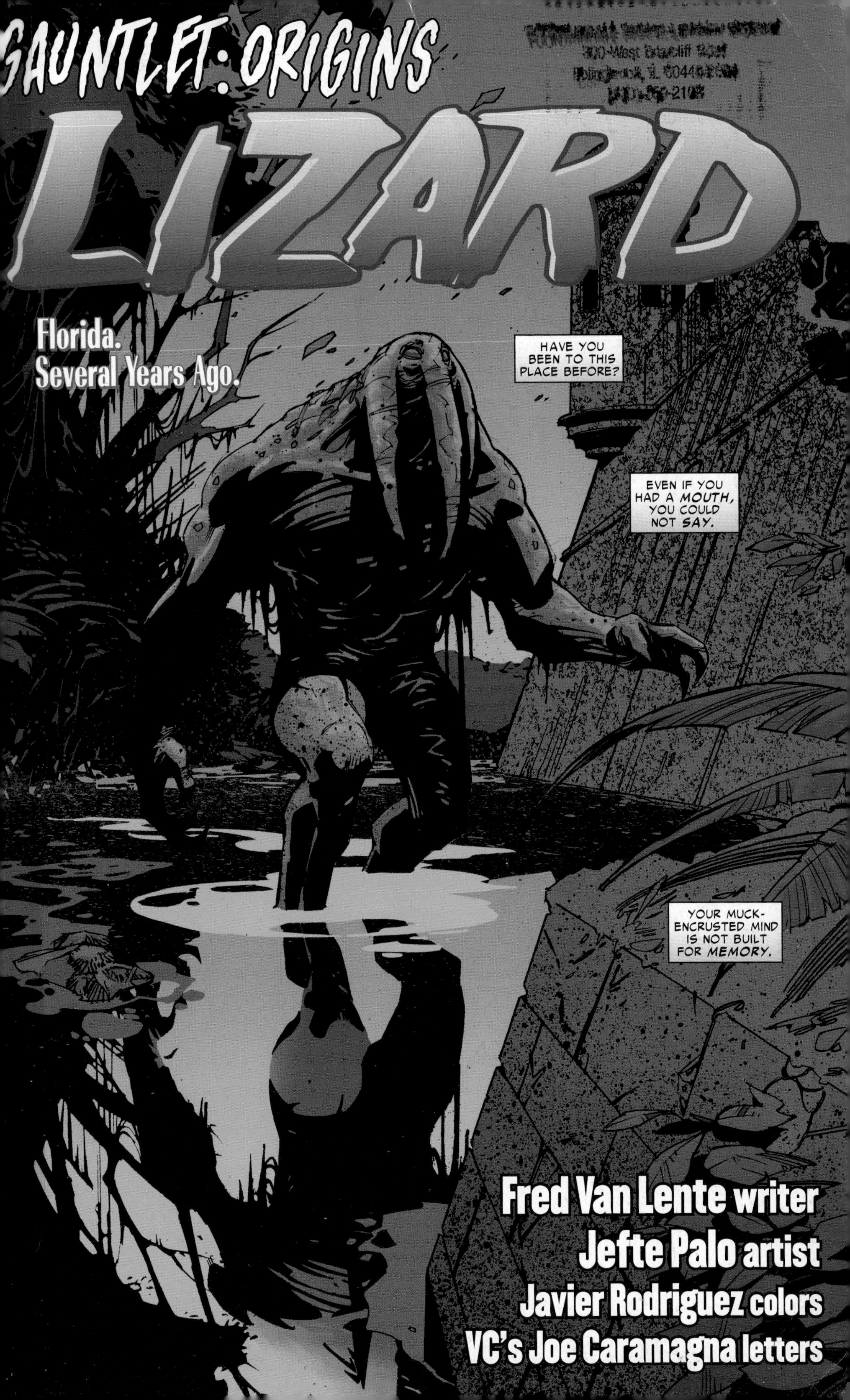
GAUNTLET: ORIGINS
LIZARD
Florida. Several Years Ago.
HAVE YOU BEEN TO THIS PLACE BEFORE?
EVEN IF YOU HAD A MOUTH, YOU COULD NOT SAY.
YOUR MUCK-ENCRUSTED MIND IS NOT BUILT FOR MEMORY.
Fred Van Lente writer
Jefte Palo artist
Javier Rodriguez colors
VC's Joe Caramagna letters

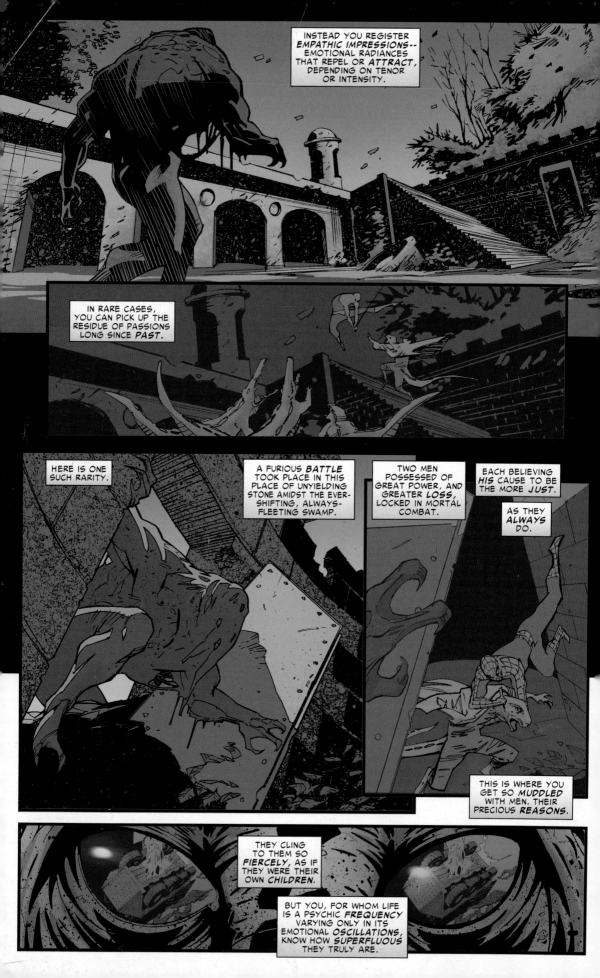

INSTEAD YOU REGISTER *EMPATHIC IMPRESSIONS*-- EMOTIONAL *RADIANCES* THAT REPEL OR *ATTRACT*, DEPENDING ON TENOR OR INTENSITY.

IN RARE CASES, YOU CAN PICK UP THE RESIDUE OF PASSIONS LONG SINCE *PAST*.

HERE IS ONE SUCH RARITY.

A FURIOUS *BATTLE* TOOK PLACE IN THIS PLACE OF UNYIELDING STONE AMIDST THE EVER-SHIFTING, ALWAYS-FLEETING SWAMP.

TWO MEN POSSESSED OF GREAT POWER, AND GREATER *LOSS*, LOCKED IN MORTAL COMBAT.

EACH BELIEVING *HIS* CAUSE TO BE THE MORE *JUST*.

AS THEY *ALWAYS* DO.

THIS IS WHERE YOU GET SO *MUDDLED* WITH MEN. THEIR PRECIOUS *REASONS*.

THEY CLING TO THEM SO *FIERCELY*, AS IF THEY WERE THEIR OWN *CHILDREN*.

BUT YOU, FOR WHOM LIFE IS A PSYCHIC *FREQUENCY* VARYING ONLY IN ITS EMOTIONAL *OSCILLATIONS*, KNOW HOW *SUPERFLUOUS* THEY TRULY ARE.

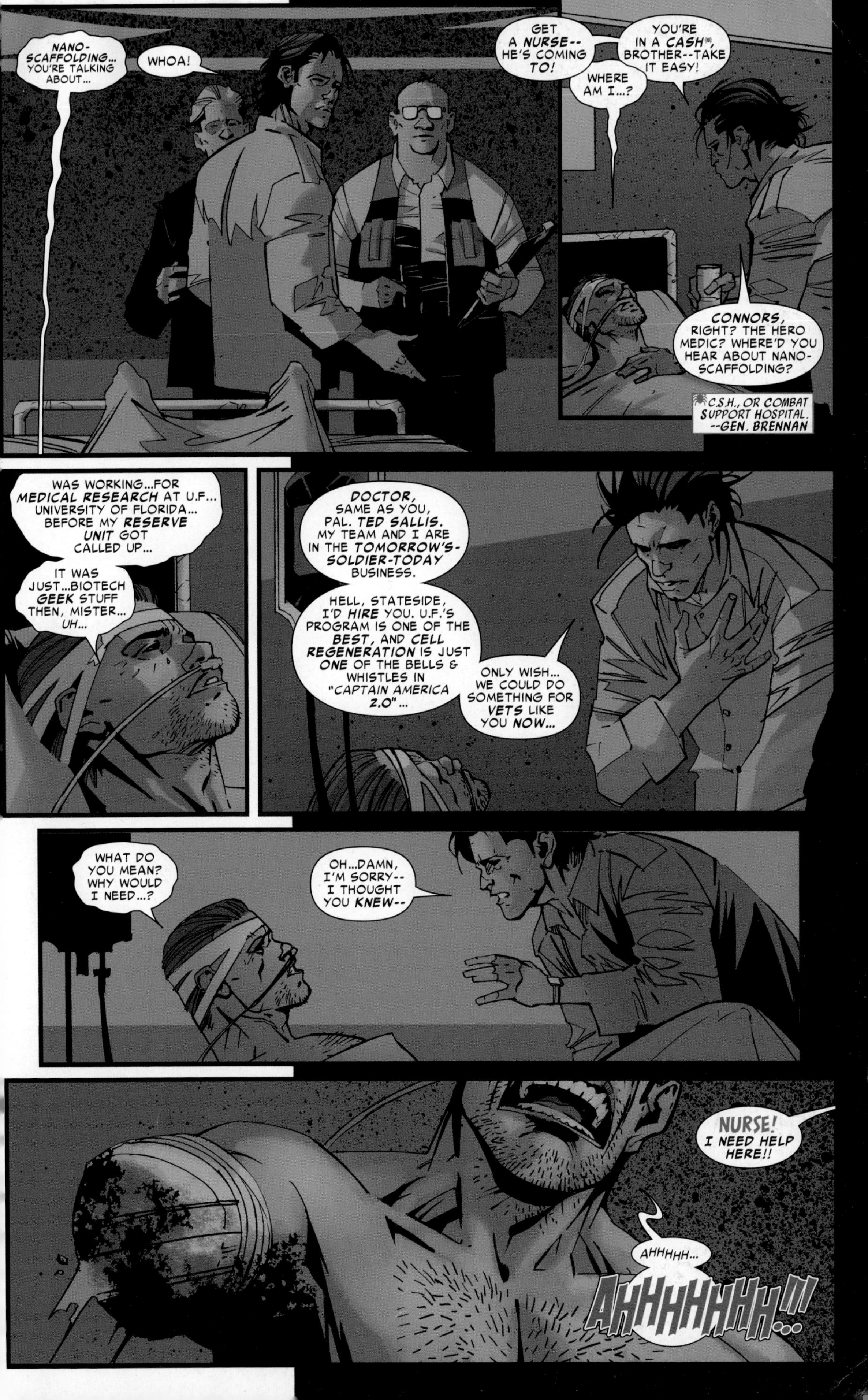

NANO-SCAFFOLDING... YOU'RE TALKING ABOUT...
WHOA!
GET A NURSE-- HE'S COMING TO!
YOU'RE IN A CASH*, BROTHER--TAKE IT EASY!
WHERE AM I...?
CONNORS, RIGHT? THE HERO MEDIC? WHERE'D YOU HEAR ABOUT NANO-SCAFFOLDING?
*C.S.H., OR COMBAT SUPPORT HOSPITAL. --GEN. BRENNAN
WAS WORKING...FOR MEDICAL RESEARCH AT U.F... UNIVERSITY OF FLORIDA... BEFORE MY RESERVE UNIT GOT CALLED UP...
IT WAS JUST...BIOTECH GEEK STUFF THEN, MISTER... UH...
DOCTOR, SAME AS YOU, PAL. TED SALLIS. MY TEAM AND I ARE IN THE TOMORROW'S-SOLDIER-TODAY BUSINESS.
HELL, STATESIDE, I'D HIRE YOU. U.F.'S PROGRAM IS ONE OF THE BEST, AND CELL REGENERATION IS JUST ONE OF THE BELLS & WHISTLES IN "CAPTAIN AMERICA 2.0"...
ONLY WISH... WE COULD DO SOMETHING FOR VETS LIKE YOU NOW...
WHAT DO YOU MEAN? WHY WOULD I NEED...?
OH...DAMN, I'M SORRY-- I THOUGHT YOU KNEW--
NURSE! I NEED HELP HERE!!
AHHHHH...
AHHHHHHH!!!..

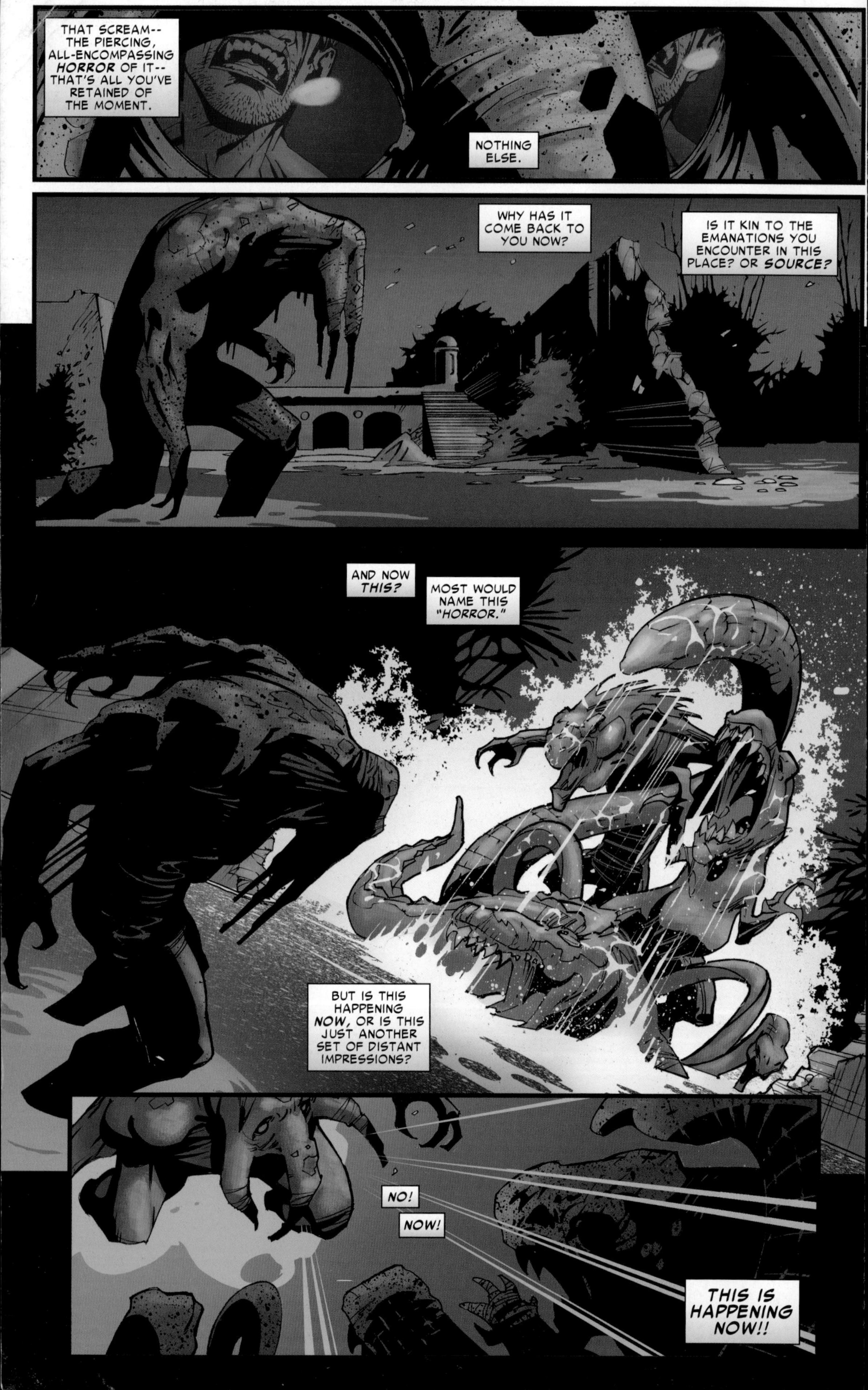

THAT SCREAM-- THE PIERCING, ALL-ENCOMPASSING *HORROR* OF IT-- THAT'S ALL YOU'VE RETAINED OF THE MOMENT.
NOTHING ELSE.
WHY HAS IT COME BACK TO YOU NOW?
IS IT KIN TO THE EMANATIONS YOU ENCOUNTER IN THIS PLACE? OR *SOURCE?*
AND NOW *THIS?*
MOST WOULD NAME THIS *"HORROR."*
BUT IS THIS HAPPENING *NOW*, OR IS THIS JUST ANOTHER SET OF DISTANT IMPRESSIONS?
NO!
NOW!
THIS IS HAPPENING NOW!!

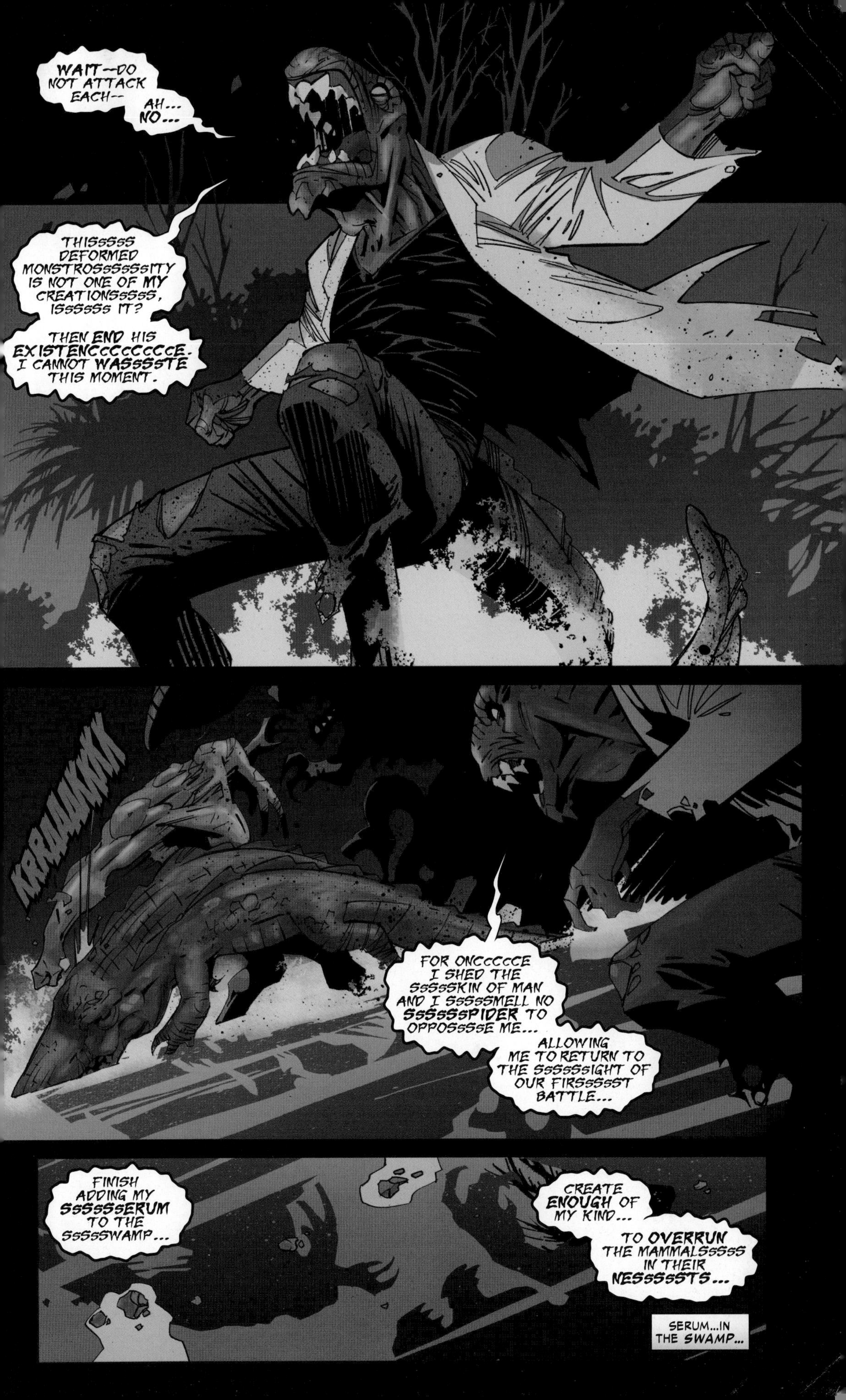

WAIT--DO NOT ATTACK EACH--
AH... NO...
THISSSSS DEFORMED MONSTROSSSSSSITY IS NOT ONE OF MY CREATIONSSSSS, ISSSSSS IT?
THEN END HIS EXISTENCCCCCCCCE. I CANNOT WASSSSTE THIS MOMENT.
KRRAAAKKK
FOR ONCCCCCE I SHED THE SSSSSKIN OF MAN AND I SSSSSMELL NO SSSSSSPIDER TO OPPOSSSSE ME...
ALLOWING ME TO RETURN TO THE SSSSSSIGHT OF OUR FIRSSSSST BATTLE...
FINISH ADDING MY SSSSSSERUM TO THE SSSSSWAMP...
CREATE ENOUGH OF MY KIND...
TO OVERRUN THE MAMMALSSSSS IN THEIR NESSSSSTS...
SERUM...IN THE SWAMP...

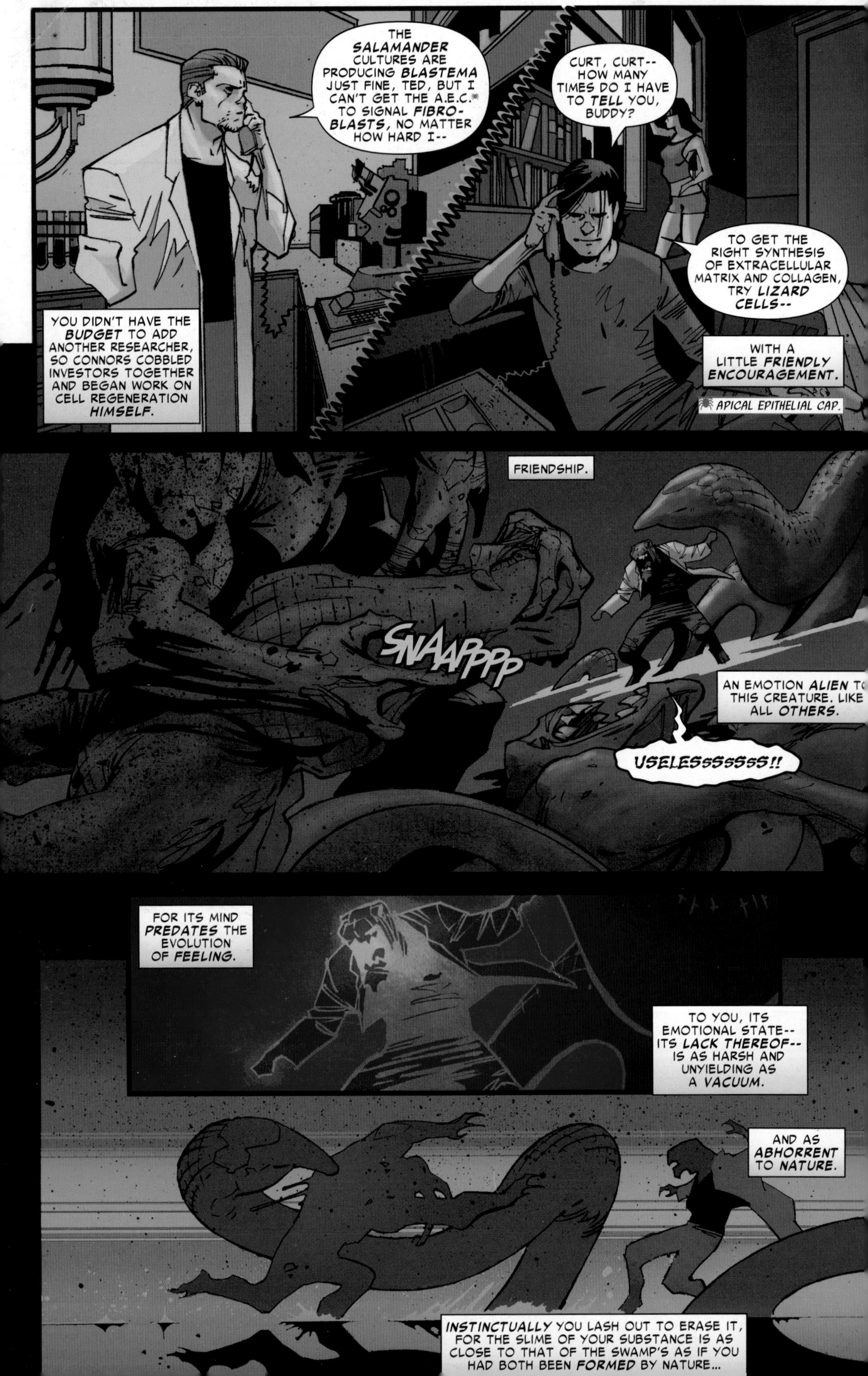
THE SALAMANDER CULTURES ARE PRODUCING BLASTEMA JUST FINE, TED, BUT I CAN'T GET THE A.E.C.* TO SIGNAL FIBRO-BLASTS, NO MATTER HOW HARD I--
CURT, CURT-- HOW MANY TIMES DO I HAVE TO TELL YOU, BUDDY?
TO GET THE RIGHT SYNTHESIS OF EXTRACELLULAR MATRIX AND COLLAGEN, TRY LIZARD CELLS--
YOU DIDN'T HAVE THE BUDGET TO ADD ANOTHER RESEARCHER, SO CONNORS COBBLED INVESTORS TOGETHER AND BEGAN WORK ON CELL REGENERATION HIMSELF.
WITH A LITTLE FRIENDLY ENCOURAGEMENT.
*APICAL EPITHELIAL CAP.
FRIENDSHIP.
SNAAPPPP
AN EMOTION ALIEN TO THIS CREATURE. LIKE ALL OTHERS.
USELESSSSSSS!!
FOR ITS MIND PREDATES THE EVOLUTION OF FEELING.
TO YOU, ITS EMOTIONAL STATE-- ITS LACK THEREOF-- IS AS HARSH AND UNYIELDING AS A VACUUM.
AND AS ABHORRENT TO NATURE.
INSTINCTUALLY YOU LASH OUT TO ERASE IT, FOR THE SLIME OF YOUR SUBSTANCE IS AS CLOSE TO THAT OF THE SWAMP'S AS IF YOU HAD BOTH BEEN FORMED BY NATURE...

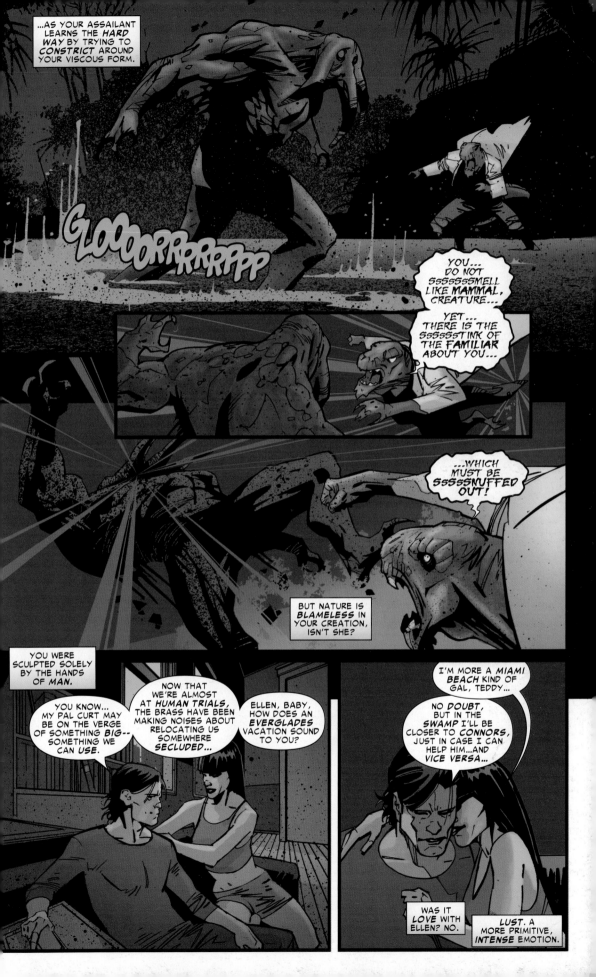

...AS YOUR ASSAILANT LEARNS THE *HARD WAY* BY TRYING TO *CONSTRICT* AROUND YOUR VISCOUS FORM.

GLOOORRRRRPPP

YOU... DO NOT SSSSSSSMELL LIKE *MAMMAL*, CREATURE...

YET... THERE IS THE SSSSSSTINK OF THE *FAMILIAR* ABOUT YOU...

...WHICH MUST BE SSSSSNUFFED OUT!

BUT NATURE IS *BLAMELESS* IN YOUR CREATION, ISN'T SHE?

YOU WERE SCULPTED SOLELY BY THE HANDS OF *MAN*.

YOU KNOW... MY PAL *CURT* MAY BE ON THE VERGE OF SOMETHING *BIG*-- SOMETHING WE CAN *USE*.

NOW THAT WE'RE ALMOST AT *HUMAN TRIALS*, THE BRASS HAVE BEEN MAKING NOISES ABOUT RELOCATING US SOMEWHERE *SECLUDED*...

ELLEN, BABY, HOW DOES AN *EVERGLADES* VACATION SOUND TO YOU?

I'M MORE A *MIAMI BEACH* KIND OF GAL, TEDDY...

NO DOUBT, BUT IN THE *SWAMP* I'LL BE CLOSER TO *CONNORS*, JUST IN CASE I CAN HELP HIM...AND *VICE VERSA*...

WAS IT *LOVE* WITH ELLEN? NO.

LUST. A MORE PRIMITIVE, *INTENSE* EMOTION.

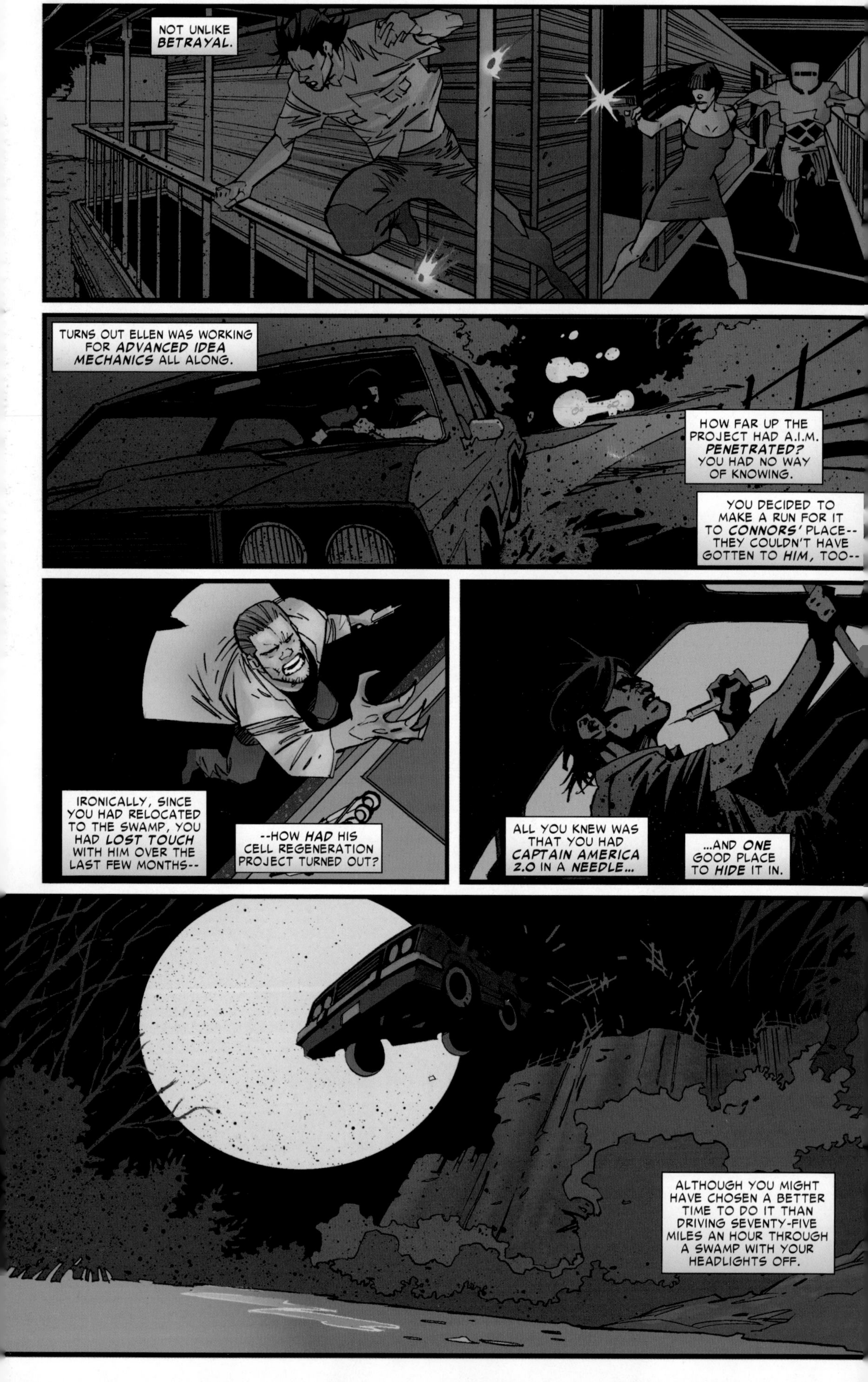

NOT UNLIKE BETRAYAL.
TURNS OUT ELLEN WAS WORKING FOR ADVANCED IDEA MECHANICS ALL ALONG.
HOW FAR UP THE PROJECT HAD A.I.M. PENETRATED? YOU HAD NO WAY OF KNOWING.
YOU DECIDED TO MAKE A RUN FOR IT TO CONNORS' PLACE--THEY COULDN'T HAVE GOTTEN TO HIM, TOO--
IRONICALLY, SINCE YOU HAD RELOCATED TO THE SWAMP, YOU HAD LOST TOUCH WITH HIM OVER THE LAST FEW MONTHS--
--HOW HAD HIS CELL REGENERATION PROJECT TURNED OUT?
ALL YOU KNEW WAS THAT YOU HAD CAPTAIN AMERICA 2.0 IN A NEEDLE...
...AND ONE GOOD PLACE TO HIDE IT IN.
ALTHOUGH YOU MIGHT HAVE CHOSEN A BETTER TIME TO DO IT THAN DRIVING SEVENTY-FIVE MILES AN HOUR THROUGH A SWAMP WITH YOUR HEADLIGHTS OFF.

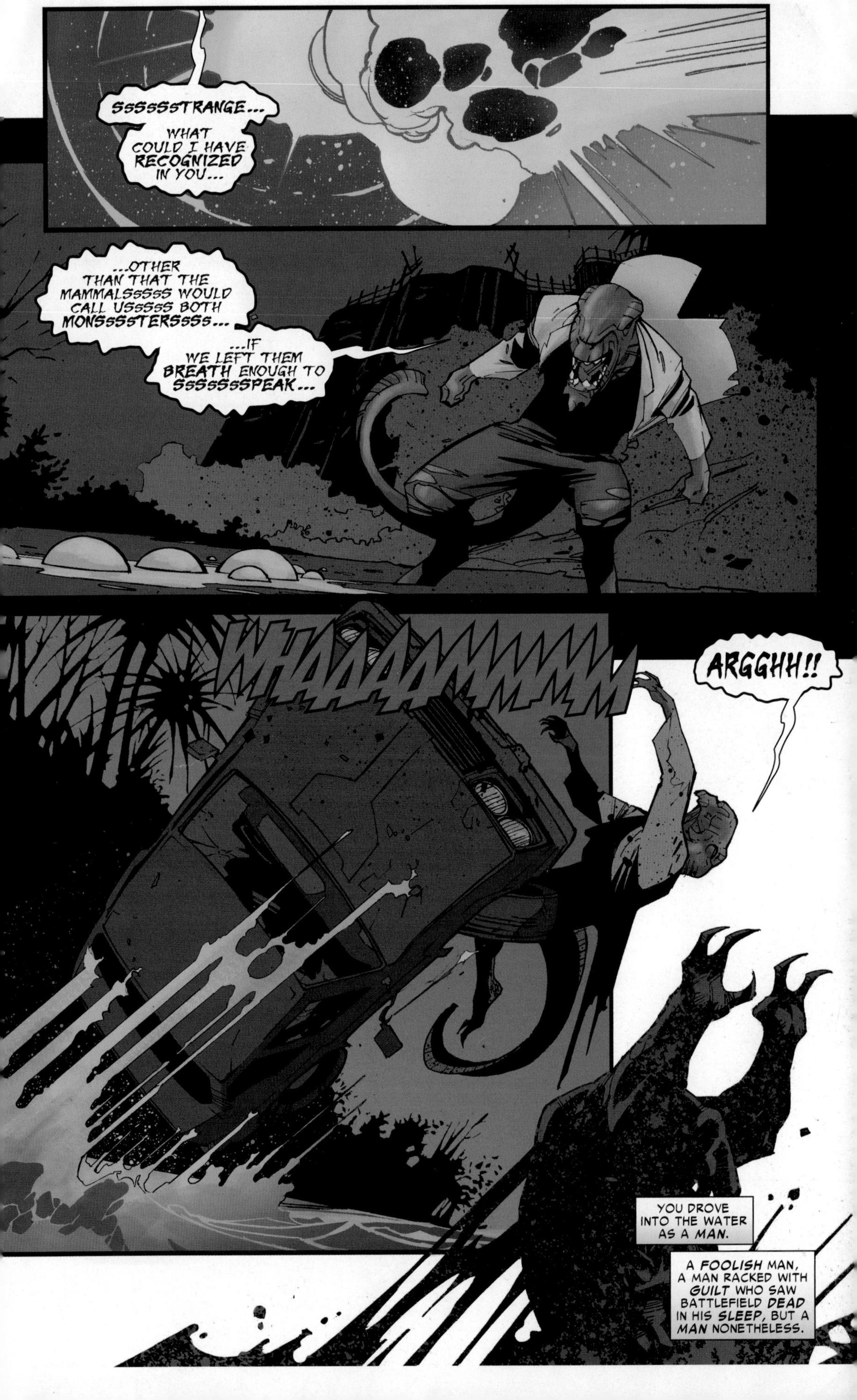
SSSSSSTRANGE... WHAT COULD I HAVE RECOGNIZED IN YOU...
...OTHER THAN THAT THE MAMMALSSSSS WOULD CALL USSSSS BOTH MONSSSSTERSSSS...
...IF WE LEFT THEM BREATH ENOUGH TO SSSSSSSPEAK...
WHAAAAMMMMM
ARGGHH!!
YOU DROVE INTO THE WATER AS A MAN.
A FOOLISH MAN, A MAN RACKED WITH GUILT WHO SAW BATTLEFIELD DEAD IN HIS SLEEP, BUT A MAN NONETHELESS.

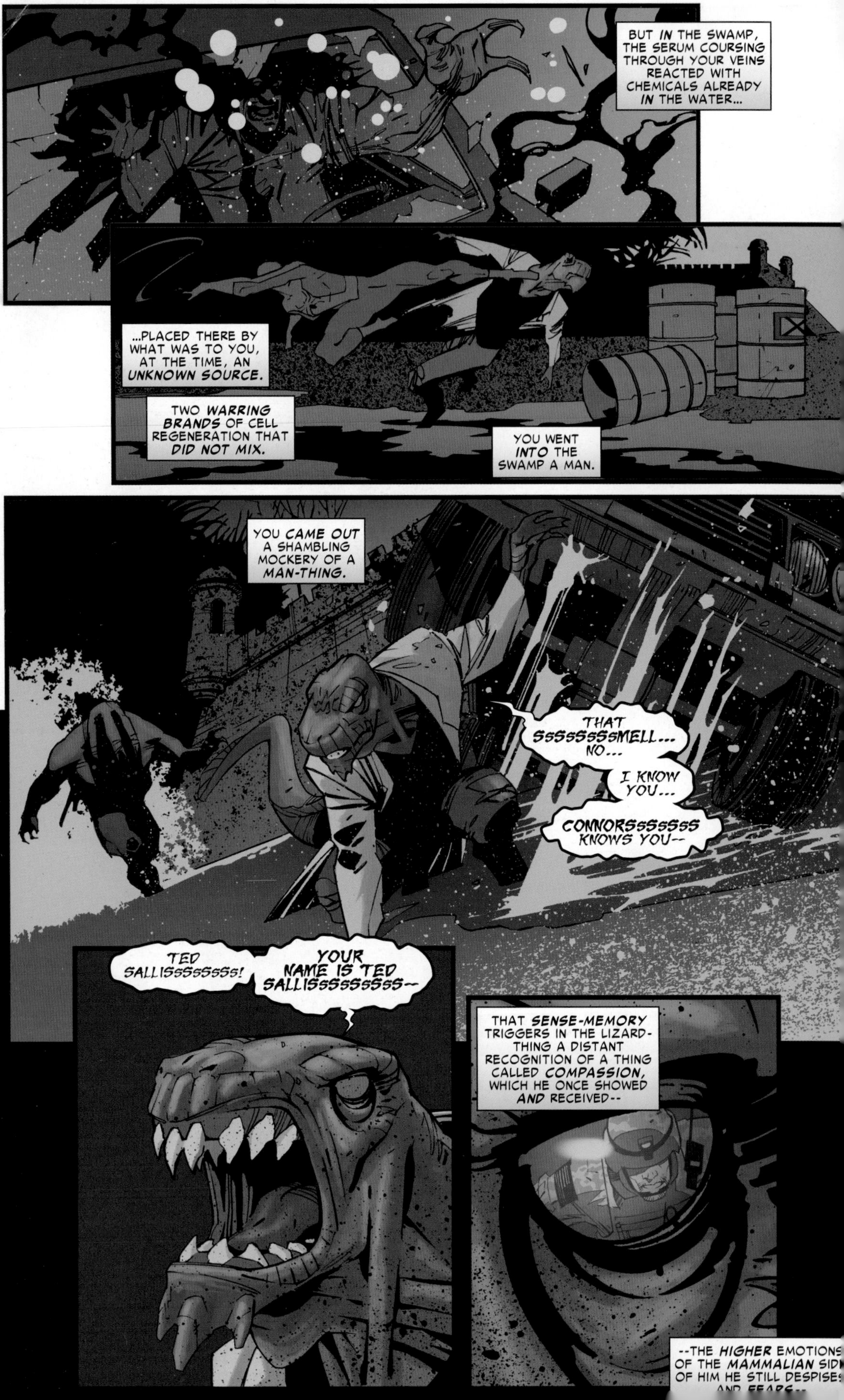
BUT *IN* THE SWAMP, THE SERUM COURSING THROUGH YOUR VEINS REACTED WITH CHEMICALS ALREADY *IN* THE WATER...
...PLACED THERE BY WHAT WAS TO YOU, AT THE TIME, AN *UNKNOWN SOURCE.*
TWO *WARRING BRANDS* OF CELL REGENERATION THAT *DID NOT MIX.*
YOU WENT *INTO* THE SWAMP A MAN.
YOU *CAME OUT* A SHAMBLING MOCKERY OF A *MAN-THING.*
THAT SSSSSSSSMELL... NO...
I KNOW YOU...
CONNORSSSSSSS KNOWS YOU--
TED SALLISSSSSSSS!
YOUR NAME IS TED SALLISSSSSSSSS--
THAT *SENSE-MEMORY* TRIGGERS IN THE LIZARD-THING A DISTANT RECOGNITION OF A THING CALLED *COMPASSION,* WHICH HE ONCE SHOWED *AND* RECEIVED--
--THE *HIGHER* EMOTIONS OF THE *MAMMALIAN* SID OF HIM HE STILL DESPISES AND *FEARS*--

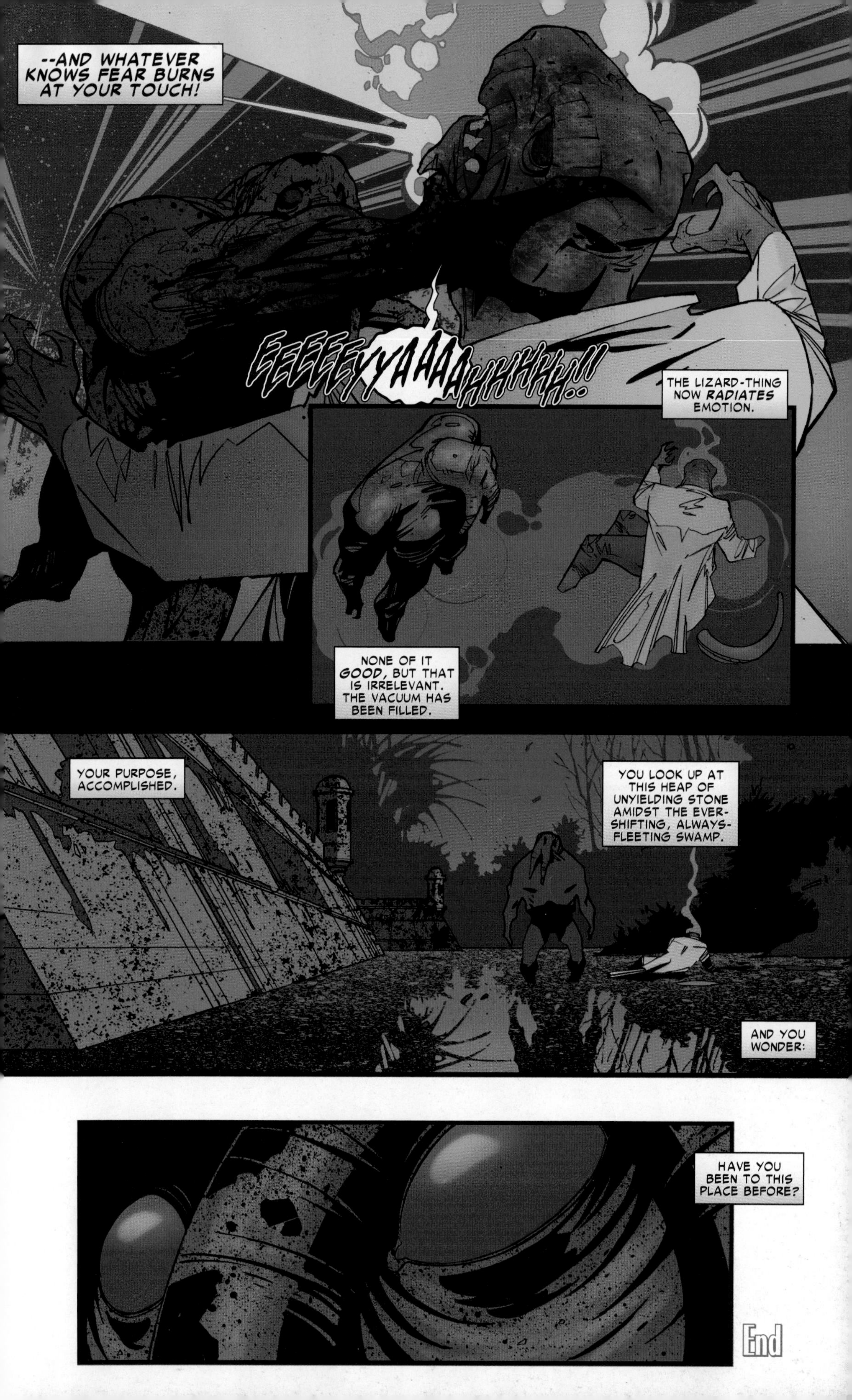
--AND WHATEVER KNOWS FEAR BURNS AT YOUR TOUCH!
EEEEEEYYAAAAAHHHHHH!!
THE LIZARD-THING NOW RADIATES EMOTION.
NONE OF IT GOOD, BUT THAT IS IRRELEVANT. THE VACUUM HAS BEEN FILLED.
YOUR PURPOSE, ACCOMPLISHED.
YOU LOOK UP AT THIS HEAP OF UNYIELDING STONE AMIDST THE EVER-SHIFTING, ALWAYS-FLEETING SWAMP.
AND YOU WONDER:
HAVE YOU BEEN TO THIS PLACE BEFORE?
End

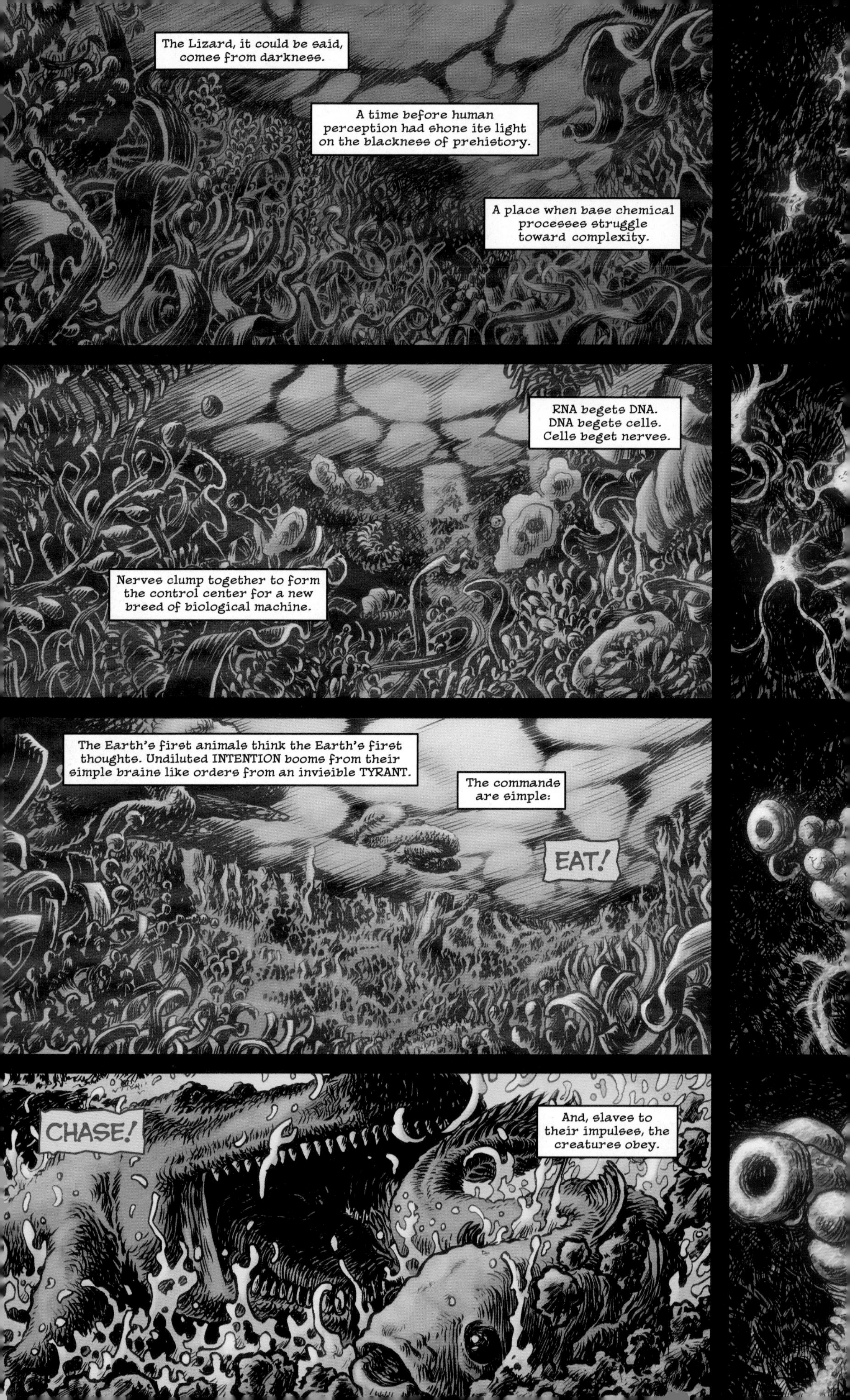
The Lizard, it could be said, comes from darkness.
A time before human perception had shone its light on the blackness of prehistory.
A place when base chemical processes struggle toward complexity.
RNA begets DNA. DNA begets cells. Cells beget nerves.
Nerves clump together to form the control center for a new breed of biological machine.
The Earth's first animals think the Earth's first thoughts. Undiluted INTENTION booms from their simple brains like orders from an invisible TYRANT.
The commands are simple:
EAT!
CHASE!
And, slaves to their impulses, the creatures obey.

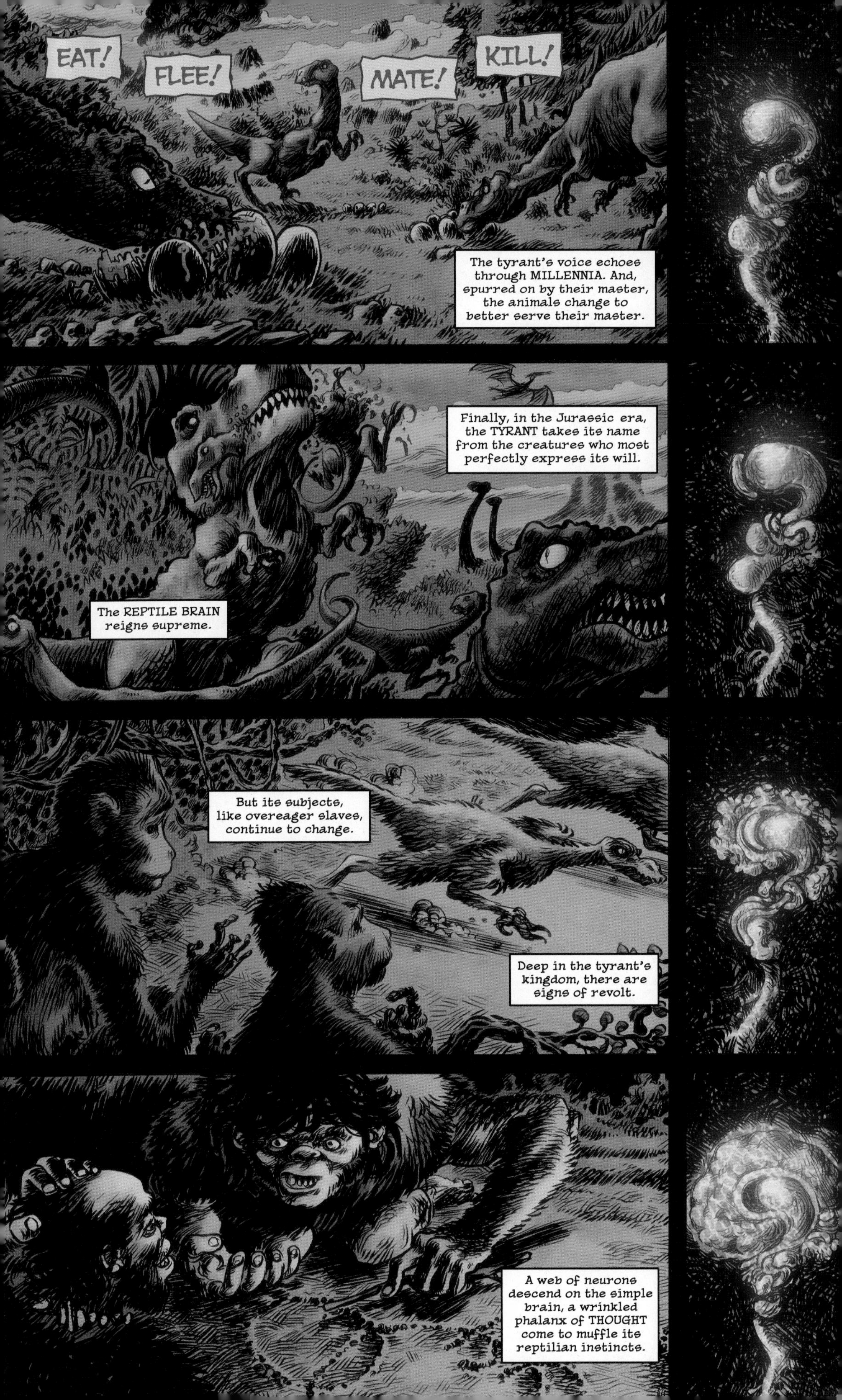

EAT!
FLEE!
MATE!
KILL!
The tyrant's voice echoes through MILLENNIA. And, spurred on by their master, the animals change to better serve their master.
Finally, in the Jurassic era, the TYRANT takes its name from the creatures who most perfectly express its will.
The REPTILE BRAIN reigns supreme.
But its subjects, like overeager slaves, continue to change.
Deep in the tyrant's kingdom, there are signs of revolt.
A web of neurons descend on the simple brain, a wrinkled phalanx of THOUGHT come to muffle its reptilian instincts.

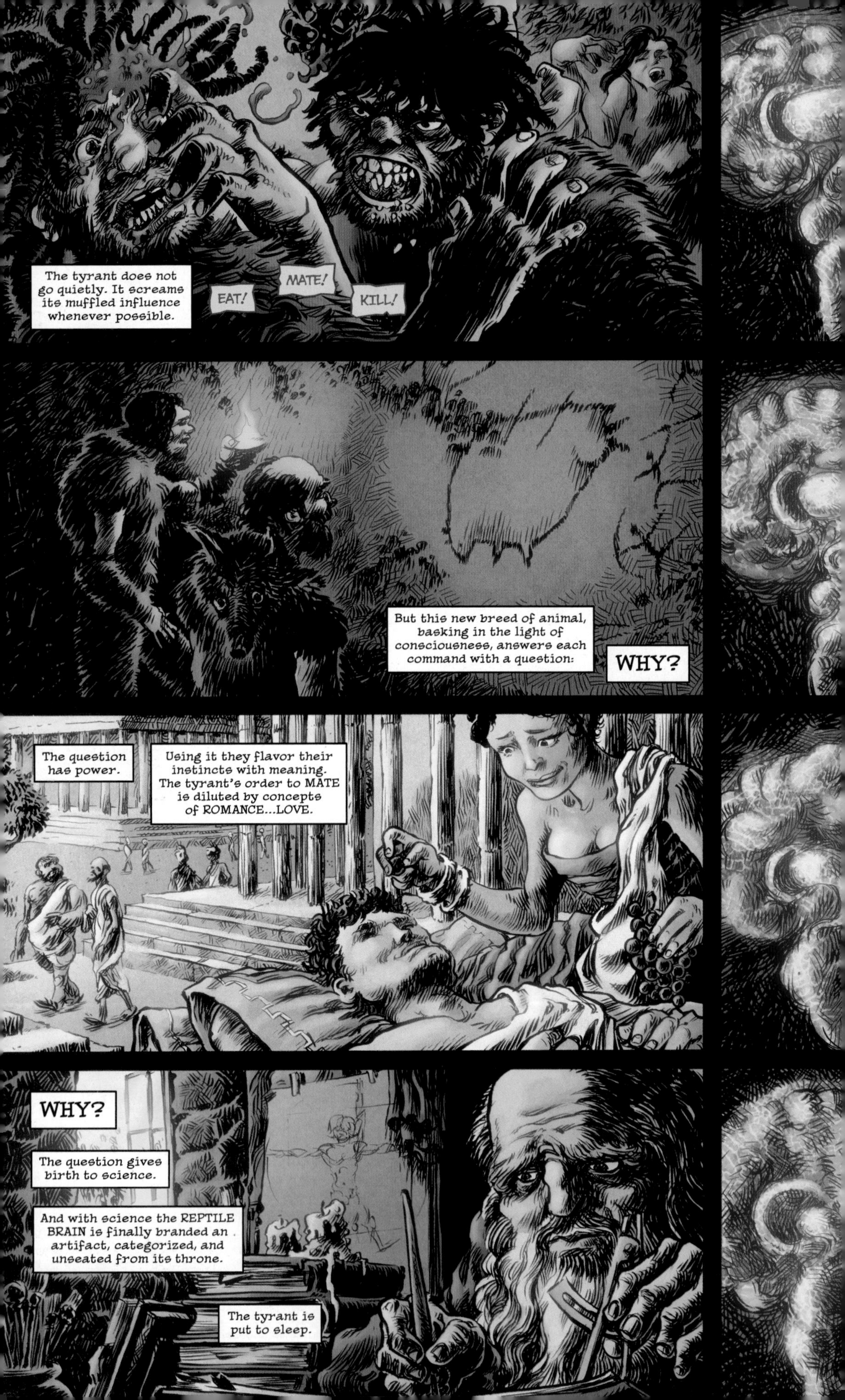
The tyrant does not go quietly. It screams its muffled influence whenever possible.
EAT!
MATE!
KILL!
But this new breed of animal, basking in the light of consciousness, answers each command with a question:
WHY?
The question has power.
Using it they flavor their instincts with meaning. The tyrant's order to MATE is diluted by concepts of ROMANCE...LOVE.
WHY?
The question gives birth to science.
And with science the REPTILE BRAIN is finally branded an artifact, categorized, and unseated from its throne.
The tyrant is put to sleep.

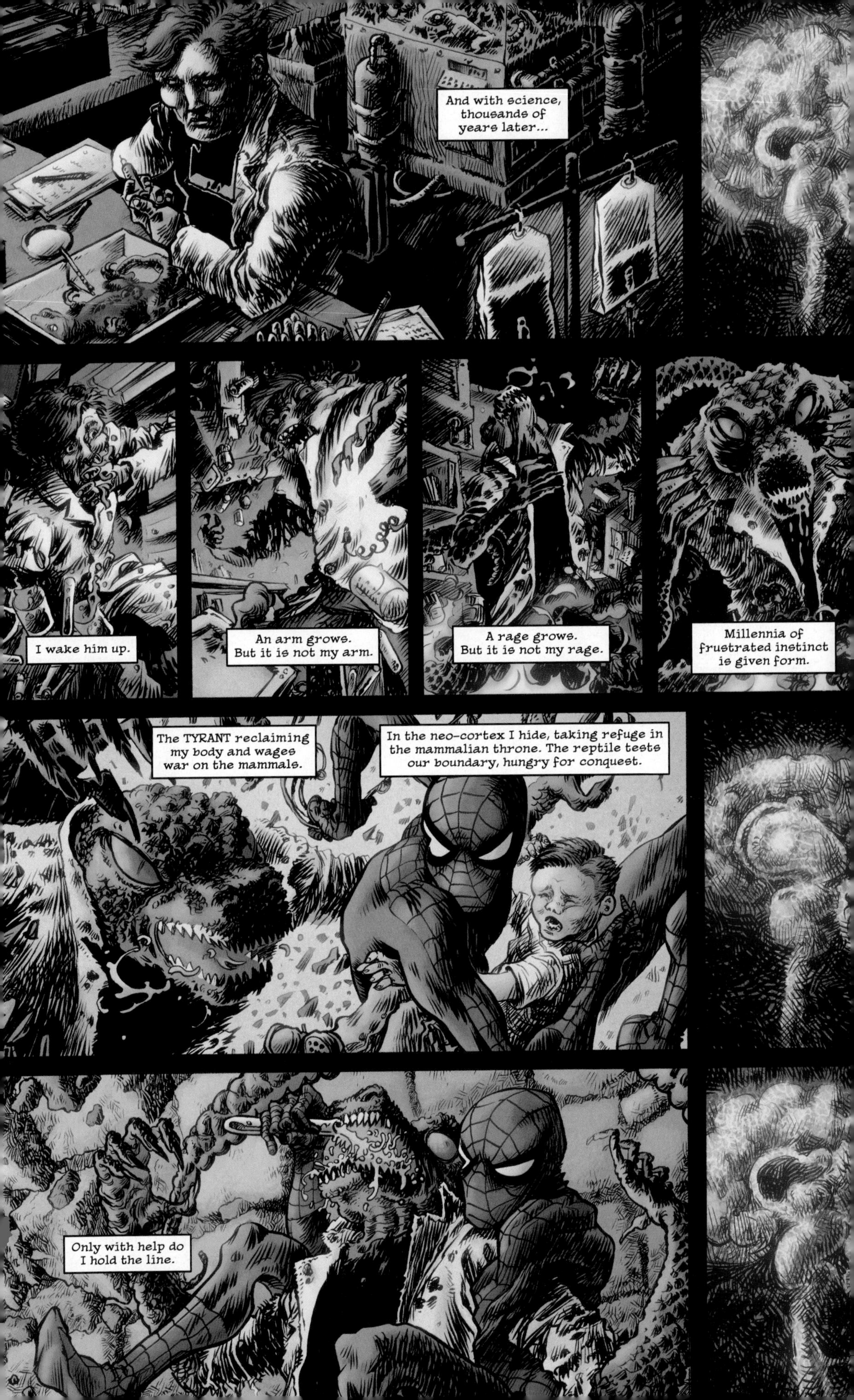

And with science, thousands of years later...
I wake him up.
An arm grows. But it is not my arm.
A rage grows. But it is not my rage.
Millennia of frustrated instinct is given form.
The TYRANT reclaiming my body and wages war on the mammals.
In the neo-cortex I hide, taking refuge in the mammalian throne. The reptile tests our boundary, hungry for conquest.
Only with help do I hold the line.

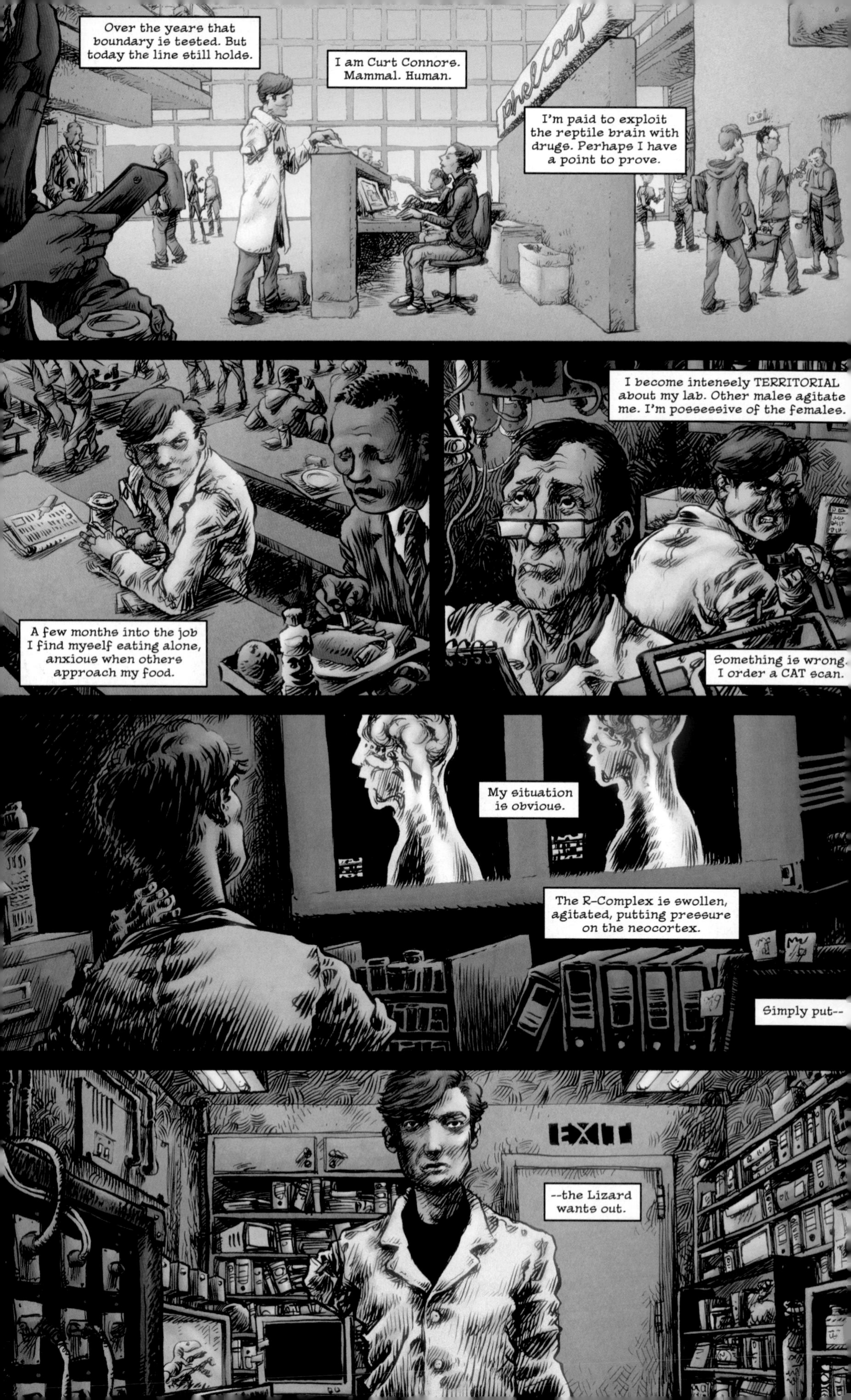
Over the years that boundary is tested. But today the line still holds.
I am Curt Connors. Mammal. Human.
phelcorp
I'm paid to exploit the reptile brain with drugs. Perhaps I have a point to prove.
A few months into the job I find myself eating alone, anxious when others approach my food.
I become intensely TERRITORIAL about my lab. Other males agitate me. I'm possessive of the females.
Something is wrong. I order a CAT scan.
My situation is obvious.
The R-Complex is swollen, agitated, putting pressure on the neocortex.
Simply put--
EXIT
--the Lizard wants out.

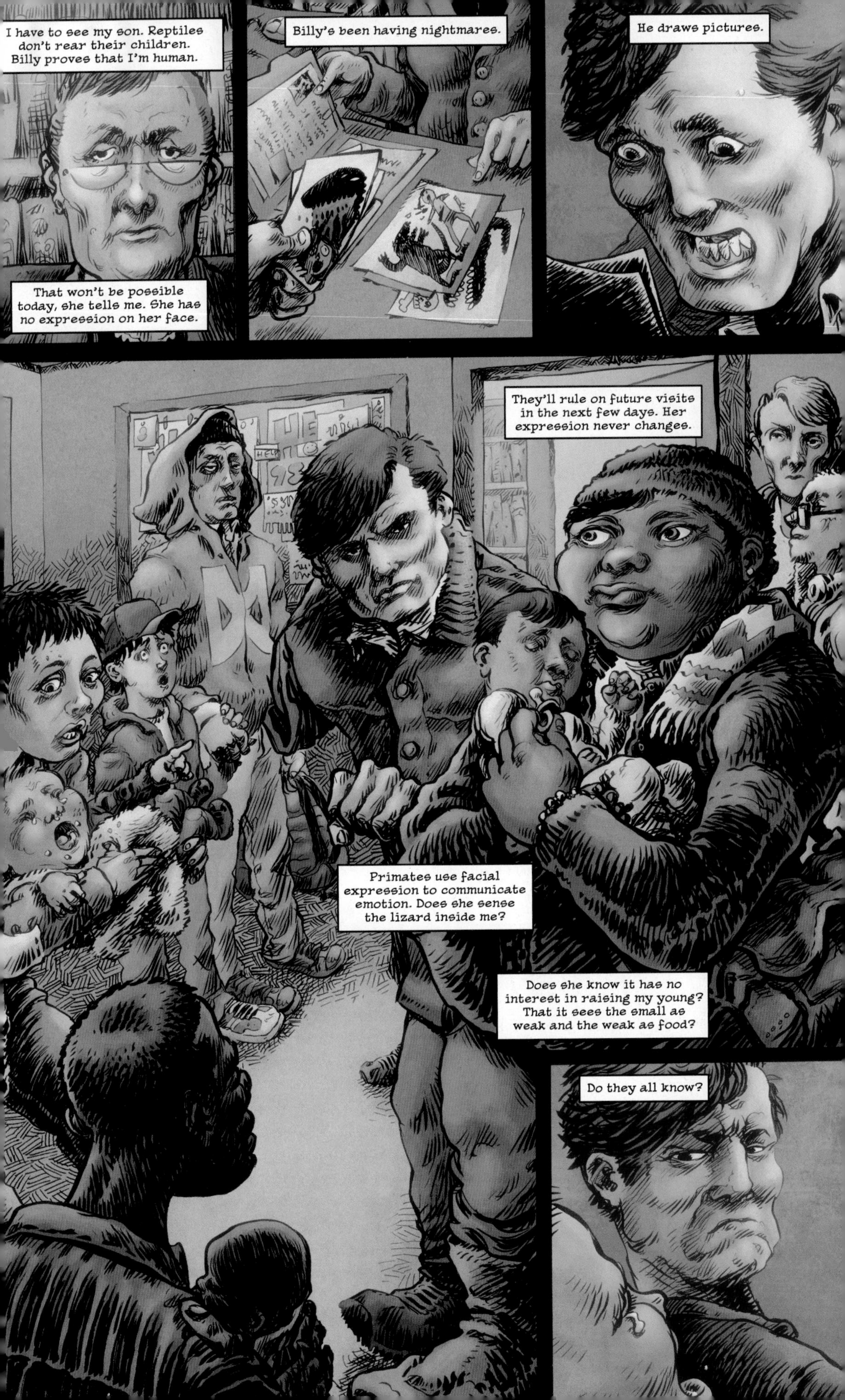
I have to see my son. Reptiles don't rear their children. Billy proves that I'm human.
That won't be possible today, she tells me. She has no expression on her face.
Billy's been having nightmares.
He draws pictures.
They'll rule on future visits in the next few days. Her expression never changes.
Primates use facial expression to communicate emotion. Does she sense the lizard inside me?
Does she know it has no interest in raising my young? That it sees the small as weak and the weak as food?
Do they all know?

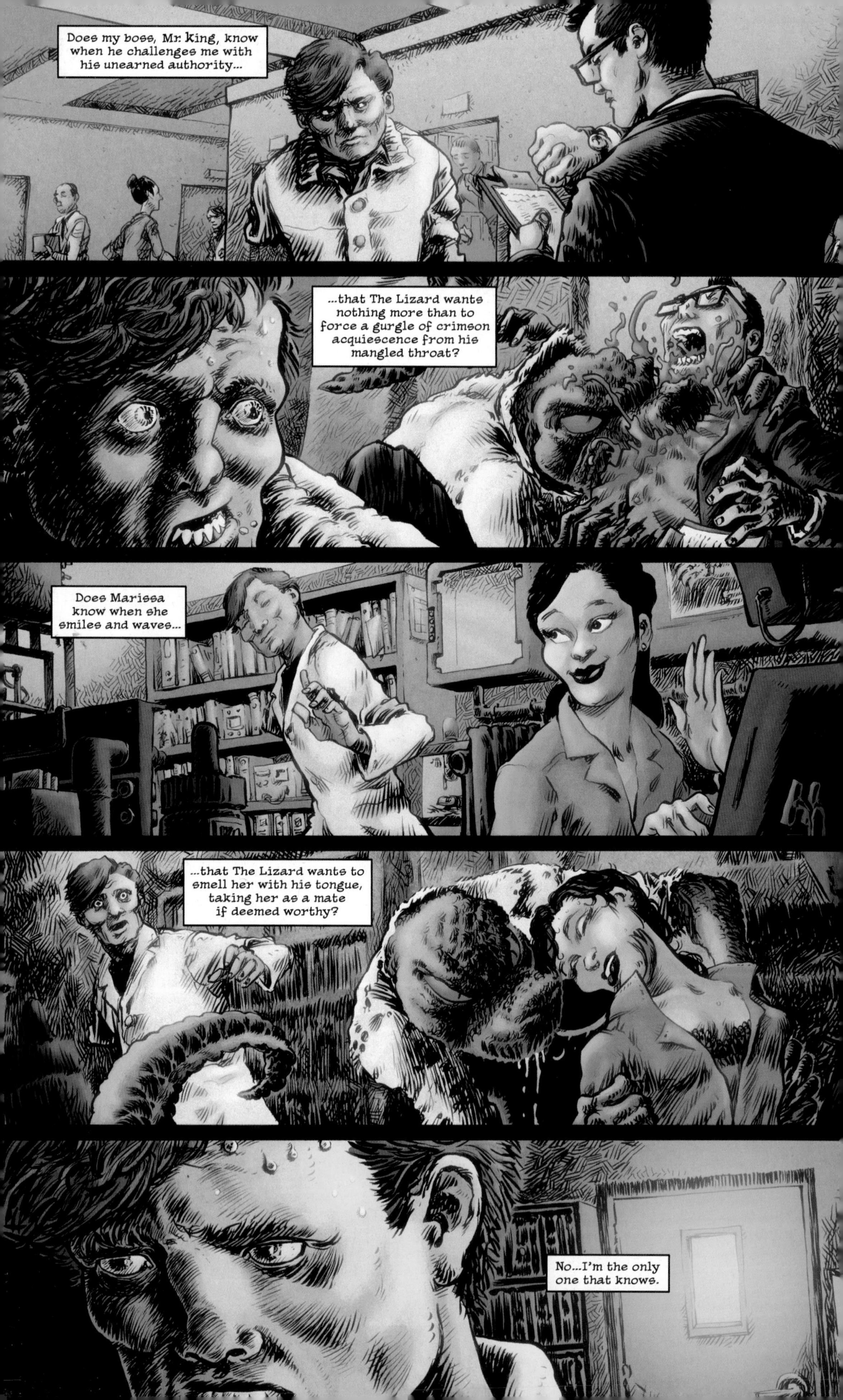
Does my boss, Mr. King, know when he challenges me with his unearned authority...
...that The Lizard wants nothing more than to force a gurgle of crimson acquiescence from his mangled throat?
Does Marissa know when she smiles and waves...
...that The Lizard wants to smell her with his tongue, taking her as a mate if deemed worthy?
No...I'm the only one that knows.

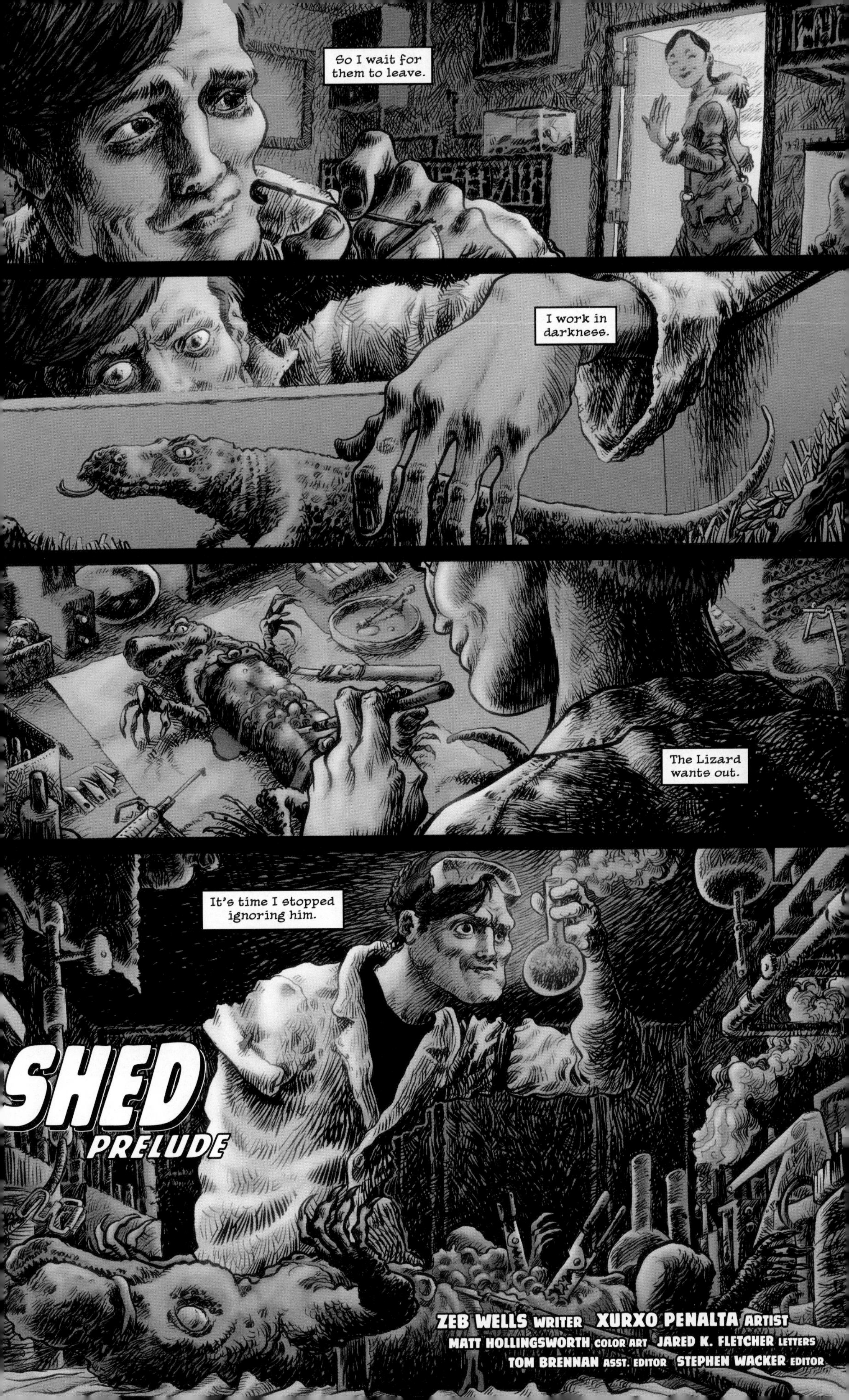
So I wait for them to leave.
I work in darkness.
The Lizard wants out.
It's time I stopped ignoring him.
SHED
PRELUDE
ZEB WELLS WRITER XURXO PENALTA ARTIST
MATT HOLLINGSWORTH COLOR ART JARED K. FLETCHER LETTERS
TOM BRENNAN ASST. EDITOR STEPHEN WACKER EDITOR

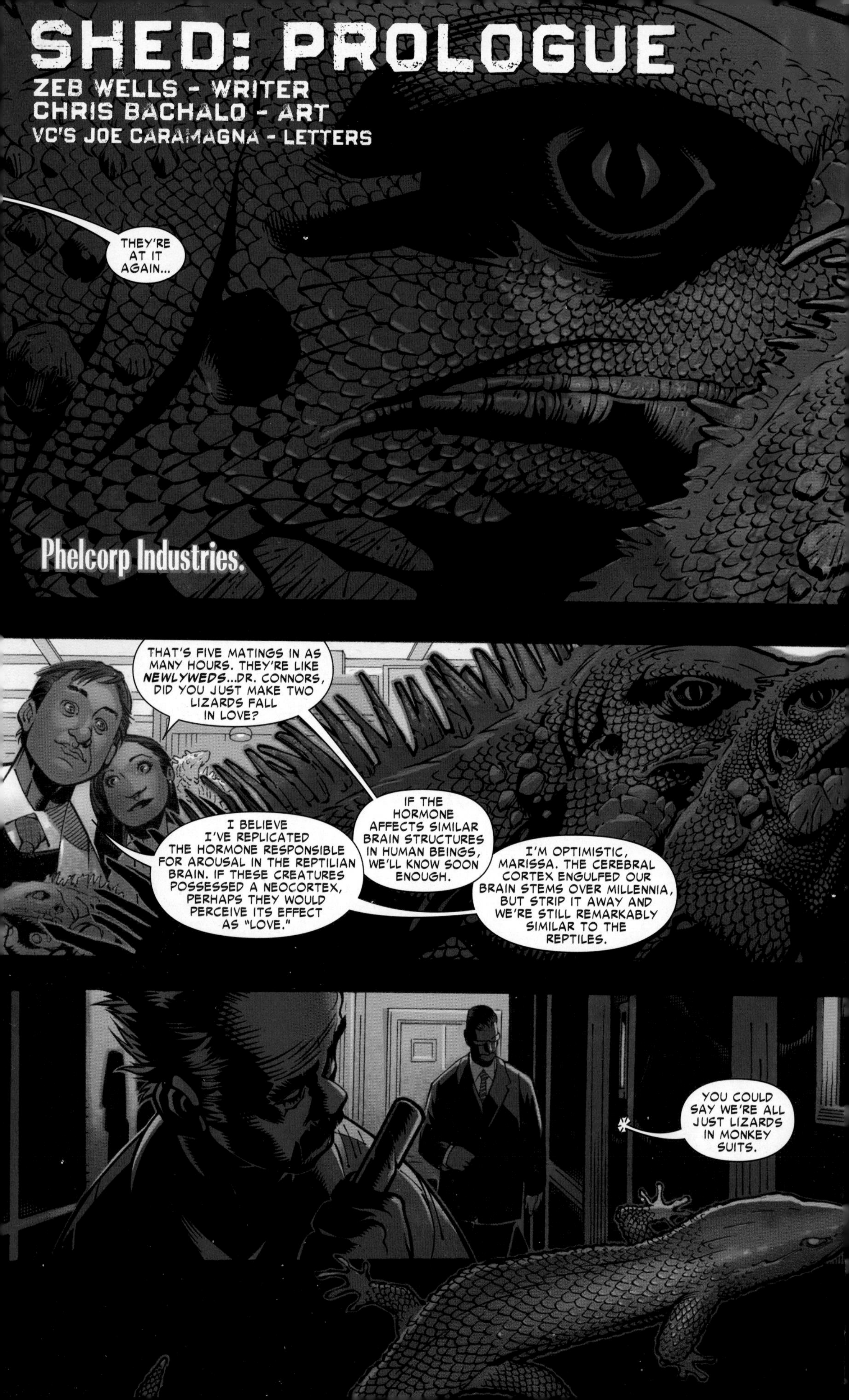

SHED: PROLOGUE
ZEB WELLS - WRITER
CHRIS BACHALO - ART
VC'S JOE CARAMAGNA - LETTERS
THEY'RE AT IT AGAIN...
Phelcorp Industries.
THAT'S FIVE MATINGS IN AS MANY HOURS. THEY'RE LIKE *NEWLYWEDS*...DR. CONNORS, DID YOU JUST MAKE TWO LIZARDS FALL IN LOVE?
I BELIEVE I'VE REPLICATED THE HORMONE RESPONSIBLE FOR AROUSAL IN THE REPTILIAN BRAIN. IF THESE CREATURES POSSESSED A NEOCORTEX, PERHAPS THEY WOULD PERCEIVE ITS EFFECT AS "LOVE."
IF THE HORMONE AFFECTS SIMILAR BRAIN STRUCTURES IN HUMAN BEINGS, WE'LL KNOW SOON ENOUGH.
I'M OPTIMISTIC, MARISSA. THE CEREBRAL CORTEX ENGULFED OUR BRAIN STEMS OVER MILLENNIA, BUT STRIP IT AWAY AND WE'RE STILL REMARKABLY SIMILAR TO THE REPTILES.
YOU COULD SAY WE'RE ALL JUST LIZARDS IN MONKEY SUITS.

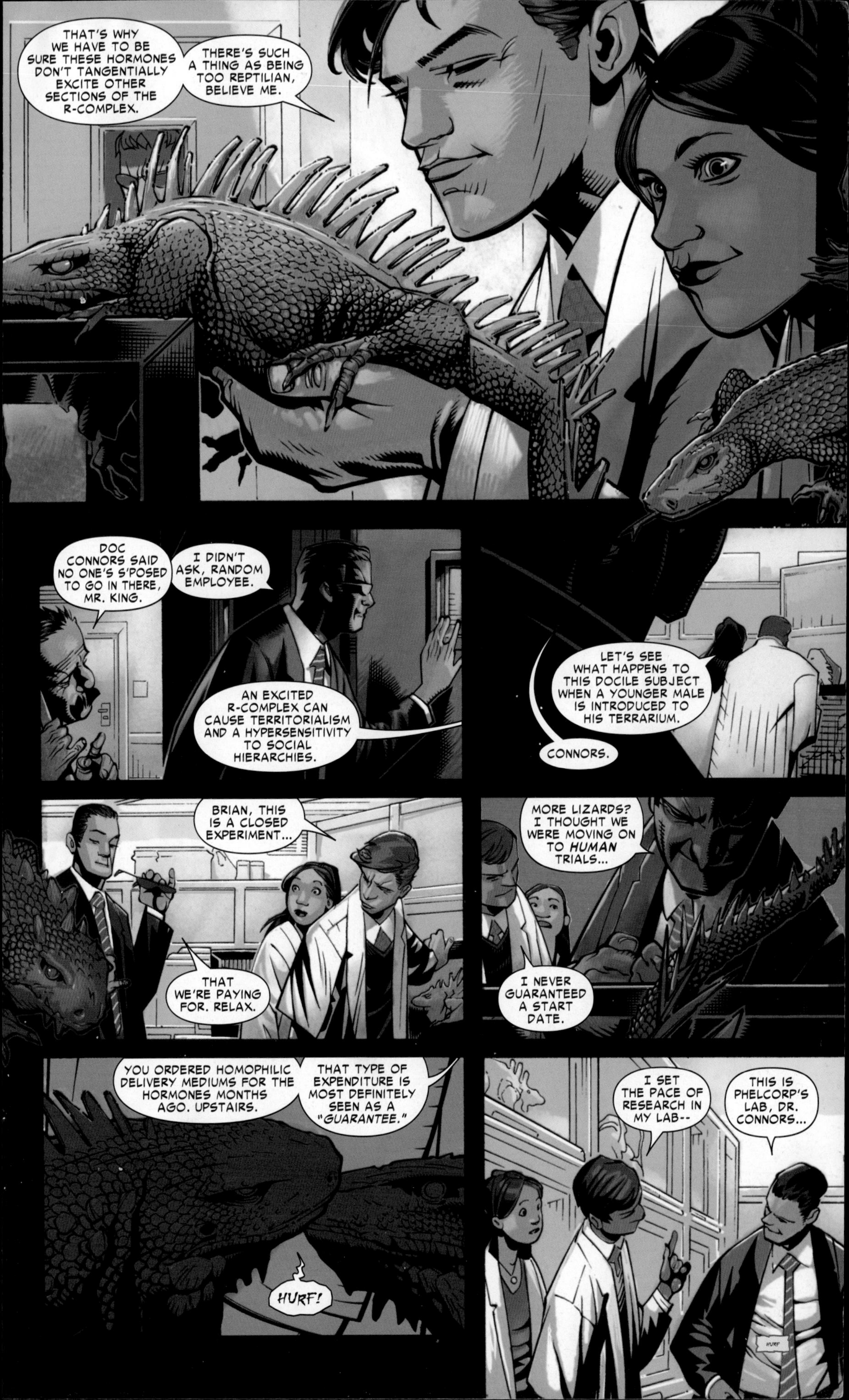
THAT'S WHY WE HAVE TO BE SURE THESE HORMONES DON'T TANGENTIALLY EXCITE OTHER SECTIONS OF THE R-COMPLEX.
THERE'S SUCH A THING AS BEING TOO REPTILIAN, BELIEVE ME.
DOC CONNORS SAID NO ONE'S S'POSED TO GO IN THERE, MR. KING.
I DIDN'T ASK, RANDOM EMPLOYEE.
AN EXCITED R-COMPLEX CAN CAUSE TERRITORIALISM AND A HYPERSENSITIVITY TO SOCIAL HIERARCHIES.
LET'S SEE WHAT HAPPENS TO THIS DOCILE SUBJECT WHEN A YOUNGER MALE IS INTRODUCED TO HIS TERRARIUM.
CONNORS.
BRIAN, THIS IS A CLOSED EXPERIMENT...
THAT WE'RE PAYING FOR. RELAX.
MORE LIZARDS? I THOUGHT WE WERE MOVING ON TO *HUMAN* TRIALS...
I NEVER GUARANTEED A START DATE.
YOU ORDERED HOMOPHILIC DELIVERY MEDIUMS FOR THE HORMONES MONTHS AGO. UPSTAIRS.
THAT TYPE OF EXPENDITURE IS MOST DEFINITELY SEEN AS A "*GUARANTEE.*"
HURF!
I SET THE PACE OF RESEARCH IN MY LAB--
THIS IS PHELCORP'S LAB, DR. CONNORS...

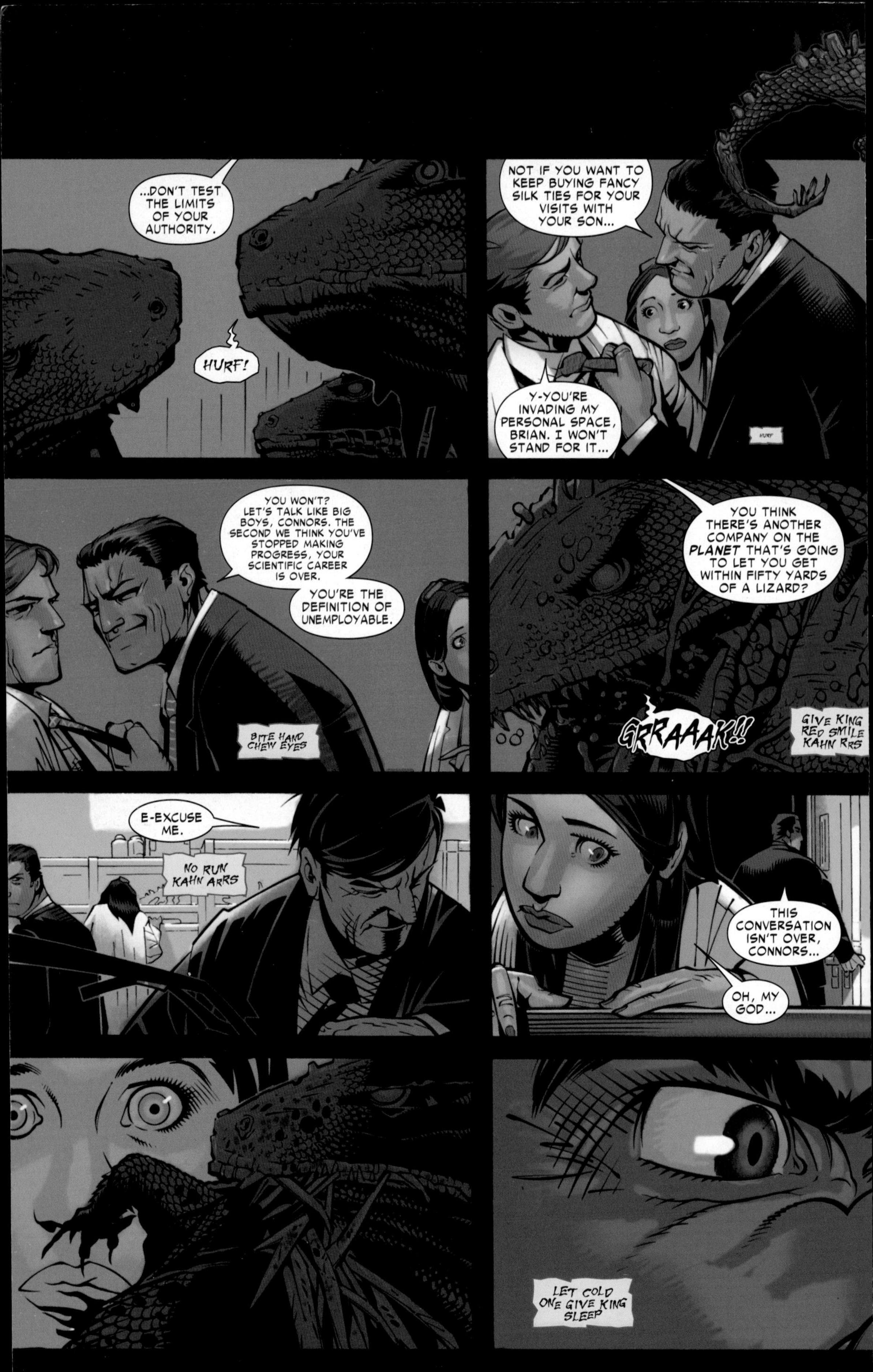
...DON'T TEST THE LIMITS OF YOUR AUTHORITY.
HURF!
NOT IF YOU WANT TO KEEP BUYING FANCY SILK TIES FOR YOUR VISITS WITH YOUR SON...
Y-YOU'RE INVADING MY PERSONAL SPACE, BRIAN. I WON'T STAND FOR IT...
HURF
YOU WON'T? LET'S TALK LIKE BIG BOYS, CONNORS. THE SECOND WE THINK YOU'VE STOPPED MAKING PROGRESS, YOUR SCIENTIFIC CAREER IS OVER.
YOU'RE THE DEFINITION OF UNEMPLOYABLE.
BITE HAND CHEW EYES
YOU THINK THERE'S ANOTHER COMPANY ON THE PLANET THAT'S GOING TO LET YOU GET WITHIN FIFTY YARDS OF A LIZARD?
GRRAAAK!!
GIVE KING RED SMILE KAHN RRS
E-EXCUSE ME.
NO RUN KAHN ARRS
THIS CONVERSATION ISN'T OVER, CONNORS...
OH, MY GOD...
LET COLD ONE GIVE KING SLEEP

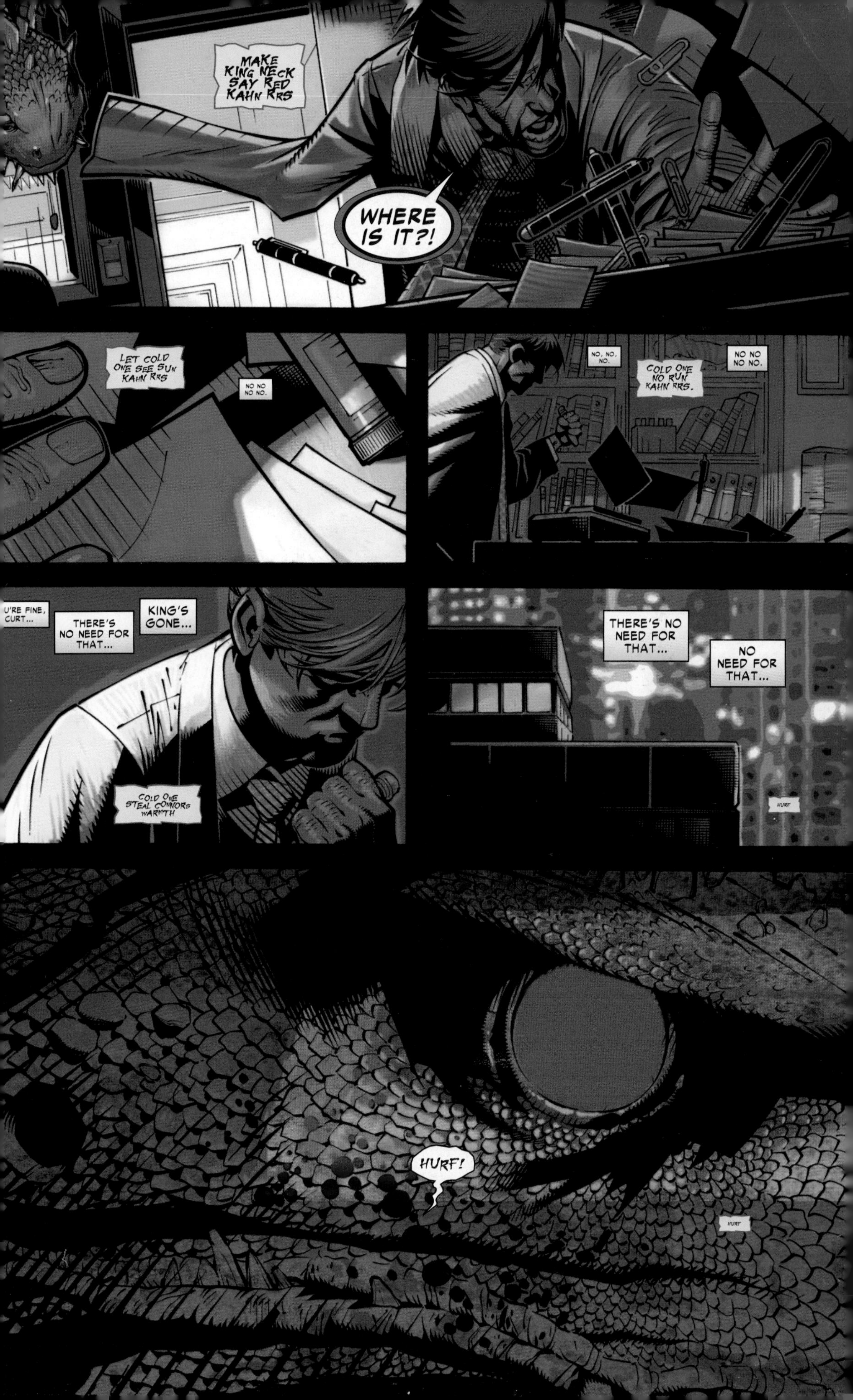
MAKE KING NECK SAY RED KAHN RRS
WHERE IS IT?!
LET COLD ONE SEE SUN KAHN RRS
NO NO NO NO.
NO, NO, NO.
COLD ONE NO RUN KAHN RRS.
NO NO NO NO.
U'RE FINE, CURT...
THERE'S NO NEED FOR THAT...
KING'S GONE...
COLD ONE STEAL CONNORS WARMTH
THERE'S NO NEED FOR THAT...
NO NEED FOR THAT...
HURF
HURF!
HURF

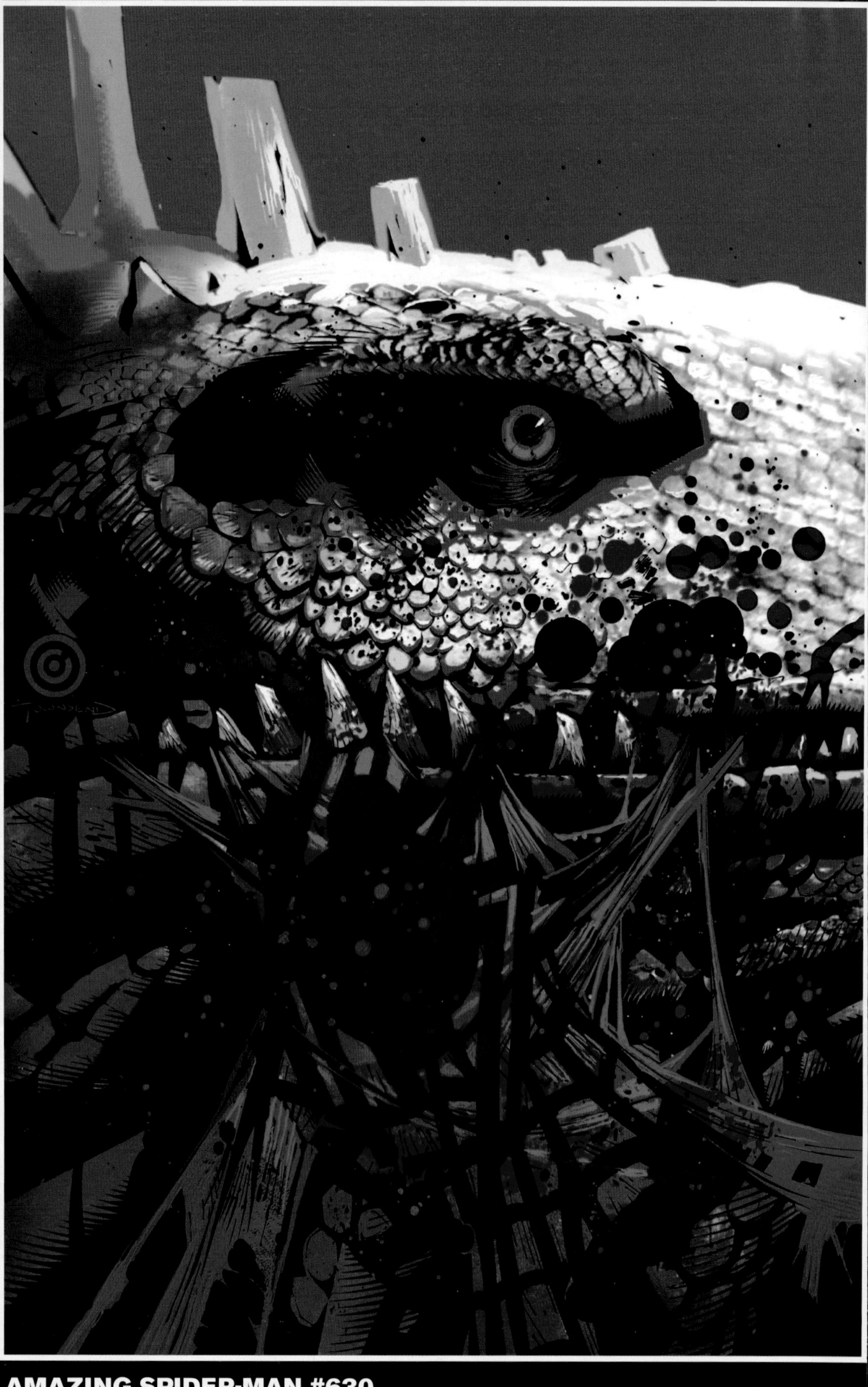

AMAZING SPIDER-MAN #630
COVER BY CHRIS BACHALO & TIM TOWNSEND

BUGLE GIRL

by
BETTY BRANT

SEARCH GO

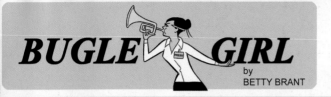

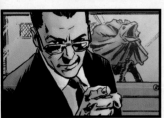

INNOVATIONS AT PHELCORP – Phelcorp executive Brian King continues to impress stockholders. His decisions have led to an increase in the company's scientific research departments. Under King's guidance, Phelcorp executives authorized the implementation of a new program studying lizards. more...

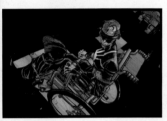

IS HOPE LOST? – It is with a heavy heart that Bugle Girl by Betty Brant reports that the NYPD has given up on the rescue efforts in the search for Mattie Franklin and Cassandra Webb. They are now pursuing a "search and recovery" operation. more...

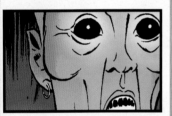

AUNT MAY – ANTI-MAY? – May Parker, local hero and beloved staple of Martin Li's F.E.A.S.T. center, has come under fire from F.E.A.S.T. regulars for "abusive language and behavior"... more...

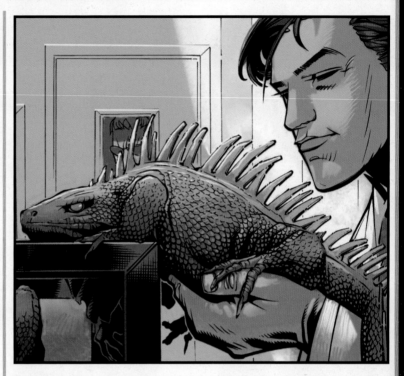

After a wartime injury, Dr. Curt Connors, once a talented and gifted surgeon, had to endure the amputation of his right arm. Devoting himself to the study of reptilian DNA, Connors attempted to create a serum that would grant his body the power to regenerate lost limbs. The result was an effect the scientist had not foreseen, as he was transformed into a reptilian-humanoid monster known as THE LIZARD. Peter Parker, the Amazing Spider-Man, intervened, stopping the creature and restoring Connors to his normal self.

Things just don't seem to be going well for Peter Parker now, though. After facing down foe after foe, Spider-Man has been drained emotionally and physically. Doctor Octopus, Electro, Mysterio, and even the Rhino have all resurfaced, challenging the web-slinger at every chance they get. Are these bouts with old enemies coincidence, or is someone orchestrating Spidey's terrible luck from behind the scenes?

Adding insult to (serious) injury, Peter's life outside of his costume is proving to be difficult, as well. His uncertainties about dating Carlie Cooper of the NYPD and a casual romance with Felicia Hardy, the BLACK CAT, are only making his personal life even more complicated.

Dealing with unemployment, an aunt who has her hands full with a new marriage, and his own exhaustion, Peter Parker has slowly started to lose steam.

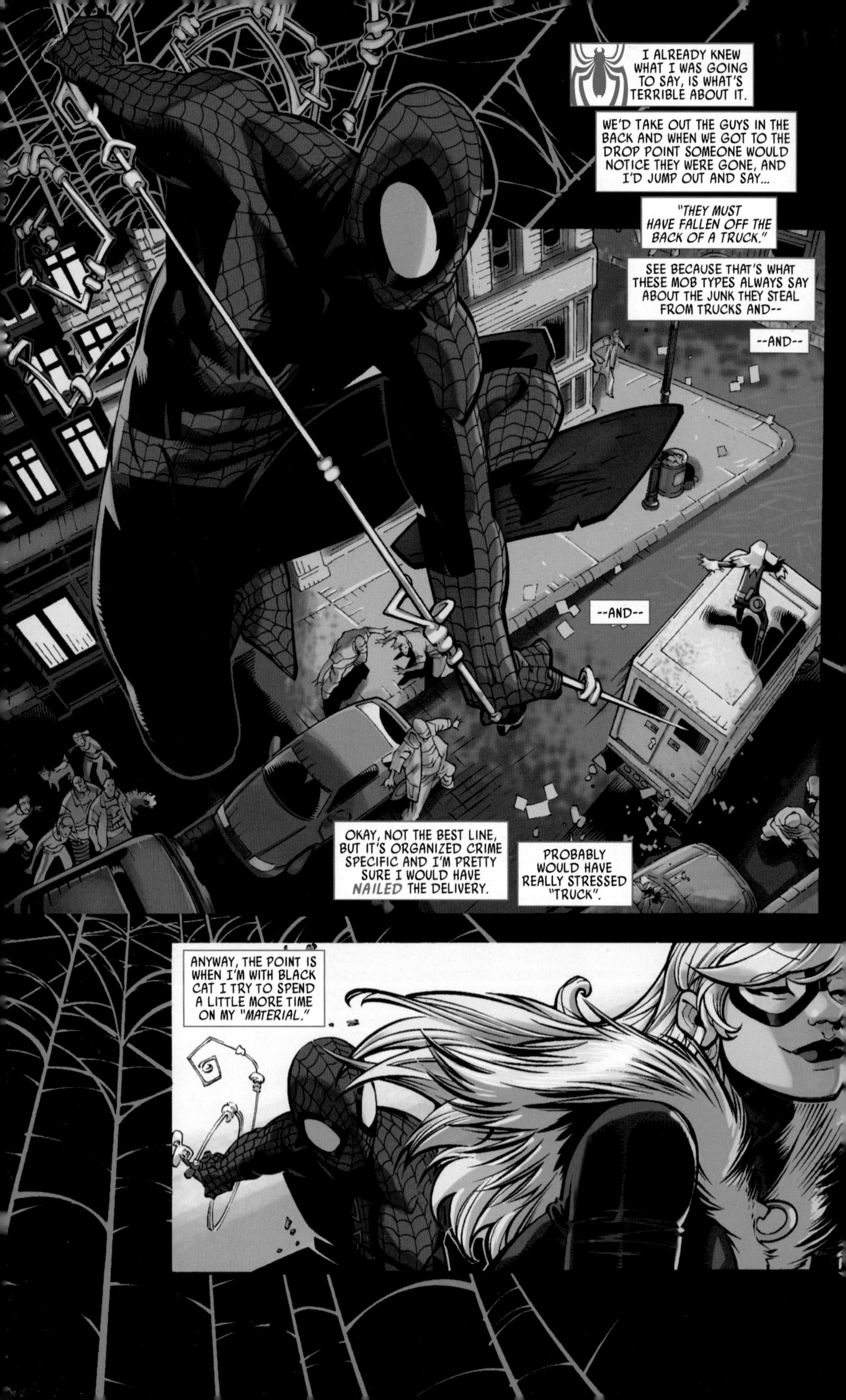
I ALREADY KNEW WHAT I WAS GOING TO SAY, IS WHAT'S TERRIBLE ABOUT IT.
WE'D TAKE OUT THE GUYS IN THE BACK AND WHEN WE GOT TO THE DROP POINT SOMEONE WOULD NOTICE THEY WERE GONE, AND I'D JUMP OUT AND SAY...
"THEY MUST HAVE FALLEN OFF THE BACK OF A TRUCK."
SEE BECAUSE THAT'S WHAT THESE MOB TYPES ALWAYS SAY ABOUT THE JUNK THEY STEAL FROM TRUCKS AND--
--AND--
--AND--
OKAY, NOT THE BEST LINE, BUT IT'S ORGANIZED CRIME SPECIFIC AND I'M PRETTY SURE I WOULD HAVE NAILED THE DELIVERY.
PROBABLY WOULD HAVE REALLY STRESSED "TRUCK".
ANYWAY, THE POINT IS WHEN I'M WITH BLACK CAT I TRY TO SPEND A LITTLE MORE TIME ON MY "MATERIAL."

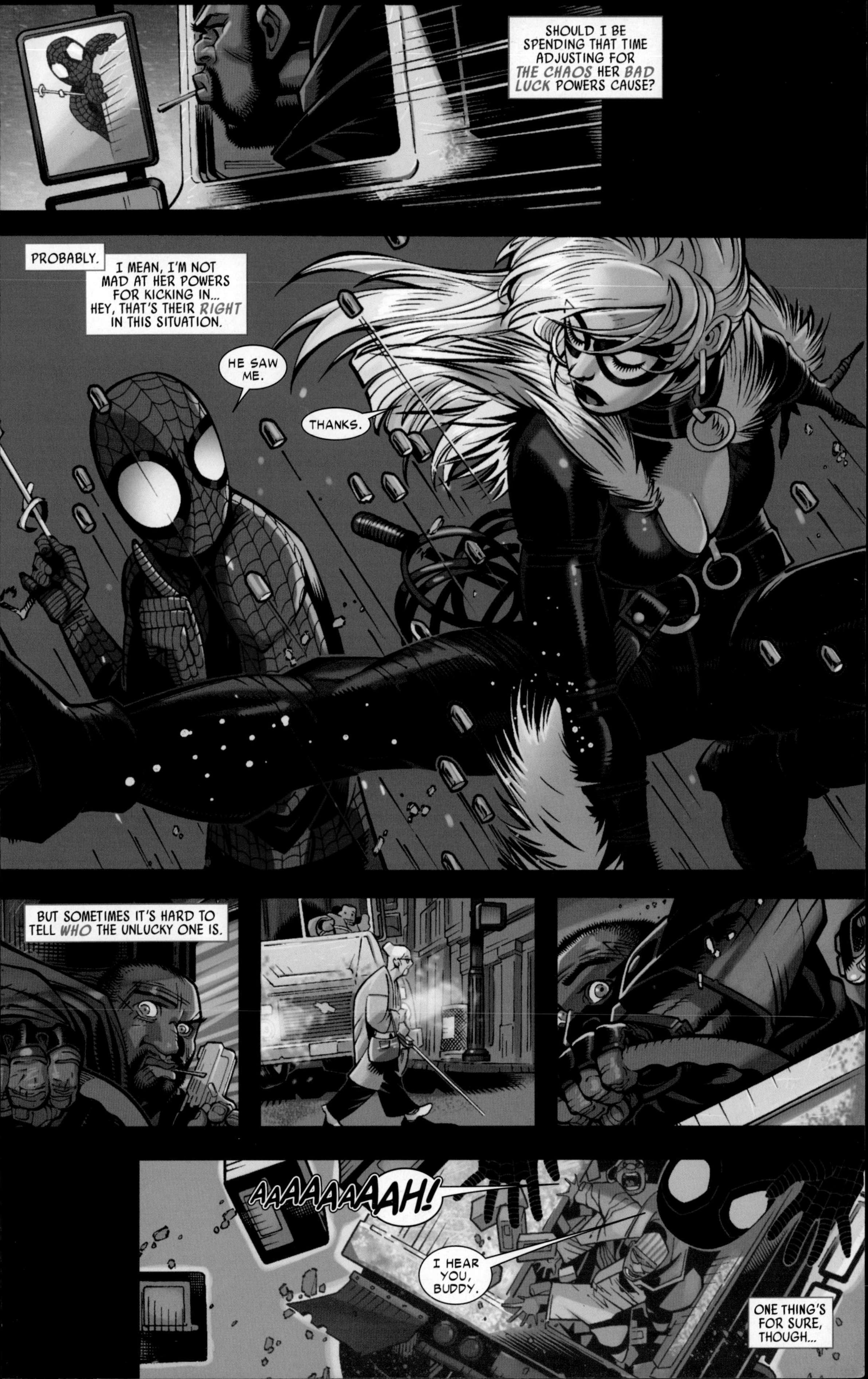
SHOULD I BE SPENDING THAT TIME ADJUSTING FOR THE CHAOS HER BAD LUCK POWERS CAUSE?
PROBABLY.
I MEAN, I'M NOT MAD AT HER POWERS FOR KICKING IN... HEY, THAT'S THEIR RIGHT IN THIS SITUATION.
HE SAW ME.
THANKS.
BUT SOMETIMES IT'S HARD TO TELL WHO THE UNLUCKY ONE IS.
AAAAAAAAAH!
I HEAR YOU, BUDDY.
ONE THING'S FOR SURE, THOUGH...

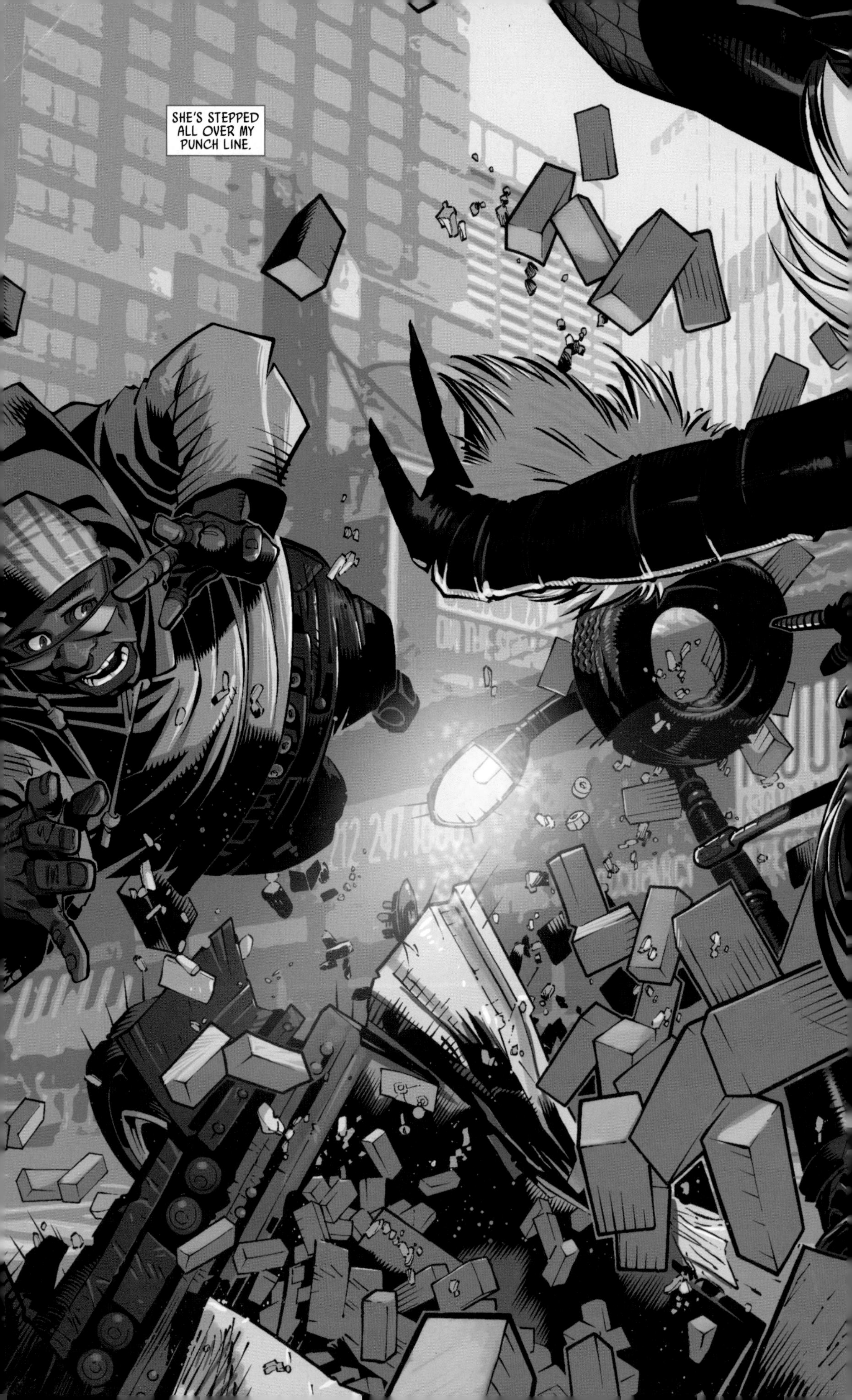
SHE'S STEPPED ALL OVER MY PUNCH LINE.

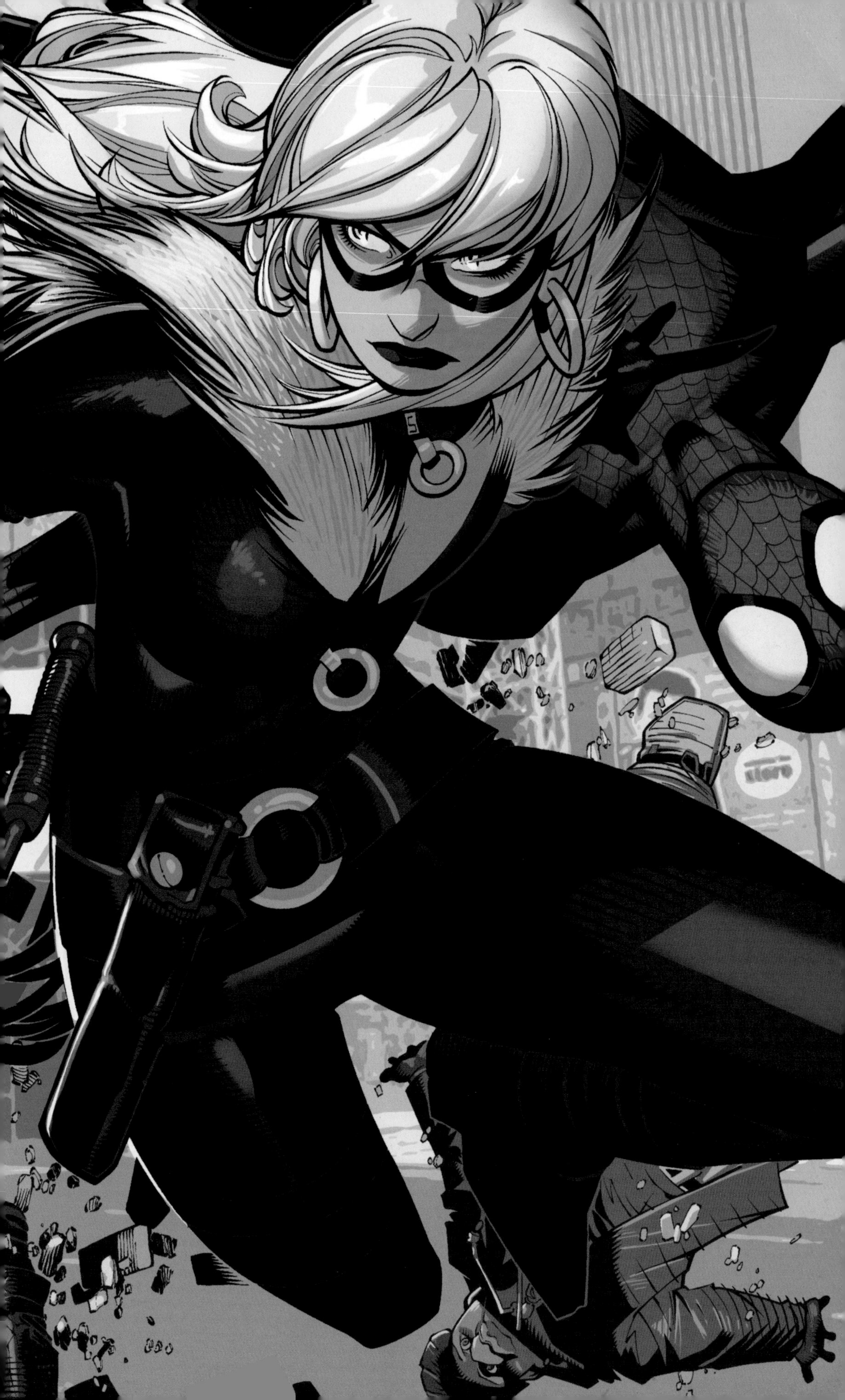

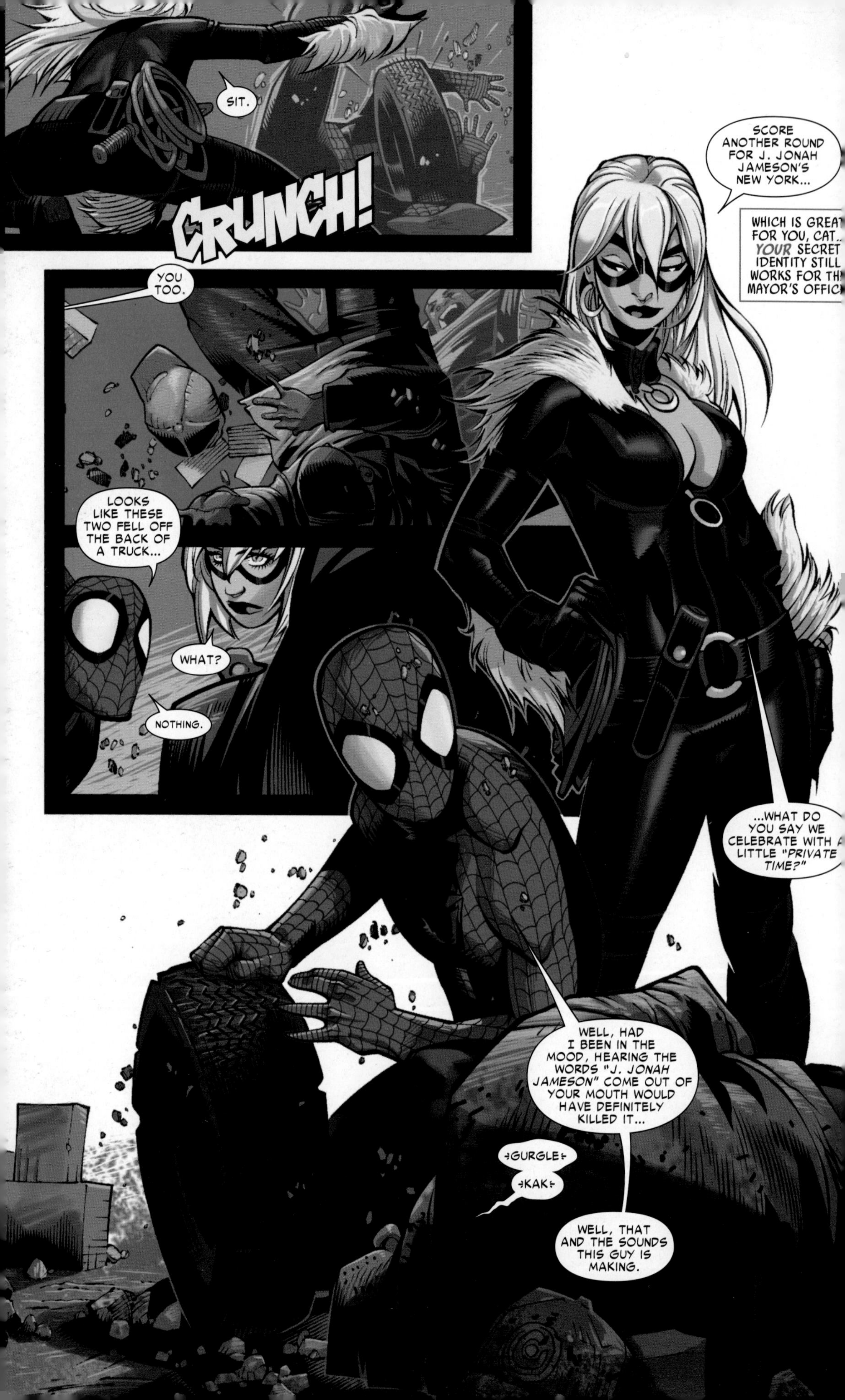
SIT.
CRUNCH!
SCORE ANOTHER ROUND FOR J. JONAH JAMESON'S NEW YORK...
YOU TOO.
WHICH IS GREAT FOR YOU, CAT... YOUR SECRET IDENTITY STILL WORKS FOR THE MAYOR'S OFFICE
LOOKS LIKE THESE TWO FELL OFF THE BACK OF A TRUCK...
WHAT?
NOTHING.
...WHAT DO YOU SAY WE CELEBRATE WITH A LITTLE "PRIVATE TIME?"
WELL, HAD I BEEN IN THE MOOD, HEARING THE WORDS "J. JONAH JAMESON" COME OUT OF YOUR MOUTH WOULD HAVE DEFINITELY KILLED IT...
GURGLE
KAK
WELL, THAT AND THE SOUNDS THIS GUY IS MAKING.

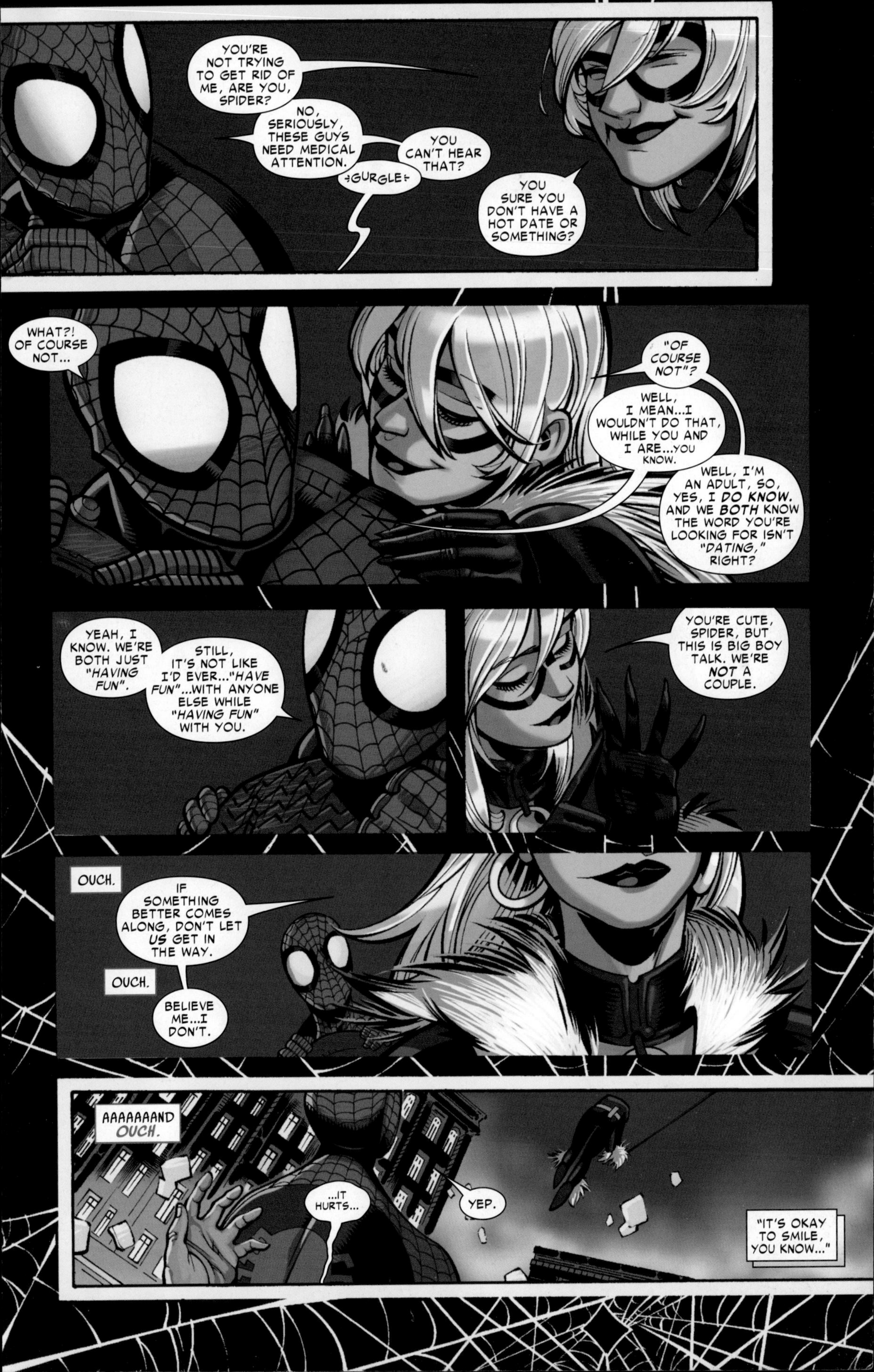
YOU'RE NOT TRYING TO GET RID OF ME, ARE YOU, SPIDER?
NO, SERIOUSLY, THESE GUYS NEED MEDICAL ATTENTION.
YOU CAN'T HEAR THAT?
GURGLE
YOU SURE YOU DON'T HAVE A HOT DATE OR SOMETHING?
WHAT?! OF COURSE NOT...
"OF COURSE NOT"?
WELL, I MEAN...I WOULDN'T DO THAT, WHILE YOU AND I ARE...YOU KNOW.
WELL, I'M AN ADULT, SO, YES, I DO KNOW. AND WE BOTH KNOW THE WORD YOU'RE LOOKING FOR ISN'T "DATING," RIGHT?
YEAH, I KNOW. WE'RE BOTH JUST "HAVING FUN".
STILL, IT'S NOT LIKE I'D EVER..."HAVE FUN"...WITH ANYONE ELSE WHILE "HAVING FUN" WITH YOU.
YOU'RE CUTE, SPIDER, BUT THIS IS BIG BOY TALK. WE'RE NOT A COUPLE.
OUCH.
IF SOMETHING BETTER COMES ALONG, DON'T LET US GET IN THE WAY.
OUCH.
BELIEVE ME...I DON'T.
AAAAAAAND OUCH.
...IT HURTS...
YEP.
"IT'S OKAY TO SMILE, YOU KNOW..."

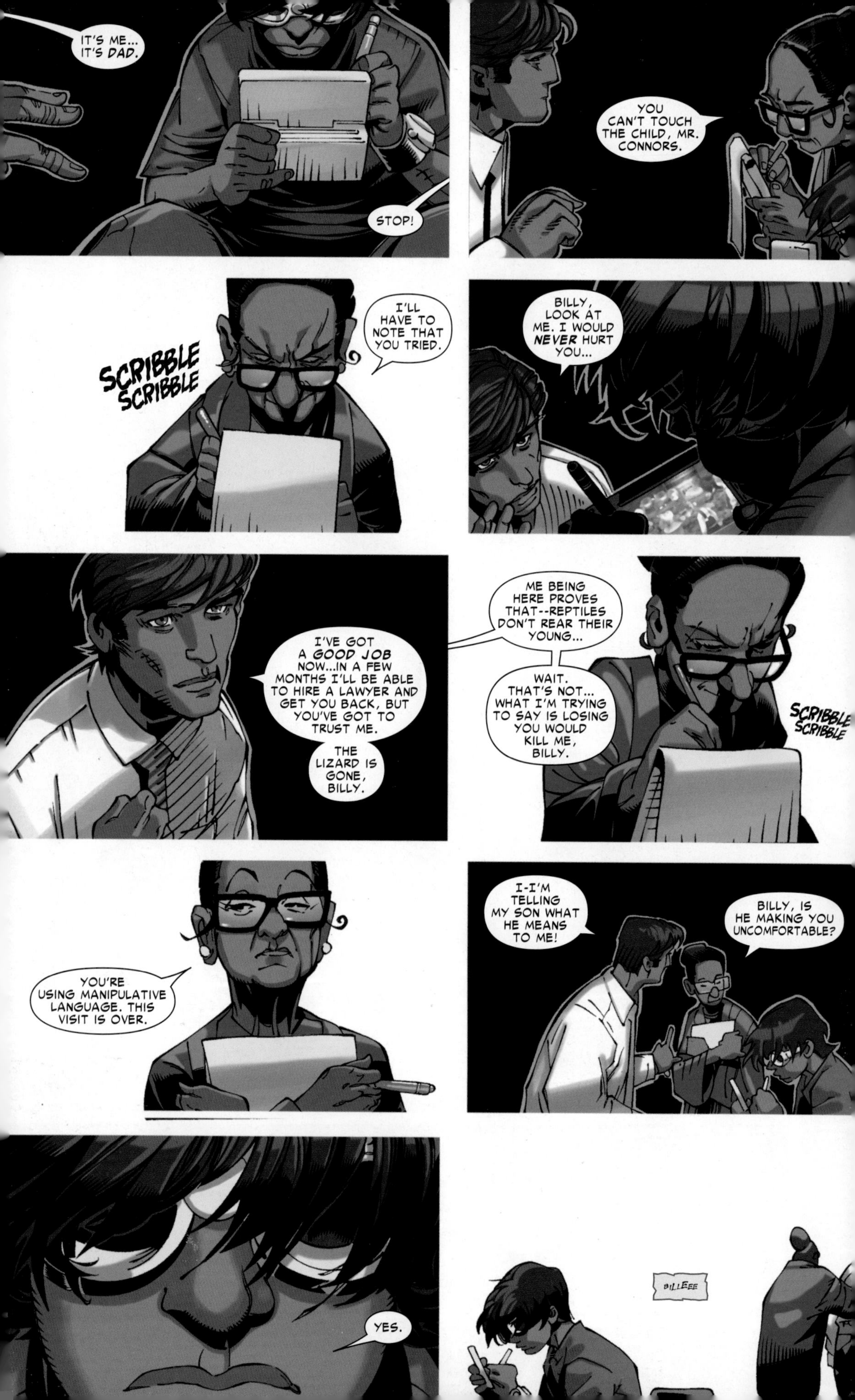
IT'S ME... IT'S DAD.
STOP!
YOU CAN'T TOUCH THE CHILD, MR. CONNORS.
SCRIBBLE SCRIBBLE
I'LL HAVE TO NOTE THAT YOU TRIED.
BILLY, LOOK AT ME. I WOULD NEVER HURT YOU...
I'VE GOT A GOOD JOB NOW...IN A FEW MONTHS I'LL BE ABLE TO HIRE A LAWYER AND GET YOU BACK, BUT YOU'VE GOT TO TRUST ME.
THE LIZARD IS GONE, BILLY.
ME BEING HERE PROVES THAT--REPTILES DON'T REAR THEIR YOUNG...
WAIT. THAT'S NOT... WHAT I'M TRYING TO SAY IS LOSING YOU WOULD KILL ME, BILLY.
SCRIBBLE SCRIBBLE
YOU'RE USING MANIPULATIVE LANGUAGE. THIS VISIT IS OVER.
I-I'M TELLING MY SON WHAT HE MEANS TO ME!
BILLY, IS HE MAKING YOU UNCOMFORTABLE?
YES.
BILLEEE

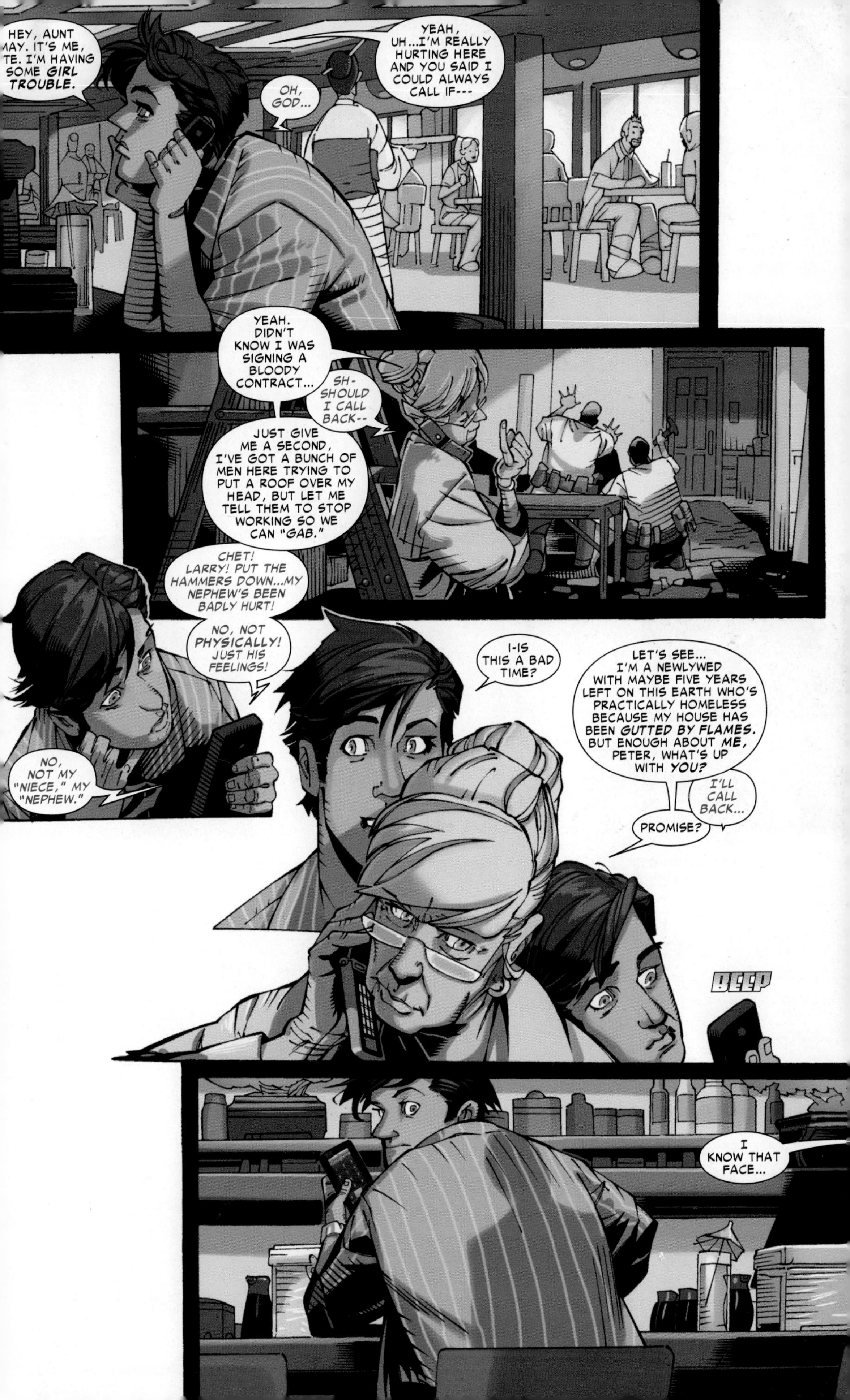
HEY, AUNT MAY. IT'S ME, TE. I'M HAVING SOME GIRL TROUBLE.
OH, GOD...
YEAH, UH...I'M REALLY HURTING HERE AND YOU SAID I COULD ALWAYS CALL IF---
YEAH. DIDN'T KNOW I WAS SIGNING A BLOODY CONTRACT...
SH-SHOULD I CALL BACK--
JUST GIVE ME A SECOND, I'VE GOT A BUNCH OF MEN HERE TRYING TO PUT A ROOF OVER MY HEAD, BUT LET ME TELL THEM TO STOP WORKING SO WE CAN "GAB."
CHET! LARRY! PUT THE HAMMERS DOWN...MY NEPHEW'S BEEN BADLY HURT!
NO, NOT PHYSICALLY! JUST HIS FEELINGS!
NO, NOT MY "NIECE," MY "NEPHEW."
I-IS THIS A BAD TIME?
LET'S SEE... I'M A NEWLYWED WITH MAYBE FIVE YEARS LEFT ON THIS EARTH WHO'S PRACTICALLY HOMELESS BECAUSE MY HOUSE HAS BEEN GUTTED BY FLAMES. BUT ENOUGH ABOUT ME, PETER, WHAT'S UP WITH YOU?
I'LL CALL BACK...
PROMISE?
BEEP
I KNOW THAT FACE...

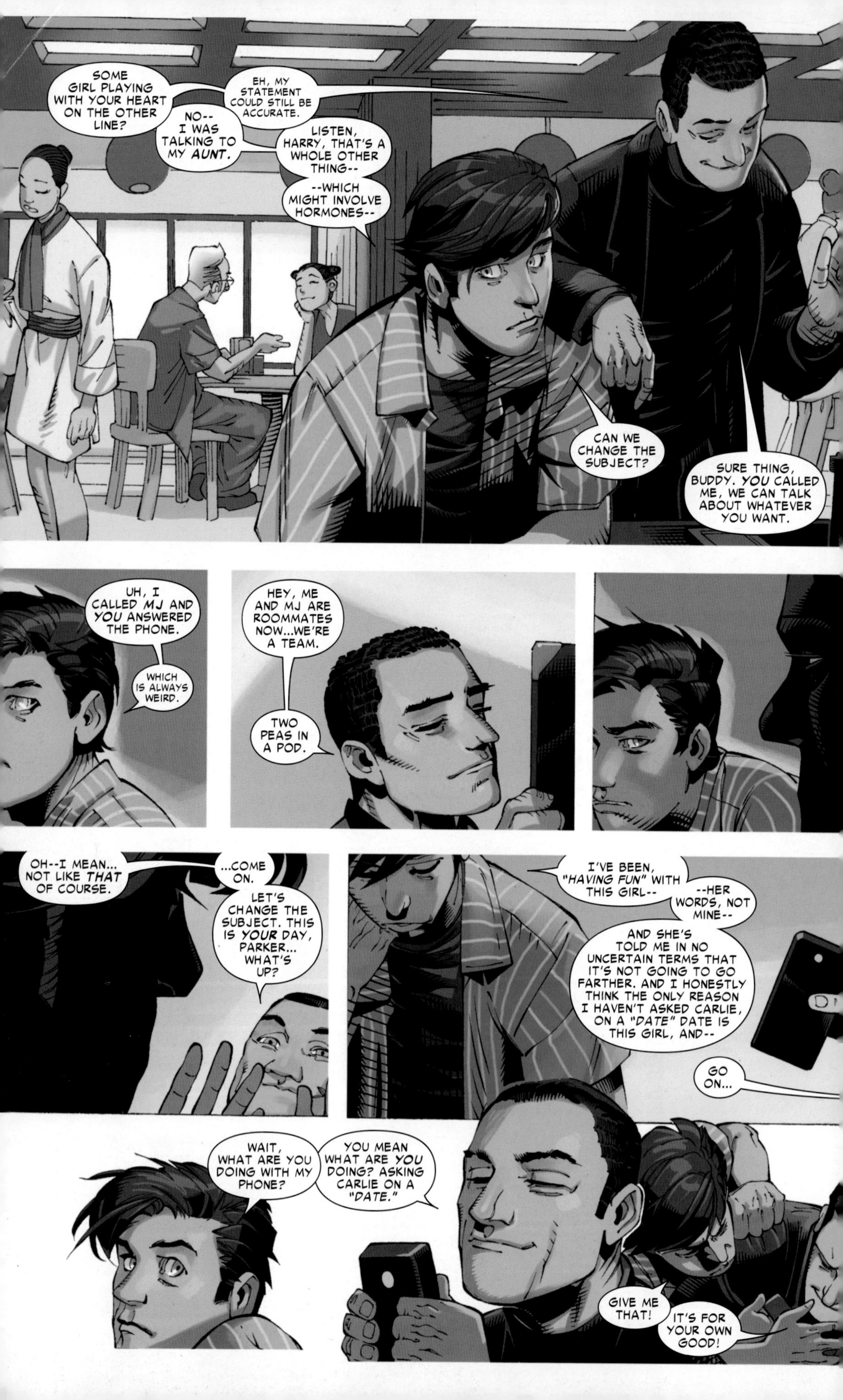
SOME GIRL PLAYING WITH YOUR HEART ON THE OTHER LINE?
EH, MY STATEMENT COULD STILL BE ACCURATE.
NO-- I WAS TALKING TO MY AUNT.
LISTEN, HARRY, THAT'S A WHOLE OTHER THING--
--WHICH MIGHT INVOLVE HORMONES--
CAN WE CHANGE THE SUBJECT?
SURE THING, BUDDY. YOU CALLED ME, WE CAN TALK ABOUT WHATEVER YOU WANT.
UH, I CALLED MJ AND YOU ANSWERED THE PHONE.
WHICH IS ALWAYS WEIRD.
HEY, ME AND MJ ARE ROOMMATES NOW...WE'RE A TEAM.
TWO PEAS IN A POD.
OH--I MEAN... NOT LIKE THAT OF COURSE.
...COME ON.
LET'S CHANGE THE SUBJECT. THIS IS YOUR DAY, PARKER... WHAT'S UP?
I'VE BEEN, "HAVING FUN" WITH THIS GIRL--
--HER WORDS, NOT MINE--
AND SHE'S TOLD ME IN NO UNCERTAIN TERMS THAT IT'S NOT GOING TO GO FARTHER. AND I HONESTLY THINK THE ONLY REASON I HAVEN'T ASKED CARLIE, ON A "DATE" DATE IS THIS GIRL, AND--
GO ON...
WAIT, WHAT ARE YOU DOING WITH MY PHONE?
YOU MEAN WHAT ARE YOU DOING? ASKING CARLIE ON A "DATE."
GIVE ME THAT!
IT'S FOR YOUR OWN GOOD!

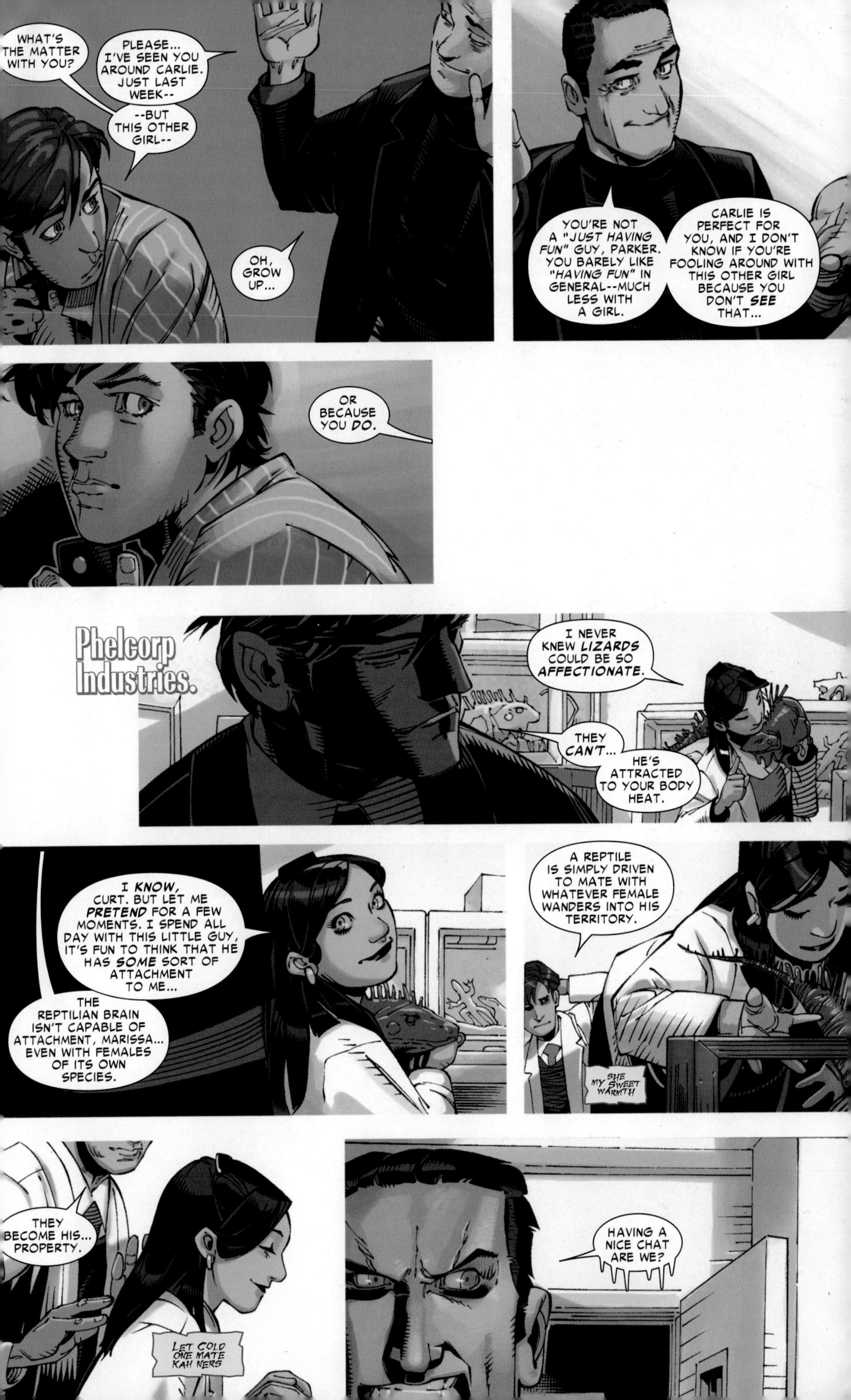
WHAT'S THE MATTER WITH YOU?
PLEASE... I'VE SEEN YOU AROUND CARLIE. JUST LAST WEEK--
--BUT THIS OTHER GIRL--
OH, GROW UP...
YOU'RE NOT A "JUST HAVING FUN" GUY, PARKER. YOU BARELY LIKE "HAVING FUN" IN GENERAL--MUCH LESS WITH A GIRL.
CARLIE IS PERFECT FOR YOU, AND I DON'T KNOW IF YOU'RE FOOLING AROUND WITH THIS OTHER GIRL BECAUSE YOU DON'T SEE THAT...
OR BECAUSE YOU DO.
Phelcorp Industries.
I NEVER KNEW LIZARDS COULD BE SO AFFECTIONATE.
THEY CAN'T...
HE'S ATTRACTED TO YOUR BODY HEAT.
I KNOW, CURT. BUT LET ME PRETEND FOR A FEW MOMENTS. I SPEND ALL DAY WITH THIS LITTLE GUY, IT'S FUN TO THINK THAT HE HAS SOME SORT OF ATTACHMENT TO ME...
THE REPTILIAN BRAIN ISN'T CAPABLE OF ATTACHMENT, MARISSA... EVEN WITH FEMALES OF ITS OWN SPECIES.
A REPTILE IS SIMPLY DRIVEN TO MATE WITH WHATEVER FEMALE WANDERS INTO HIS TERRITORY.
SHE MY SWEET WARMTH
THEY BECOME HIS... PROPERTY.
LET COLD ONE MATE KAH NERS
HAVING A NICE CHAT ARE WE?

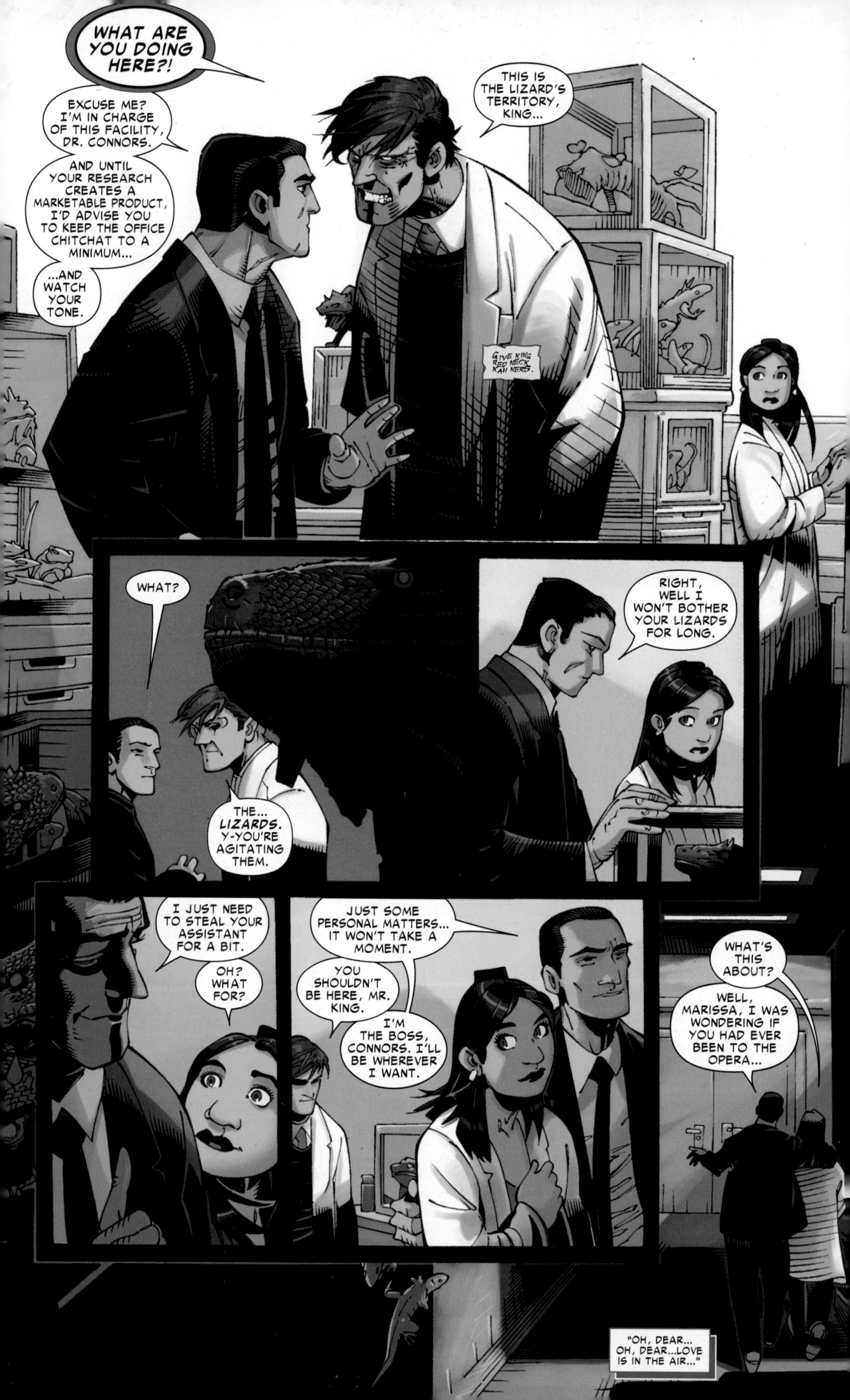
WHAT ARE YOU DOING HERE?!
EXCUSE ME? I'M IN CHARGE OF THIS FACILITY, DR. CONNORS.
AND UNTIL YOUR RESEARCH CREATES A MARKETABLE PRODUCT, I'D ADVISE YOU TO KEEP THE OFFICE CHITCHAT TO A MINIMUM...
...AND WATCH YOUR TONE.
THIS IS THE LIZARD'S TERRITORY, KING...
GIVE KING RED NECK KAHNERS.
WHAT?
THE... LIZARDS. Y-YOU'RE AGITATING THEM.
RIGHT, WELL I WON'T BOTHER YOUR LIZARDS FOR LONG.
I JUST NEED TO STEAL YOUR ASSISTANT FOR A BIT.
OH? WHAT FOR?
JUST SOME PERSONAL MATTERS... IT WON'T TAKE A MOMENT.
YOU SHOULDN'T BE HERE, MR. KING.
I'M THE BOSS, CONNORS. I'LL BE WHEREVER I WANT.
WHAT'S THIS ABOUT?
WELL, MARISSA, I WAS WONDERING IF YOU HAD EVER BEEN TO THE OPERA...
"OH, DEAR... OH, DEAR...LOVE IS IN THE AIR..."

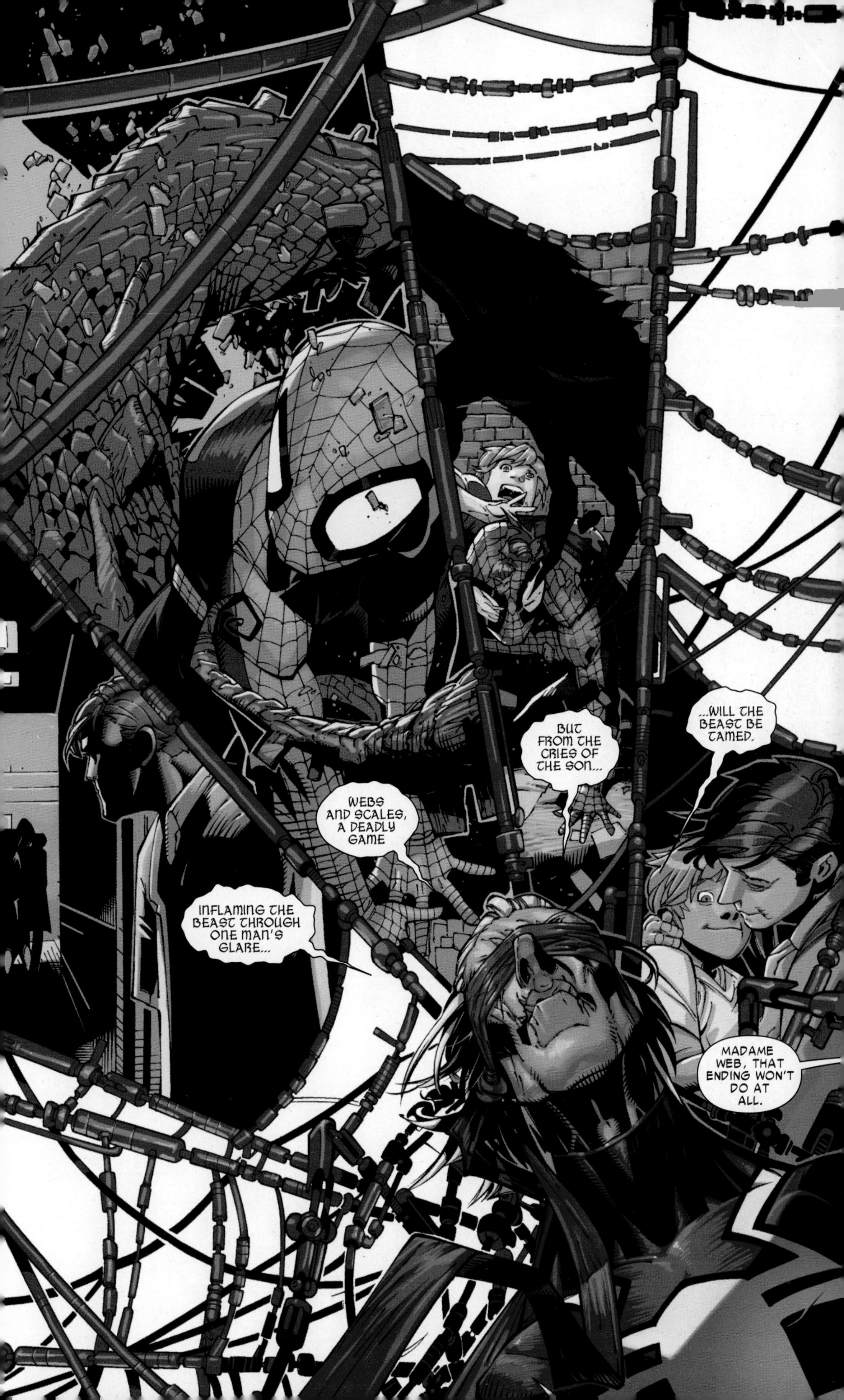
INFLAMING THE BEAST THROUGH ONE MAN'S GLARE...
WEBS AND SCALES, A DEADLY GAME
BUT FROM THE CRIES OF THE SON...
...WILL THE BEAST BE TAMED.
MADAME WEB, THAT ENDING WON'T DO AT ALL.

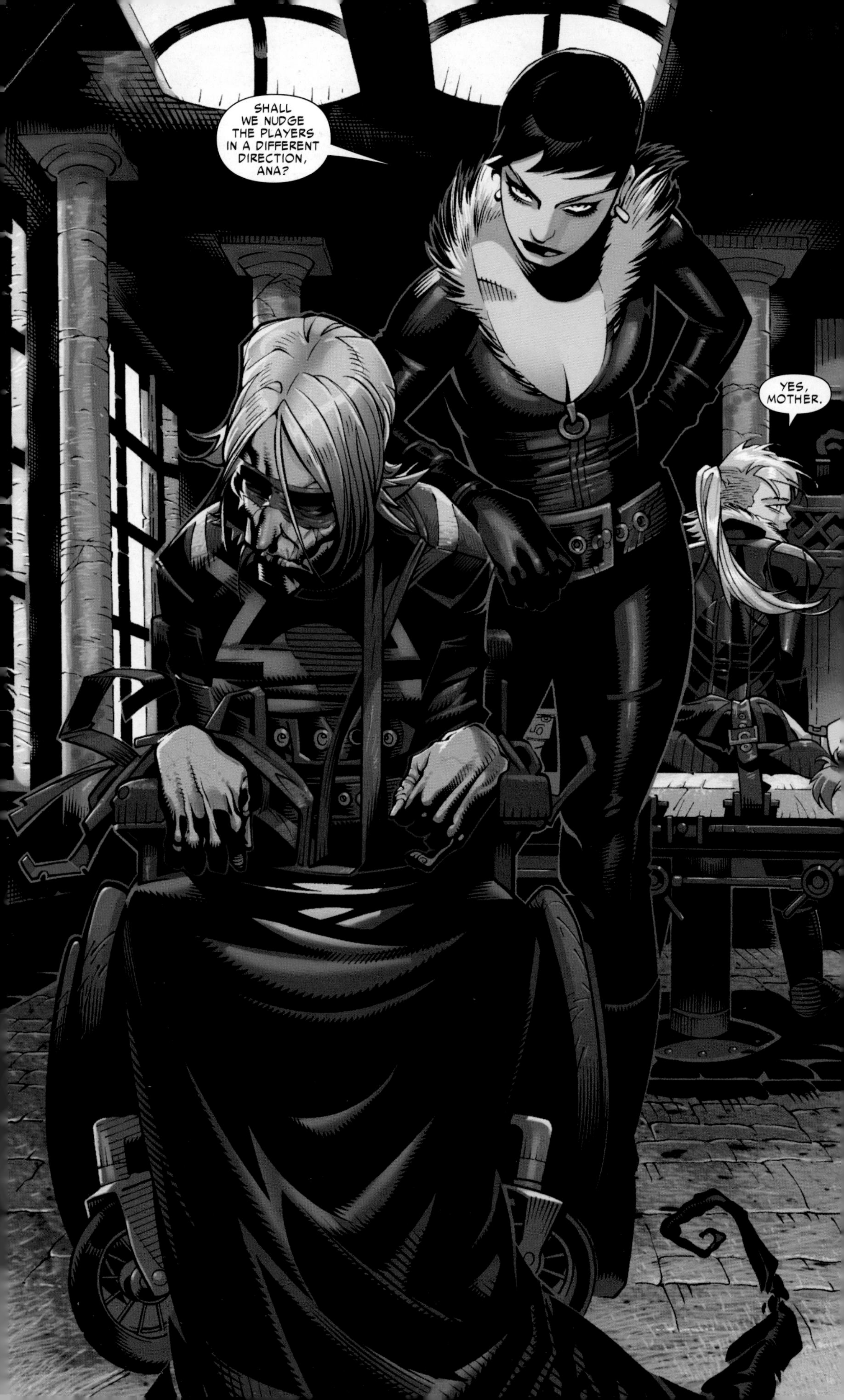
SHALL WE NUDGE THE PLAYERS IN A DIFFERENT DIRECTION, ANA?
YES, MOTHER.

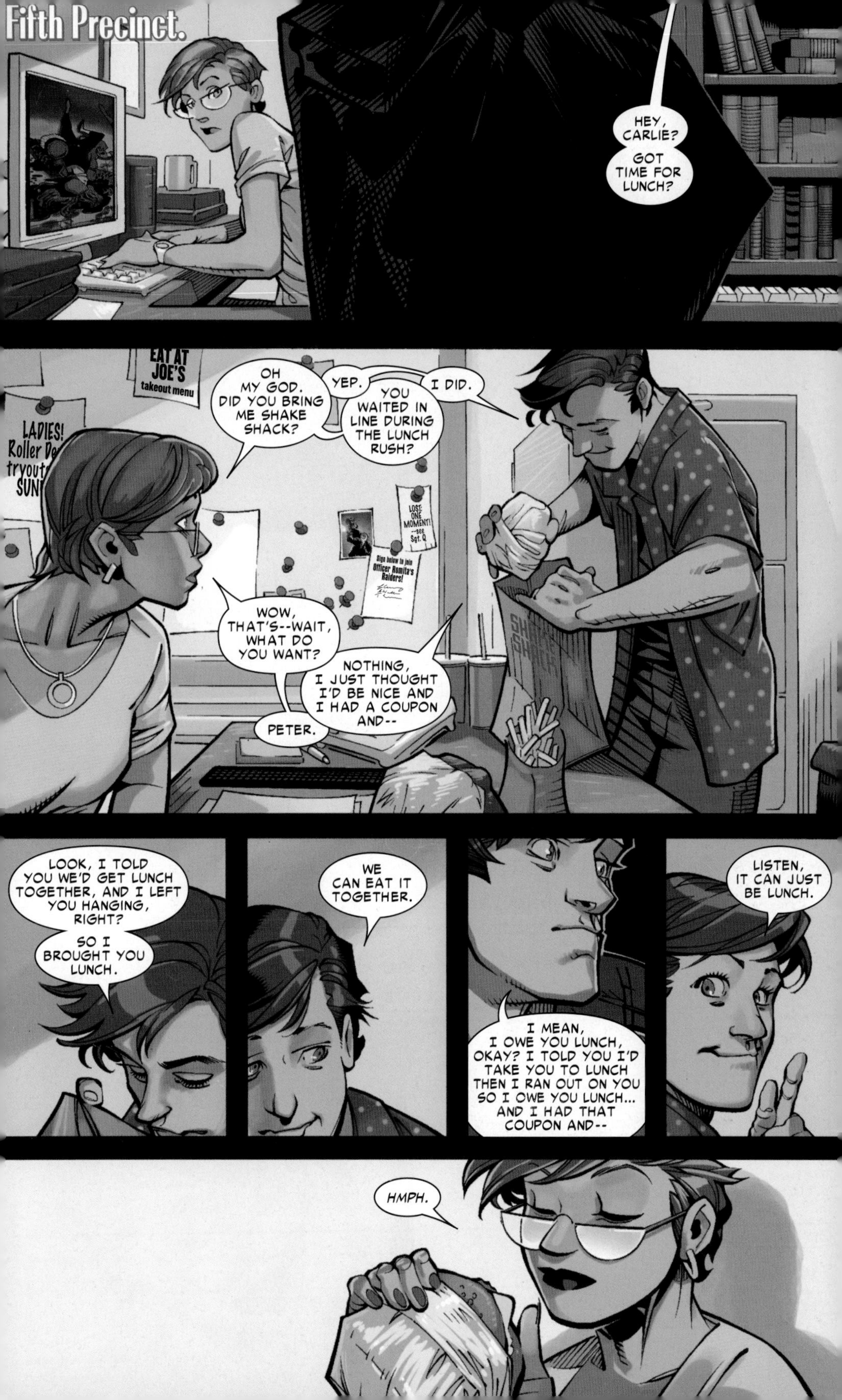
Fifth Precinct.
HEY, CARLIE?
GOT TIME FOR LUNCH?
EAT AT JOE'S takeout menu
LADIES! Roller De tryout SUN
OH MY GOD. DID YOU BRING ME SHAKE SHACK?
YEP.
YOU WAITED IN LINE DURING THE LUNCH RUSH?
I DID.
LOST: ONE MOMENT! --see Sgt. Q
Sign below to join Officer Romita's Raiders!
WOW, THAT'S--WAIT, WHAT DO YOU WANT?
NOTHING, I JUST THOUGHT I'D BE NICE AND I HAD A COUPON AND--
PETER.
LOOK, I TOLD YOU WE'D GET LUNCH TOGETHER, AND I LEFT YOU HANGING, RIGHT?
SO I BROUGHT YOU LUNCH.
WE CAN EAT IT TOGETHER.
I MEAN, I OWE YOU LUNCH, OKAY? I TOLD YOU I'D TAKE YOU TO LUNCH THEN I RAN OUT ON YOU SO I OWE YOU LUNCH... AND I HAD THAT COUPON AND--
LISTEN, IT CAN JUST BE LUNCH.
HMPH.

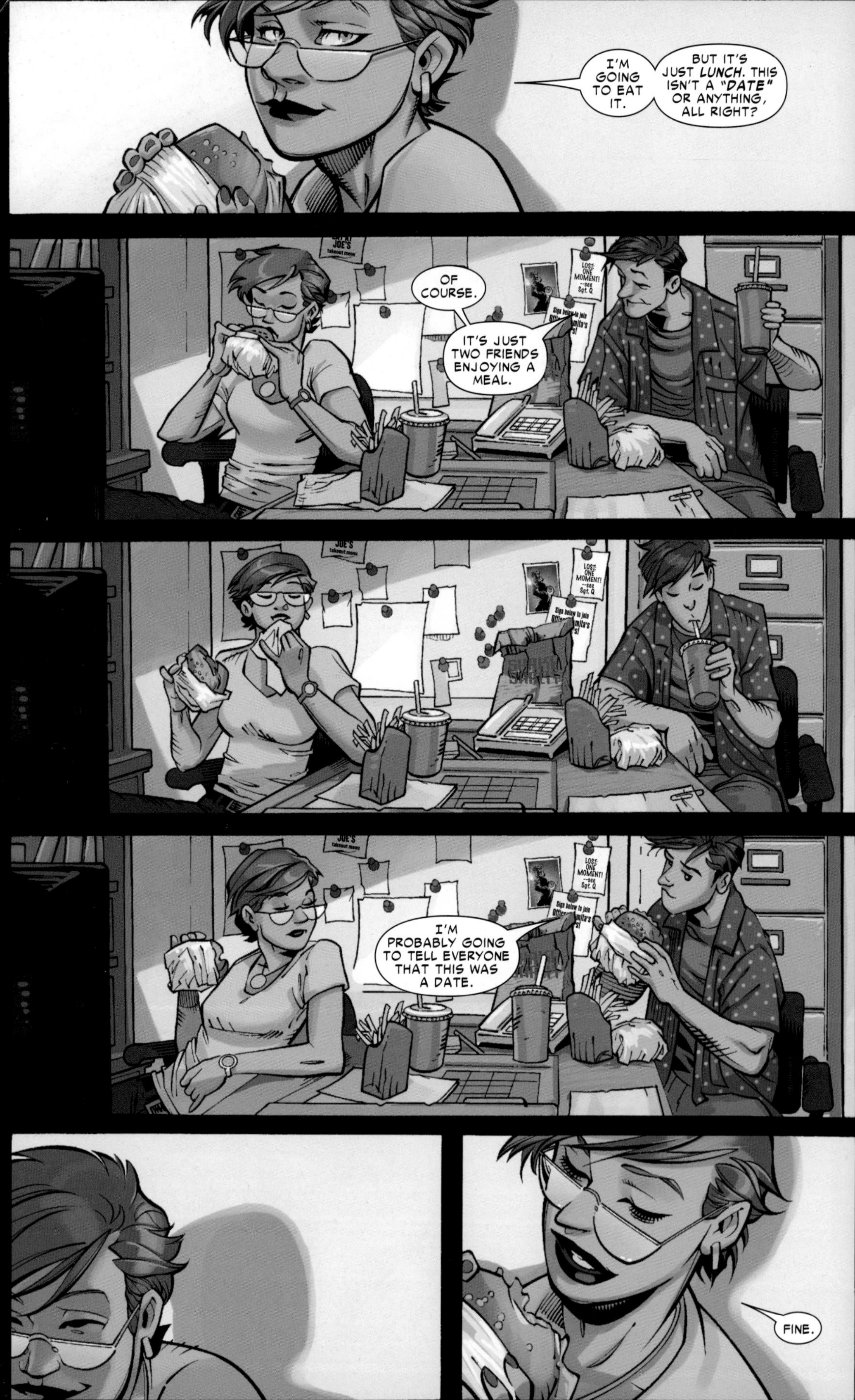
I'M GOING TO EAT IT.
BUT IT'S JUST LUNCH. THIS ISN'T A "DATE" OR ANYTHING, ALL RIGHT?
JOE'S takeout menu
LOST: ONE MOMENT! --see Sgt. Q
OF COURSE.
IT'S JUST TWO FRIENDS ENJOYING A MEAL.
I'M PROBABLY GOING TO TELL EVERYONE THAT THIS WAS A DATE.
FINE.

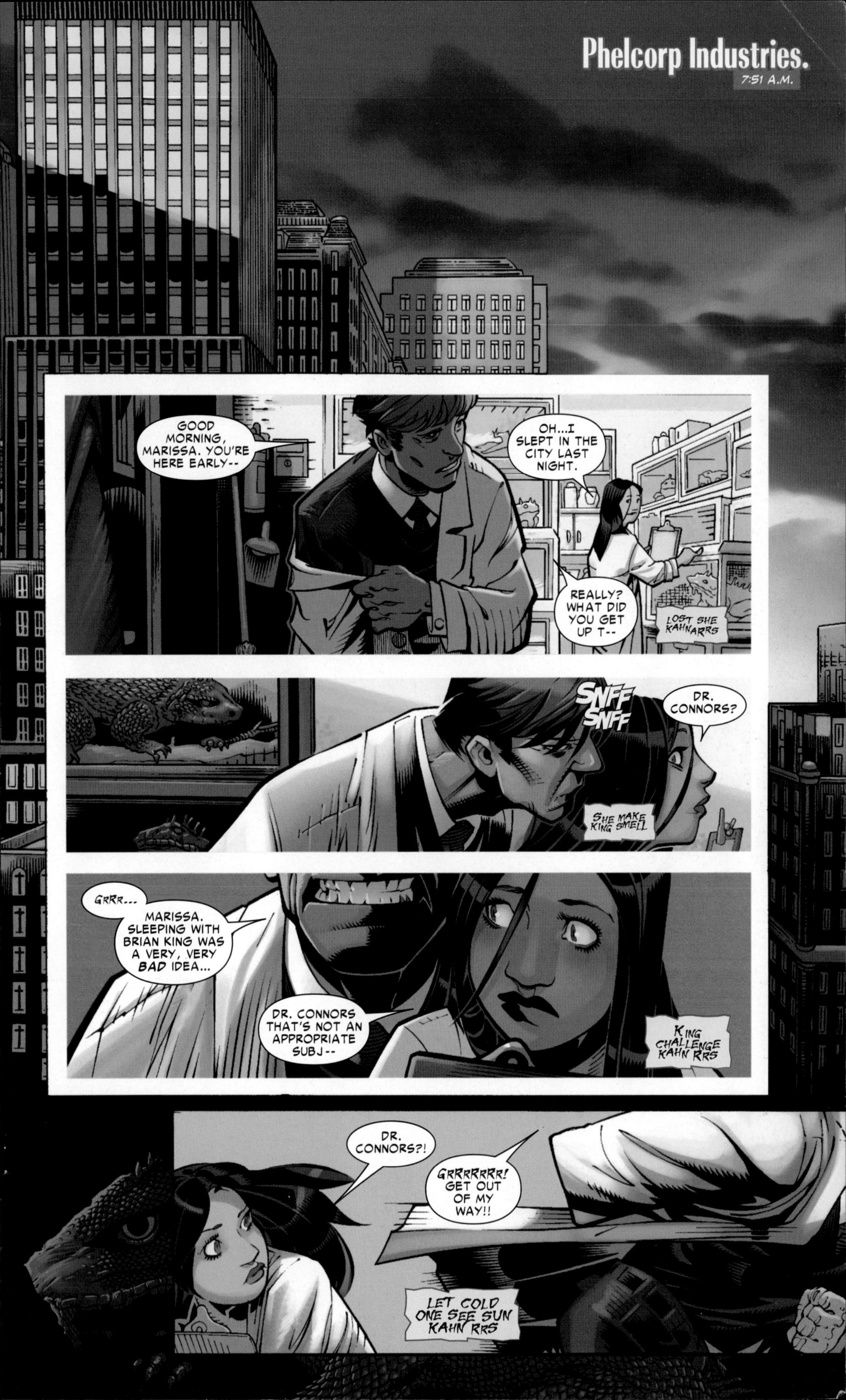
Phelcorp Industries.
7:51 A.M.
GOOD MORNING, MARISSA. YOU'RE HERE EARLY--
OH...I SLEPT IN THE CITY LAST NIGHT.
REALLY? WHAT DID YOU GET UP T--
LOST SHE KAHNARRS
SNFF SNFF
DR. CONNORS?
SHE MAKE KING SMELL
GRRR...
MARISSA. SLEEPING WITH BRIAN KING WAS A VERY, VERY BAD IDEA...
DR. CONNORS THAT'S NOT AN APPROPRIATE SUBJ--
KING CHALLENGE KAHN RRS
DR. CONNORS?!
GRRRRRRR! GET OUT OF MY WAY!!
LET COLD ONE SEE SUN KAHN RRS

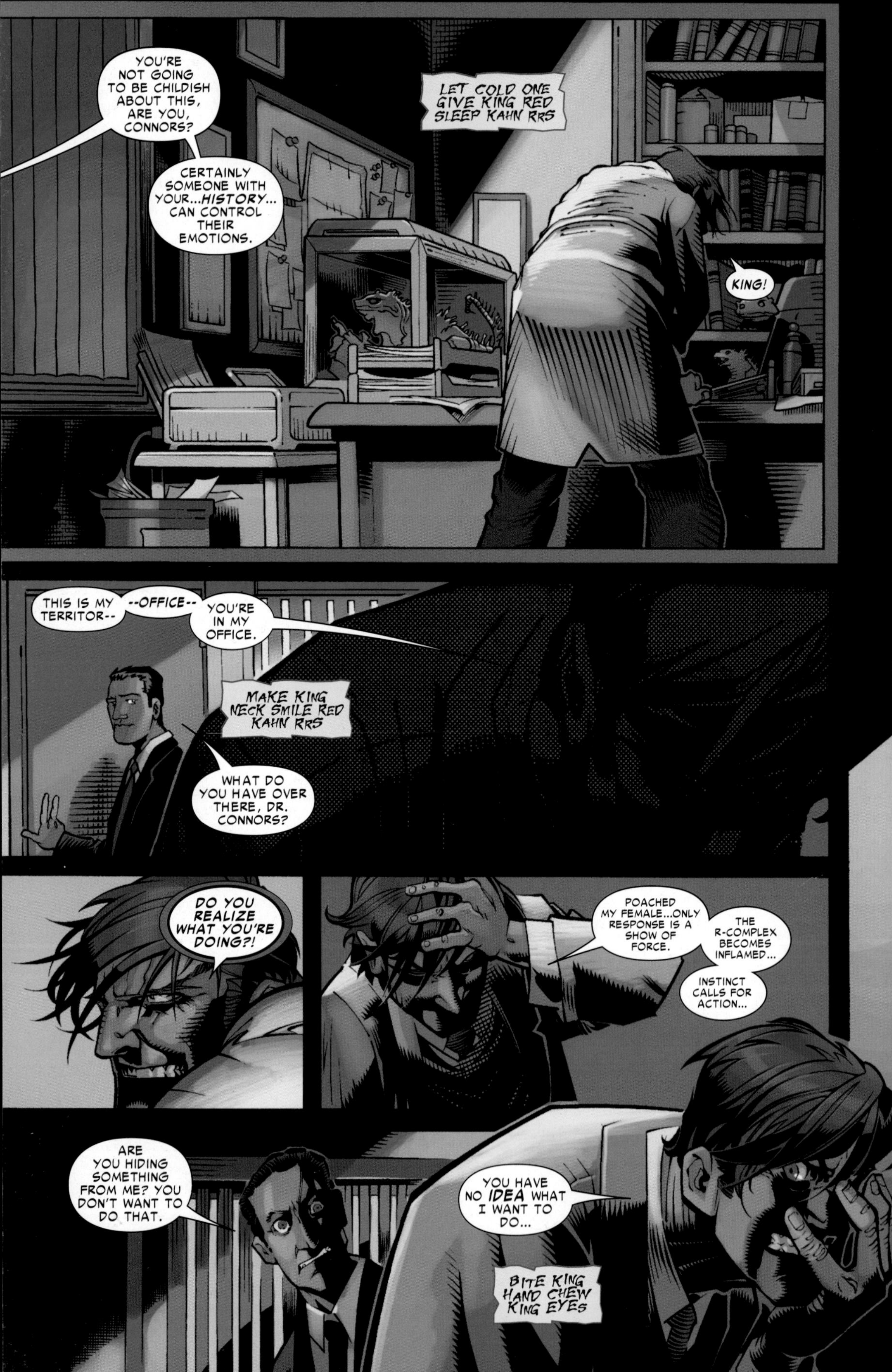
YOU'RE NOT GOING TO BE CHILDISH ABOUT THIS, ARE YOU, CONNORS?
CERTAINLY SOMEONE WITH YOUR...HISTORY... CAN CONTROL THEIR EMOTIONS.
LET COLD ONE GIVE KING RED SLEEP KAHN RRS
KING!
THIS IS MY TERRITOR--
--OFFICE--
YOU'RE IN MY OFFICE.
MAKE KING NECK SMILE RED KAHN RRS
WHAT DO YOU HAVE OVER THERE, DR. CONNORS?
DO YOU REALIZE WHAT YOU'RE DOING?!
POACHED MY FEMALE...ONLY RESPONSE IS A SHOW OF FORCE.
THE R-COMPLEX BECOMES INFLAMED...
INSTINCT CALLS FOR ACTION...
ARE YOU HIDING SOMETHING FROM ME? YOU DON'T WANT TO DO THAT.
YOU HAVE NO IDEA WHAT I WANT TO DO...
BITE KING HAND CHEW KING EYES

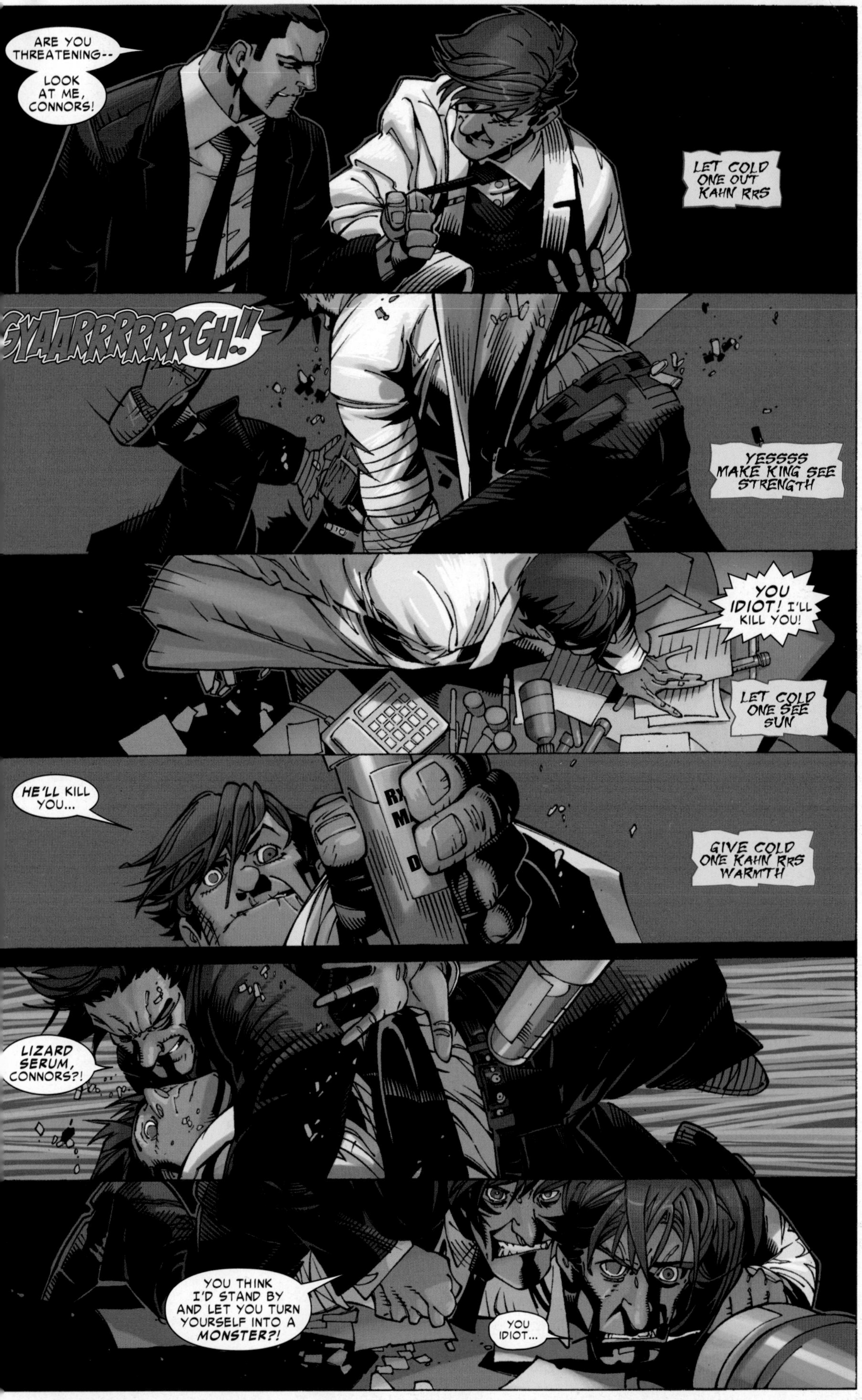
ARE YOU THREATENING--
LOOK AT ME, CONNORS!
LET COLD ONE OUT KAHN RRS
GYAARRRRRRGH!!
YESSSS MAKE KING SEE STRENGTH
YOU IDIOT! I'LL KILL YOU!
LET COLD ONE SEE SUN
HE'LL KILL YOU...
GIVE COLD ONE KAHN RRS WARMTH
LIZARD SERUM, CONNORS?!
YOU THINK I'D STAND BY AND LET YOU TURN YOURSELF INTO A MONSTER?!
YOU IDIOT...

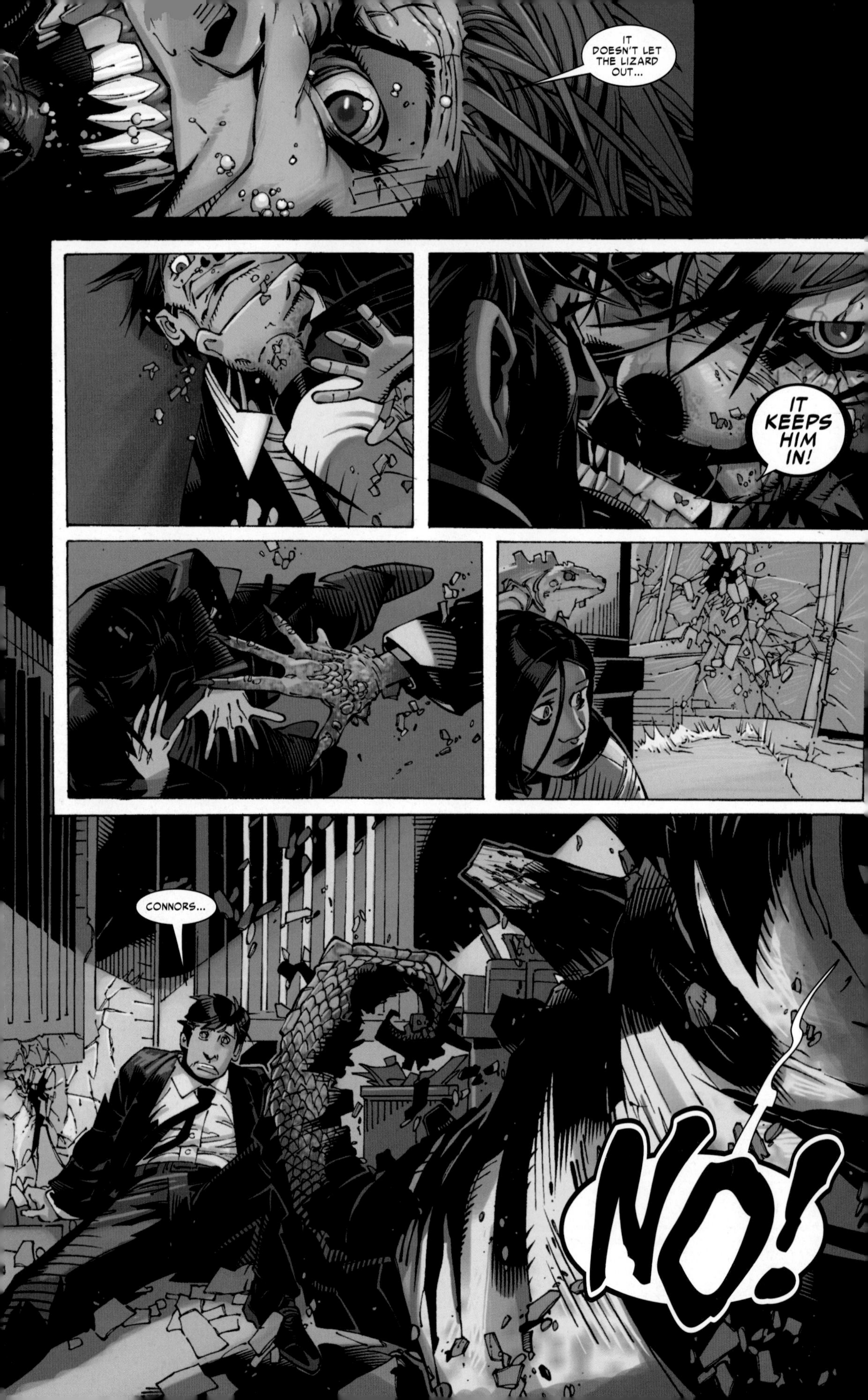
IT DOESN'T LET THE LIZARD OUT...
IT KEEPS HIM IN!
CONNORS...
NO!

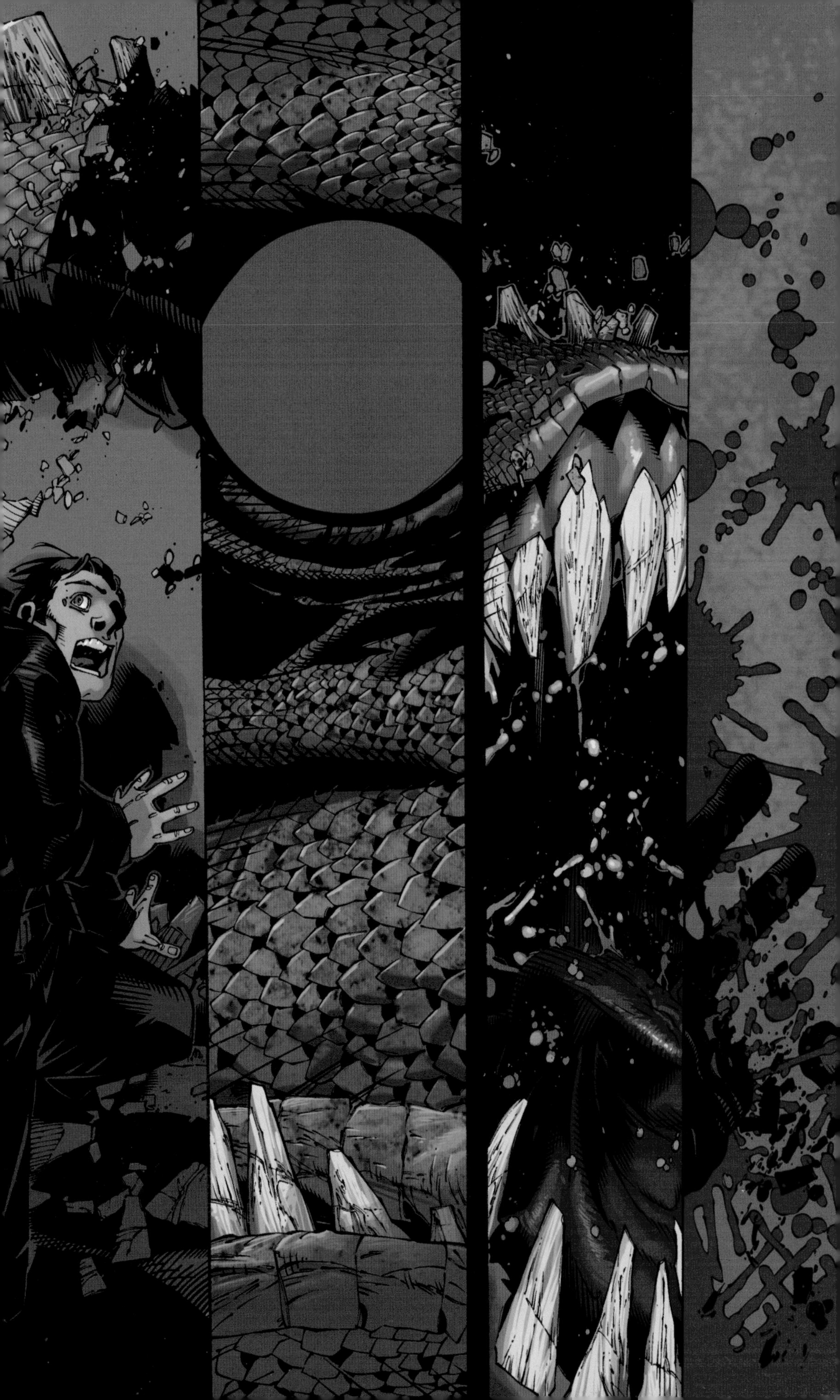

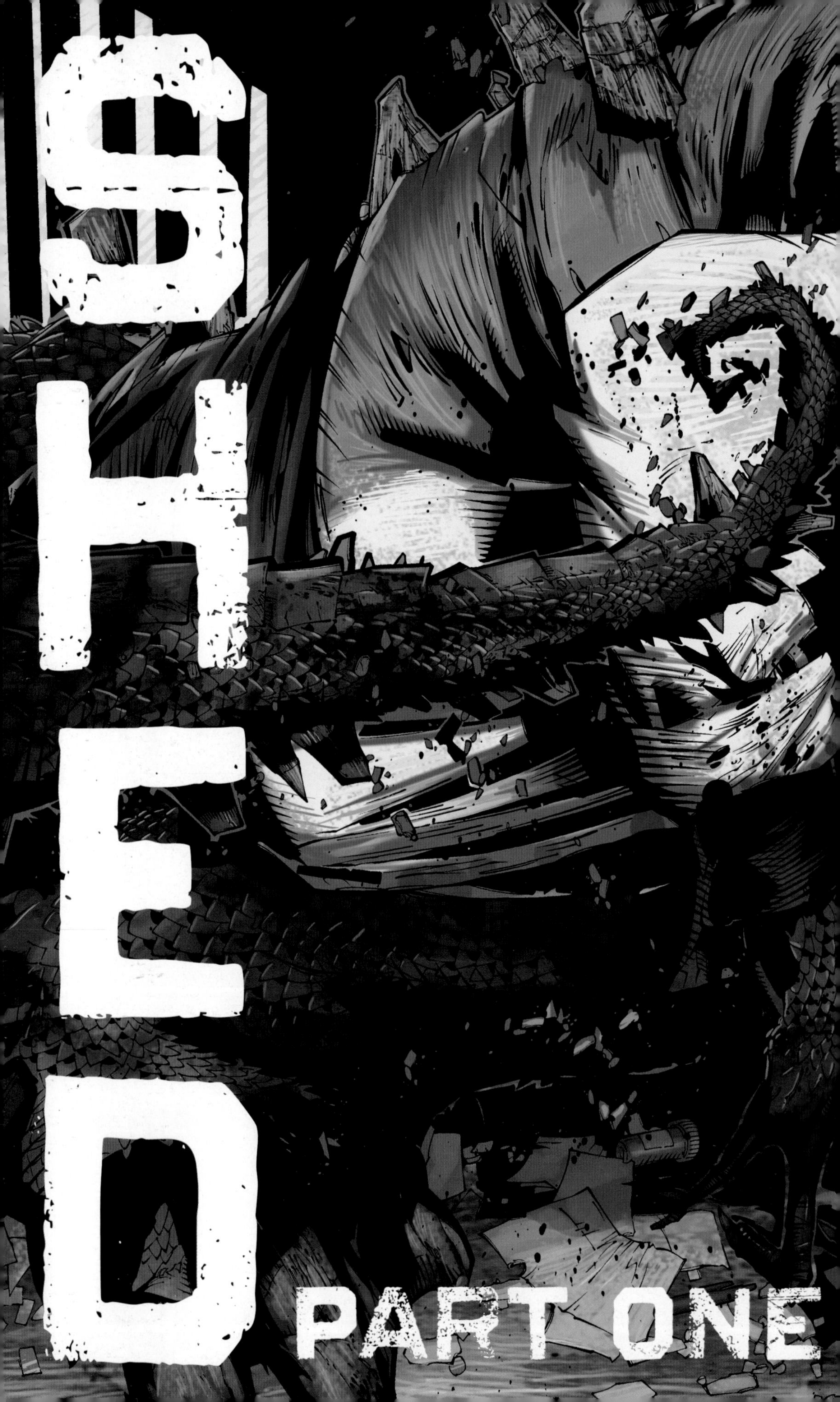
SHED
PART ONE

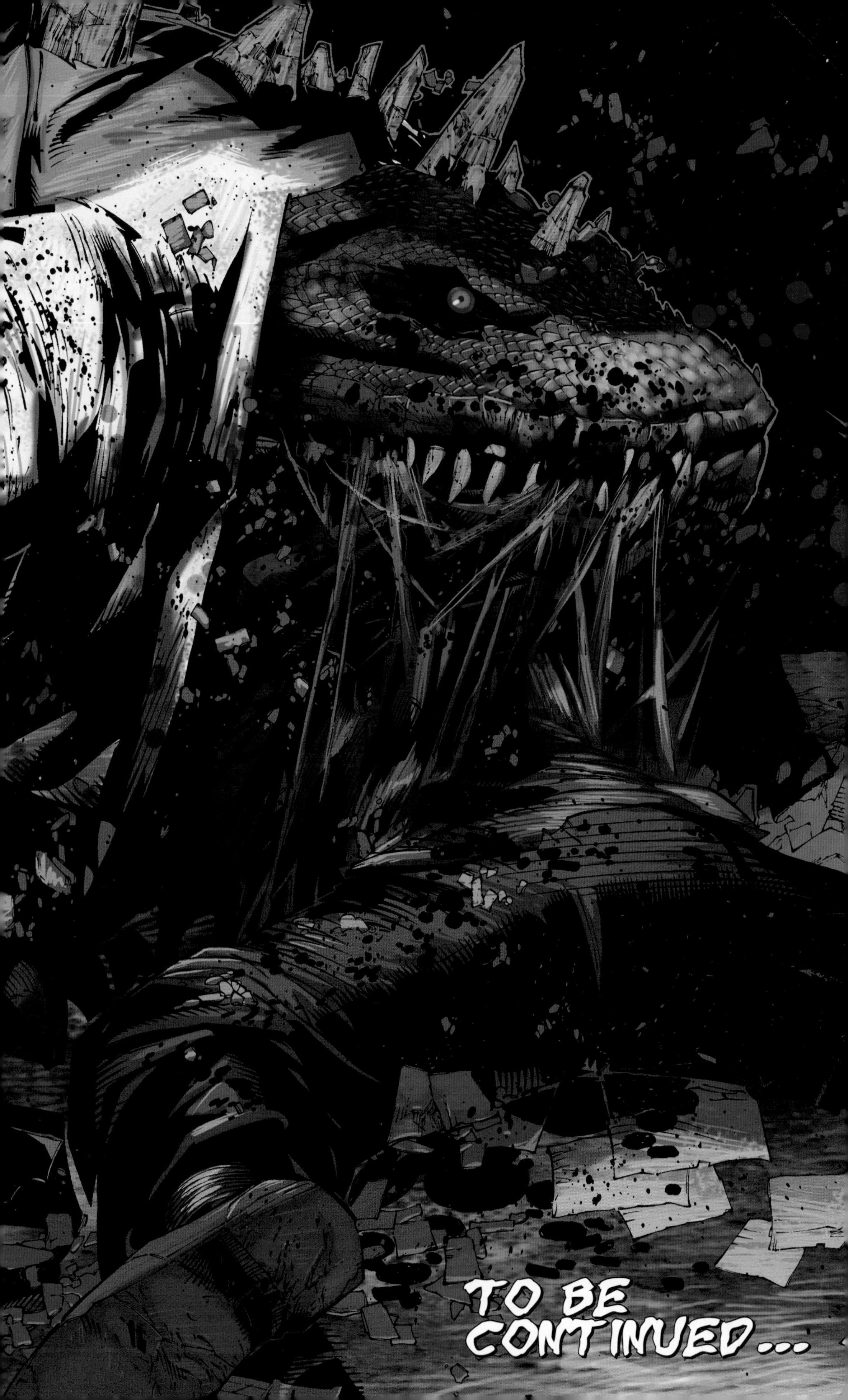
TO BE CONTINUED...

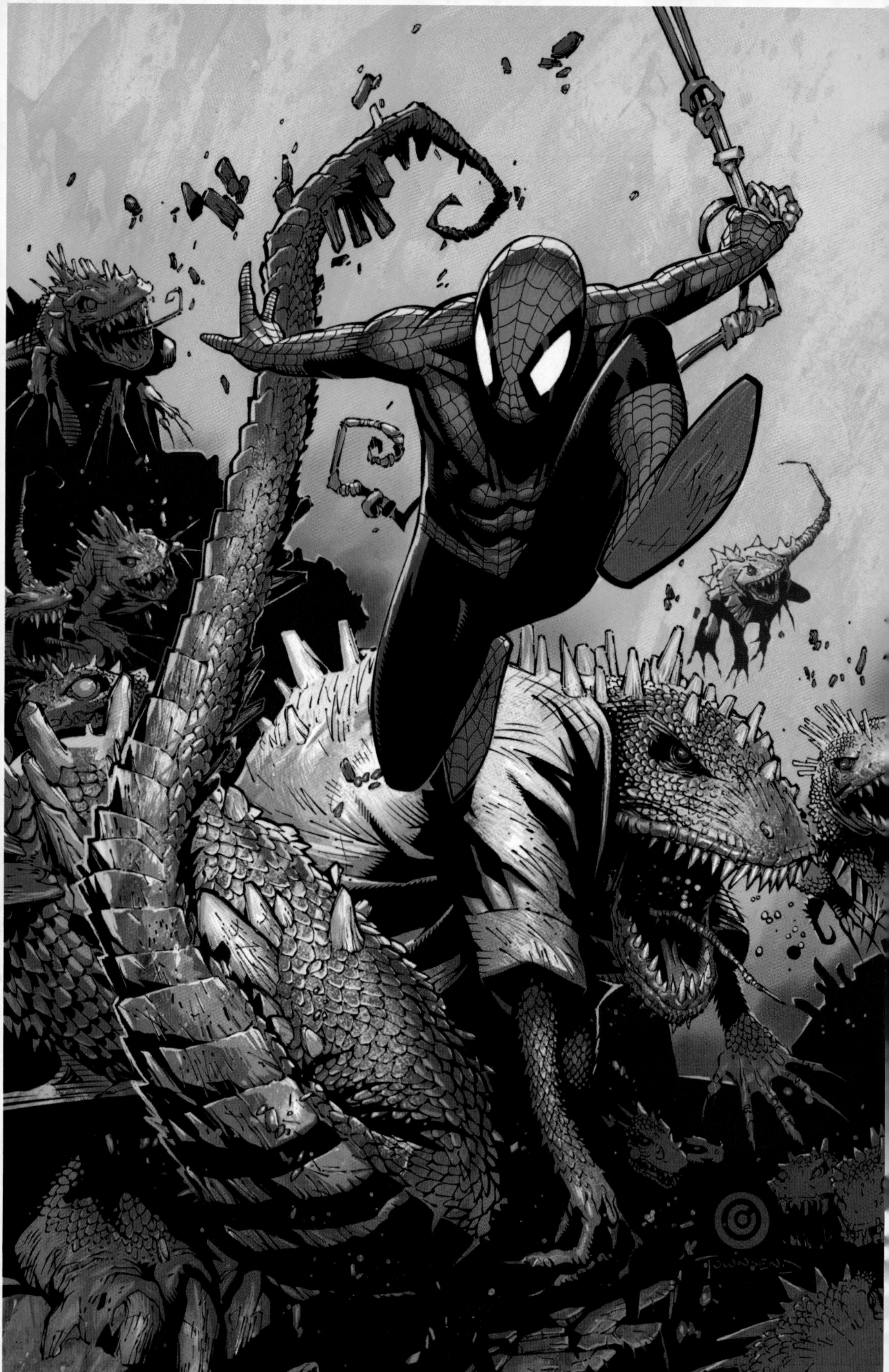

G SPIDER
Y CHRIS B

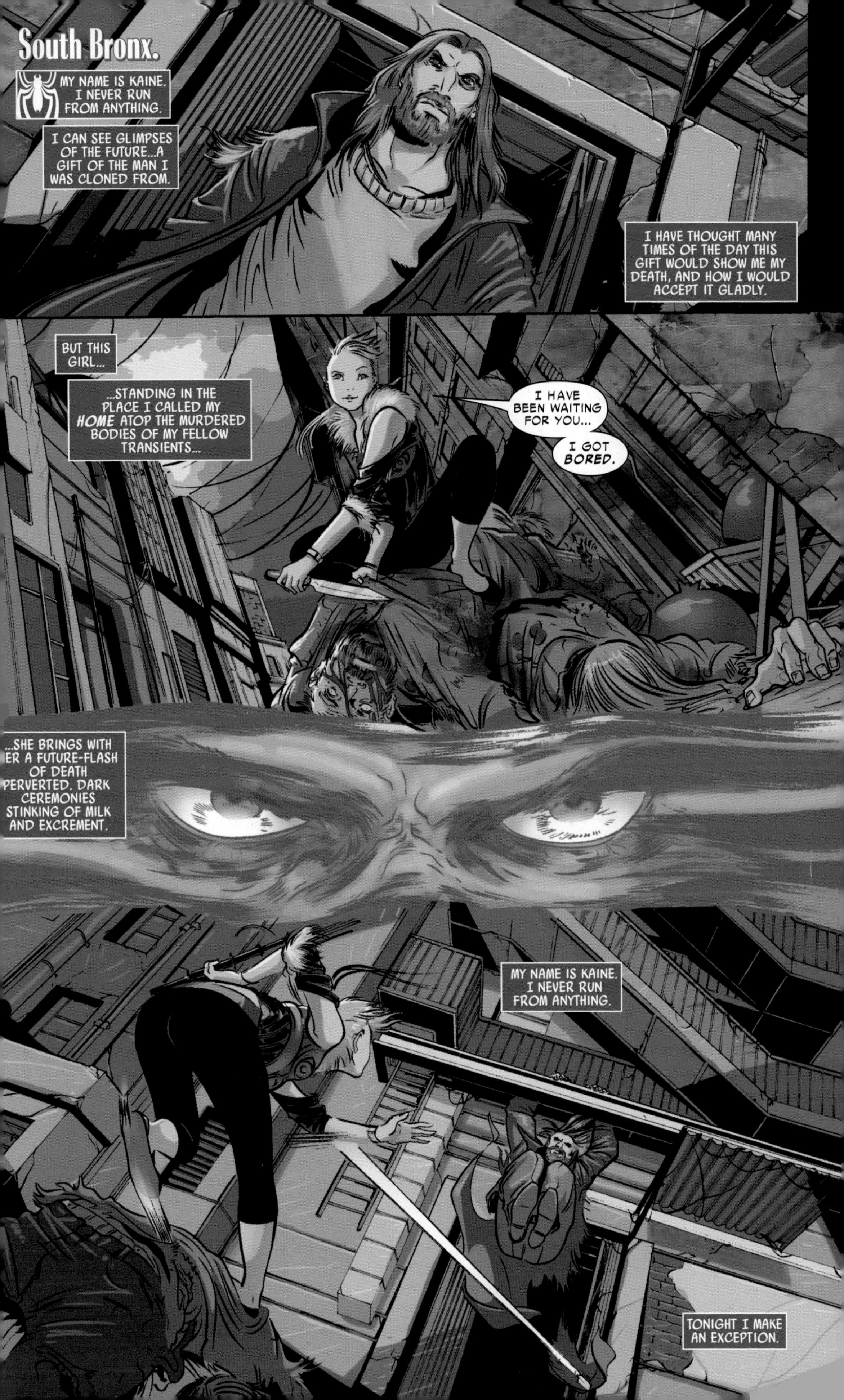
South Bronx.
MY NAME IS KAINE. I NEVER RUN FROM ANYTHING.
I CAN SEE GLIMPSES OF THE FUTURE...A GIFT OF THE MAN I WAS CLONED FROM.
I HAVE THOUGHT MANY TIMES OF THE DAY THIS GIFT WOULD SHOW ME MY DEATH, AND HOW I WOULD ACCEPT IT GLADLY.
BUT THIS GIRL...
...STANDING IN THE PLACE I CALLED MY HOME ATOP THE MURDERED BODIES OF MY FELLOW TRANSIENTS...
I HAVE BEEN WAITING FOR YOU...
I GOT BORED.
...SHE BRINGS WITH ER A FUTURE-FLASH OF DEATH PERVERTED. DARK CEREMONIES STINKING OF MILK AND EXCREMENT.
MY NAME IS KAINE. I NEVER RUN FROM ANYTHING.
TONIGHT I MAKE AN EXCEPTION.

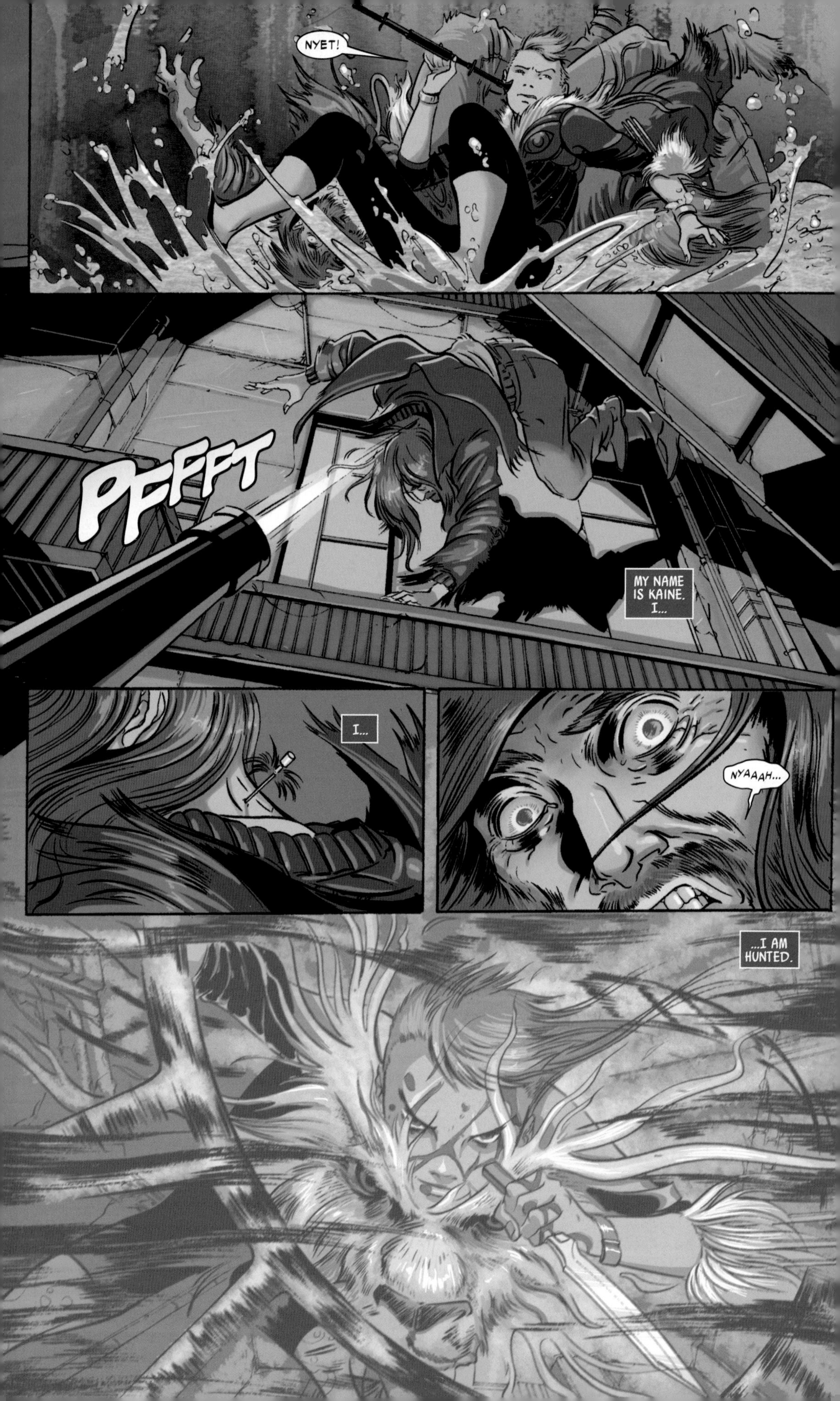
NYET!
PFFFT
MY NAME IS KAINE. I...
I...
NYAAAH...
...I AM HUNTED.

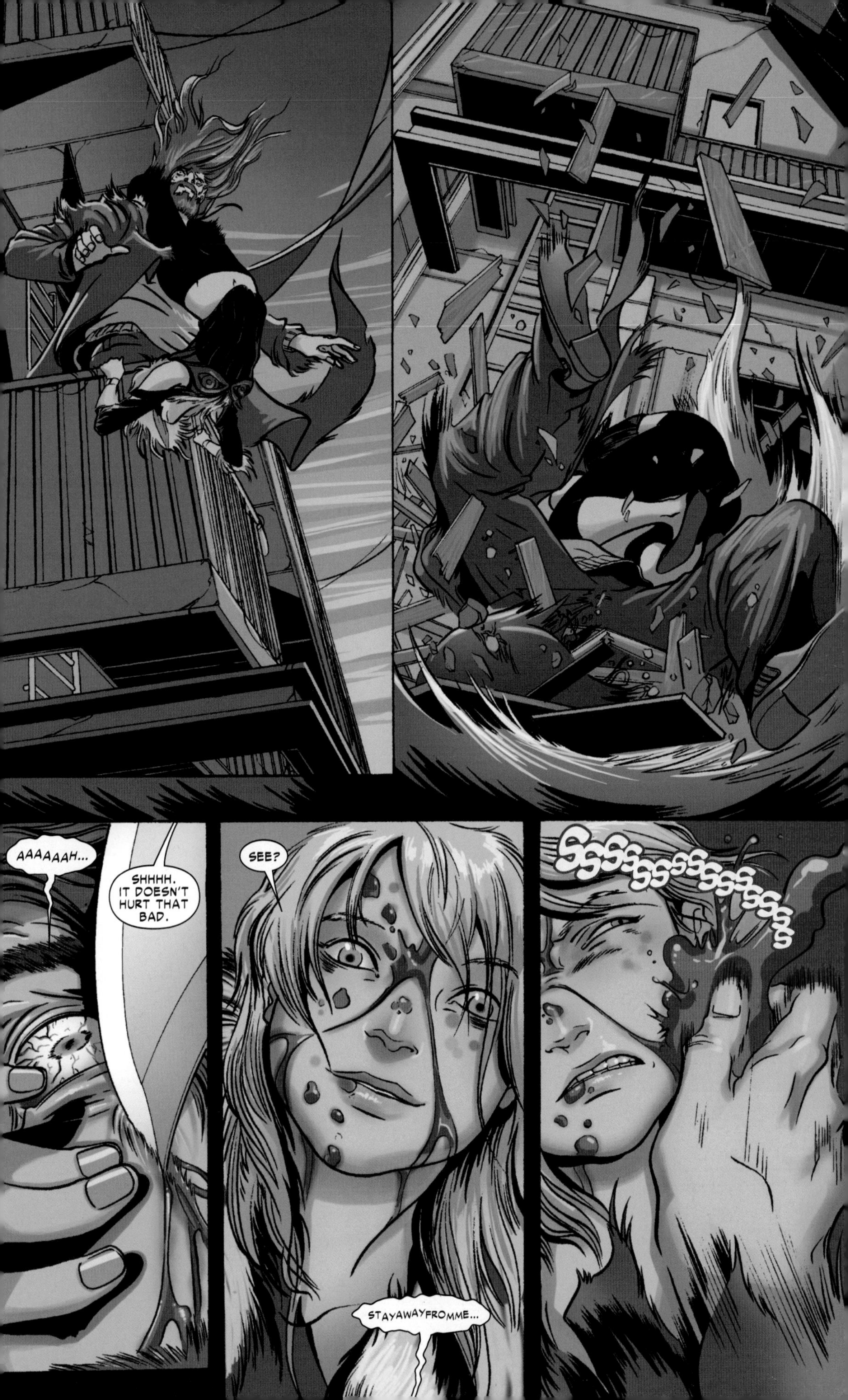
AAAAAAH...
SHHHH. IT DOESN'T HURT THAT BAD.
SEE?
STAYAWAYFROMME...
SSSSSSSSSSSSSSSS

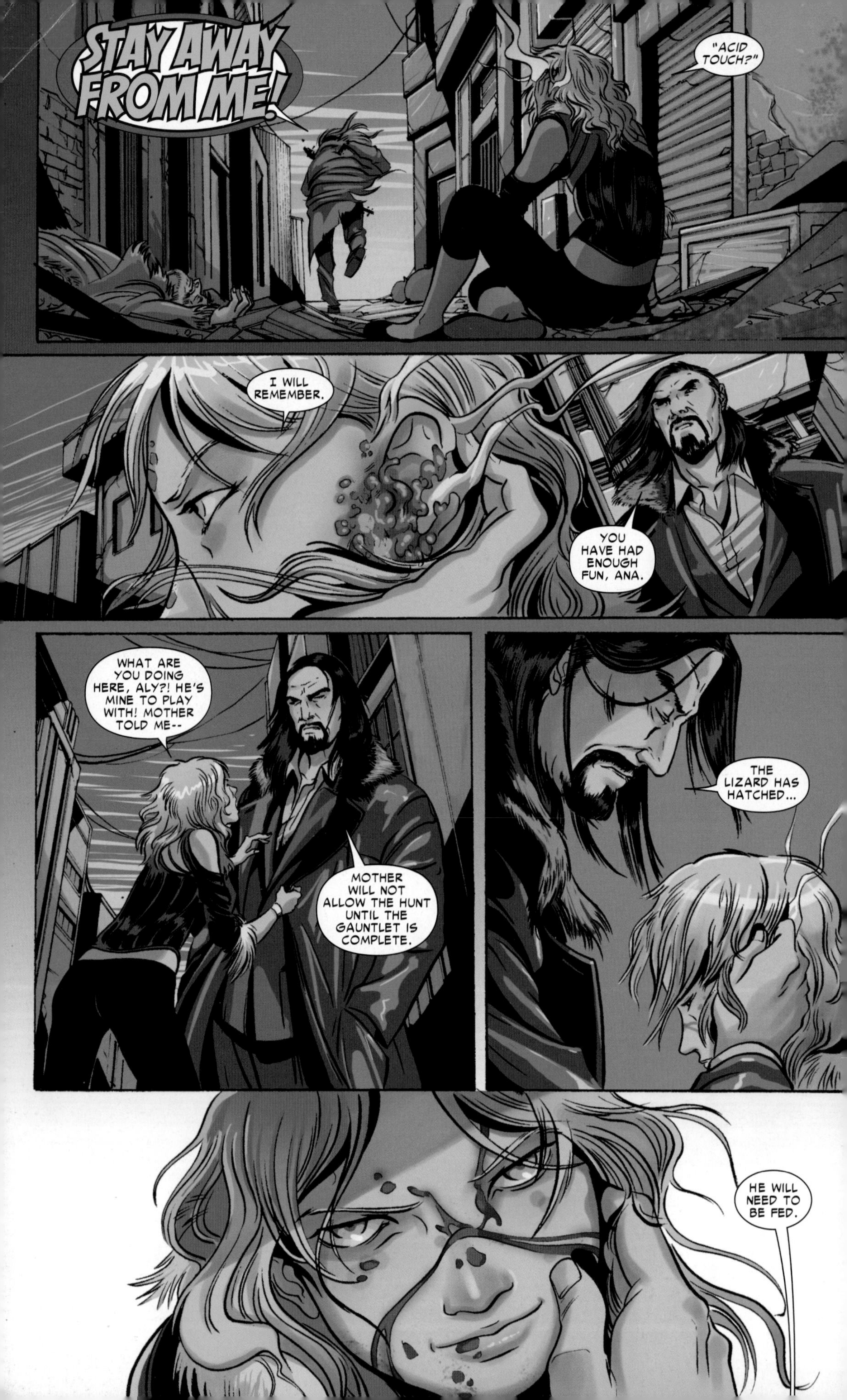
STAY AWAY FROM ME!
"ACID TOUCH?"
I WILL REMEMBER.
YOU HAVE HAD ENOUGH FUN, ANA.
WHAT ARE YOU DOING HERE, ALY?! HE'S MINE TO PLAY WITH! MOTHER TOLD ME--
MOTHER WILL NOT ALLOW THE HUNT UNTIL THE GAUNTLET IS COMPLETE.
THE LIZARD HAS HATCHED...
HE WILL NEED TO BE FED.

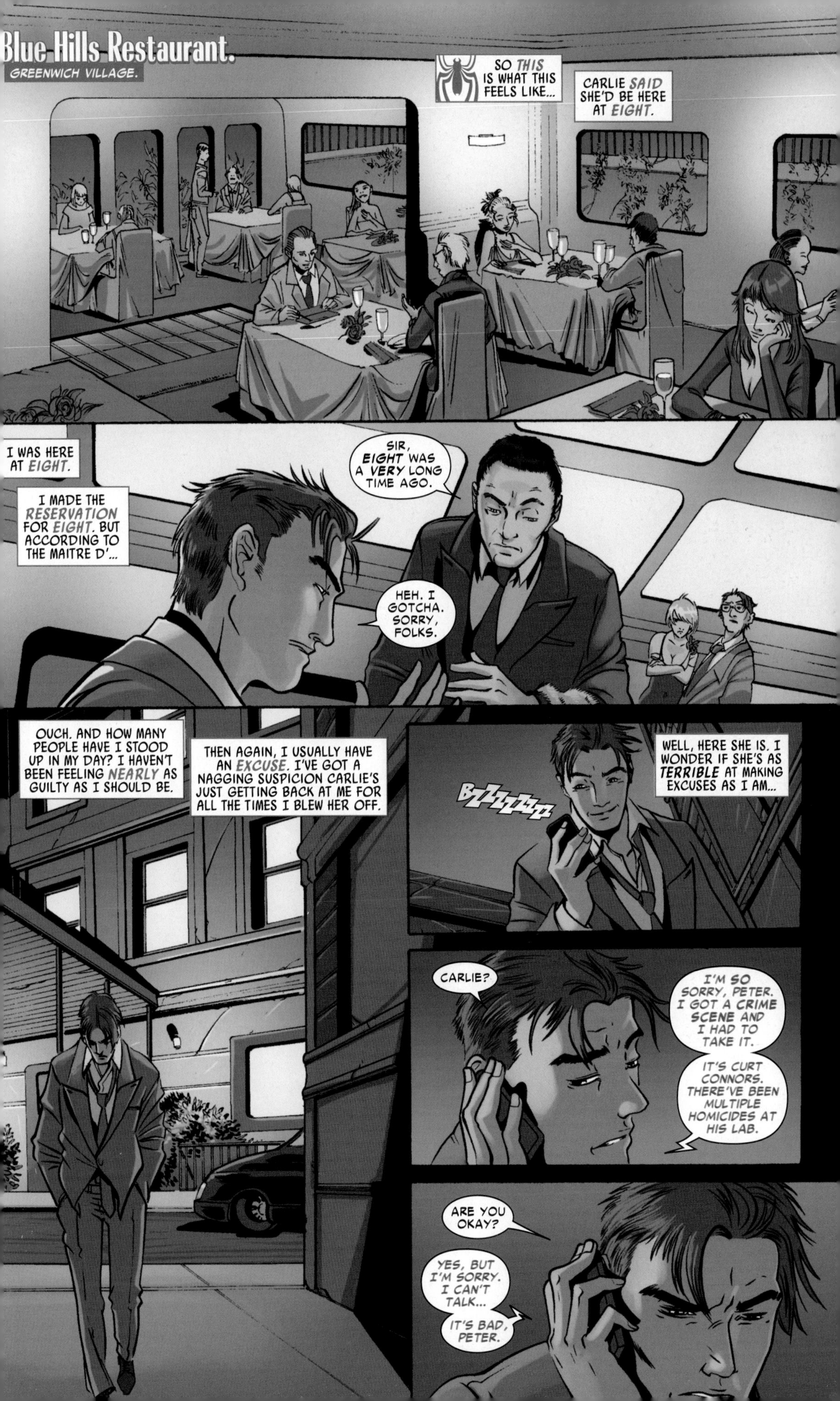
Blue Hills Restaurant.
GREENWICH VILLAGE.
SO THIS IS WHAT THIS FEELS LIKE...
CARLIE SAID SHE'D BE HERE AT EIGHT.
I WAS HERE AT EIGHT.
I MADE THE RESERVATION FOR EIGHT. BUT ACCORDING TO THE MAITRE D'...
SIR, EIGHT WAS A VERY LONG TIME AGO.
HEH. I GOTCHA. SORRY, FOLKS.
OUCH. AND HOW MANY PEOPLE HAVE I STOOD UP IN MY DAY? I HAVEN'T BEEN FEELING NEARLY AS GUILTY AS I SHOULD BE.
THEN AGAIN, I USUALLY HAVE AN EXCUSE. I'VE GOT A NAGGING SUSPICION CARLIE'S JUST GETTING BACK AT ME FOR ALL THE TIMES I BLEW HER OFF.
BZZZZZZZ
WELL, HERE SHE IS. I WONDER IF SHE'S AS TERRIBLE AT MAKING EXCUSES AS I AM...
CARLIE?
I'M SO SORRY, PETER. I GOT A CRIME SCENE AND I HAD TO TAKE IT.
IT'S CURT CONNORS. THERE'VE BEEN MULTIPLE HOMICIDES AT HIS LAB.
ARE YOU OKAY?
YES, BUT I'M SORRY. I CAN'T TALK...
IT'S BAD, PETER.

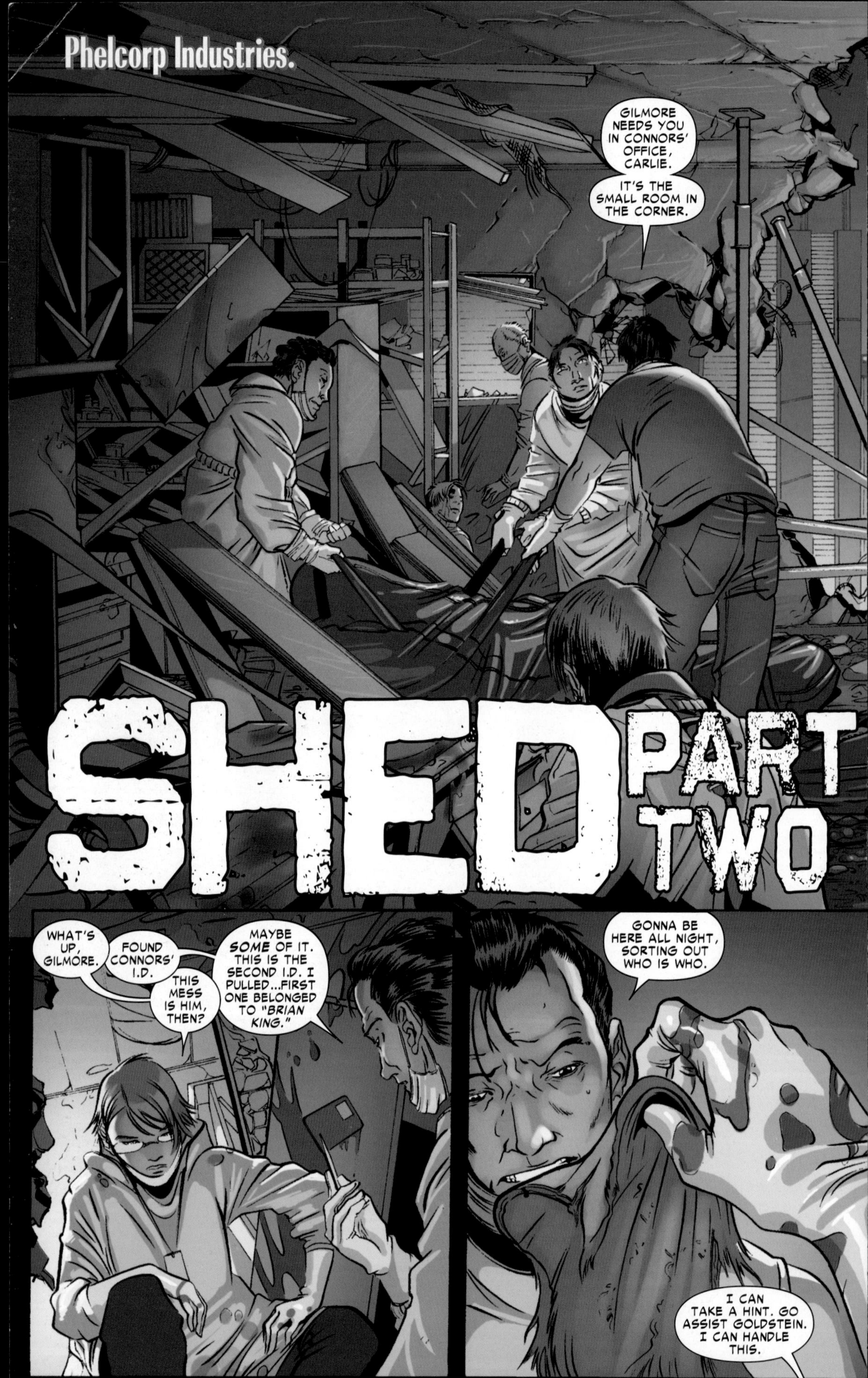
Phelcorp Industries.
GILMORE NEEDS YOU IN CONNORS' OFFICE, CARLIE.
IT'S THE SMALL ROOM IN THE CORNER.
SHED PART TWO
WHAT'S UP, GILMORE.
FOUND CONNORS' I.D.
THIS MESS IS HIM, THEN?
MAYBE *SOME* OF IT. THIS IS THE SECOND I.D. I PULLED...FIRST ONE BELONGED TO "*BRIAN KING.*"
GONNA BE HERE ALL NIGHT, SORTING OUT WHO IS WHO.
I CAN TAKE A HINT. GO ASSIST GOLDSTEIN. I CAN HANDLE THIS.

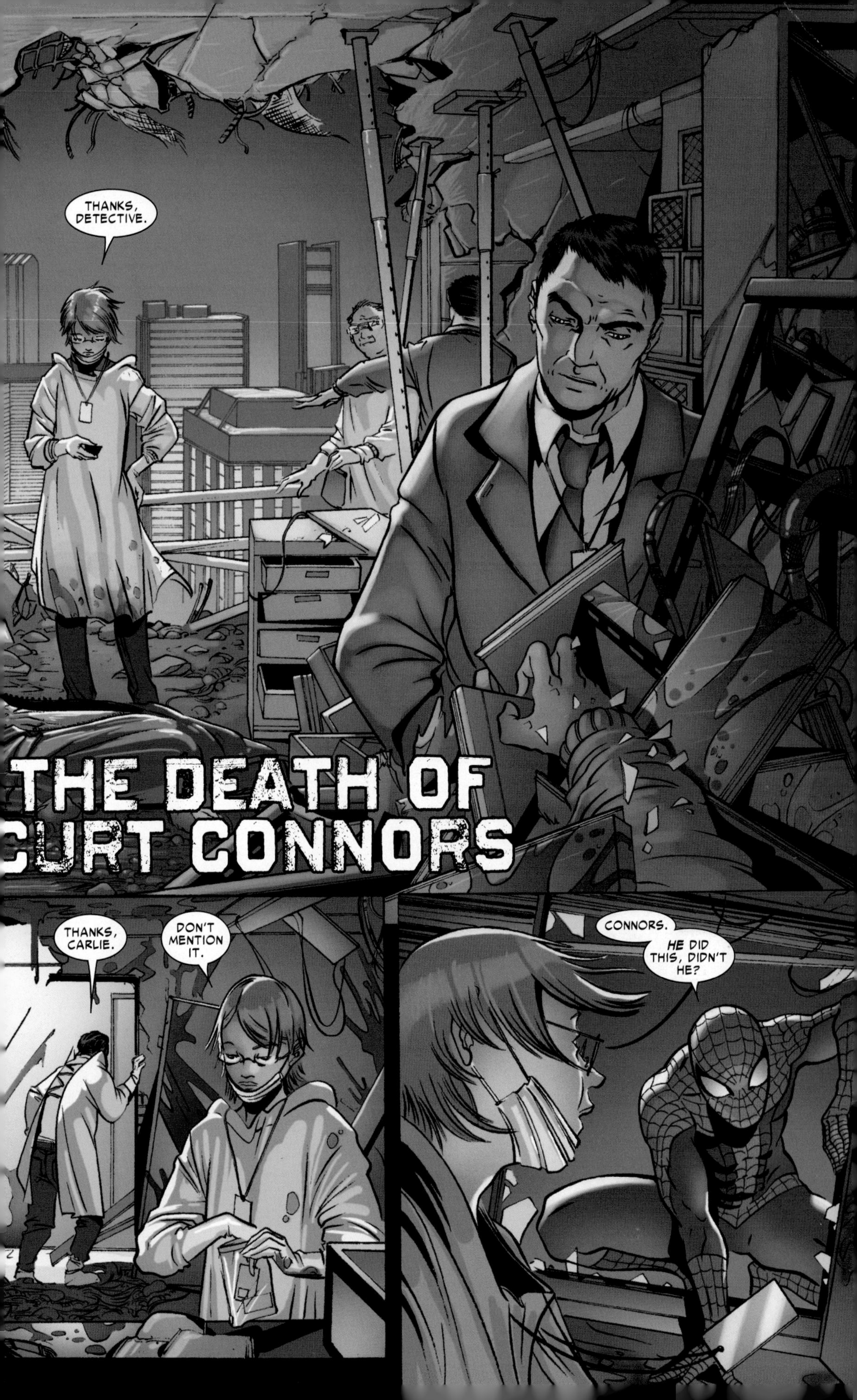
THANKS, DETECTIVE.
THE DEATH OF CURT CONNORS
THANKS, CARLIE.
DON'T MENTION IT.
CONNORS.
HE DID THIS, DIDN'T HE?

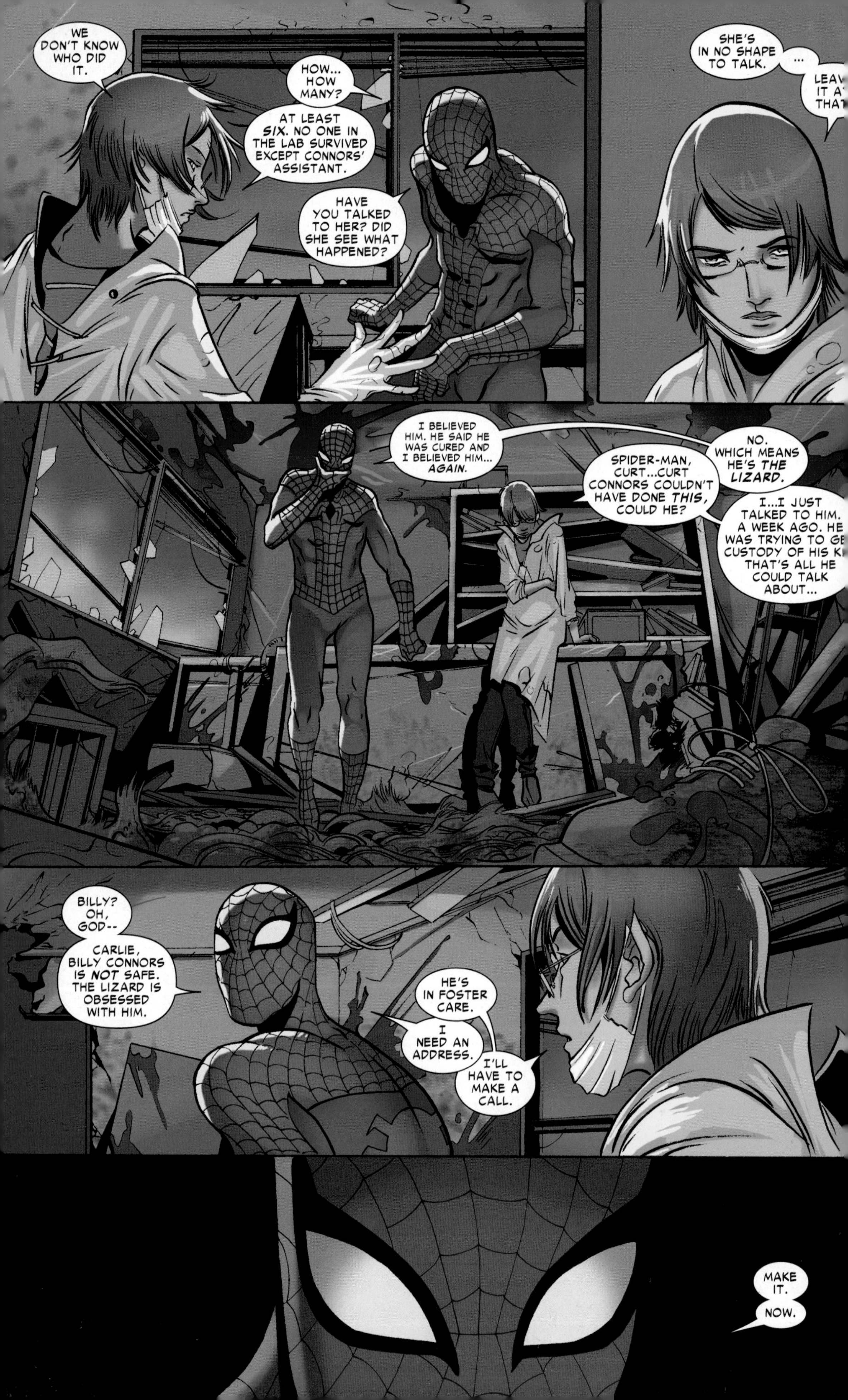

WE DON'T KNOW WHO DID IT.
HOW... HOW MANY?
AT LEAST SIX. NO ONE IN THE LAB SURVIVED EXCEPT CONNORS' ASSISTANT.
HAVE YOU TALKED TO HER? DID SHE SEE WHAT HAPPENED?
SHE'S IN NO SHAPE TO TALK.
...
LEAV IT A THA
SPIDER-MAN, CURT...CURT CONNORS COULDN'T HAVE DONE THIS, COULD HE?
NO. WHICH MEANS HE'S THE LIZARD.
I BELIEVED HIM. HE SAID HE WAS CURED AND I BELIEVED HIM... AGAIN.
I...I JUST TALKED TO HIM. A WEEK AGO. HE WAS TRYING TO GE CUSTODY OF HIS K THAT'S ALL HE COULD TALK ABOUT...
BILLY? OH, GOD--
CARLIE, BILLY CONNORS IS NOT SAFE. THE LIZARD IS OBSESSED WITH HIM.
HE'S IN FOSTER CARE.
I NEED AN ADDRESS.
I'LL HAVE TO MAKE A CALL.
MAKE IT.
NOW.

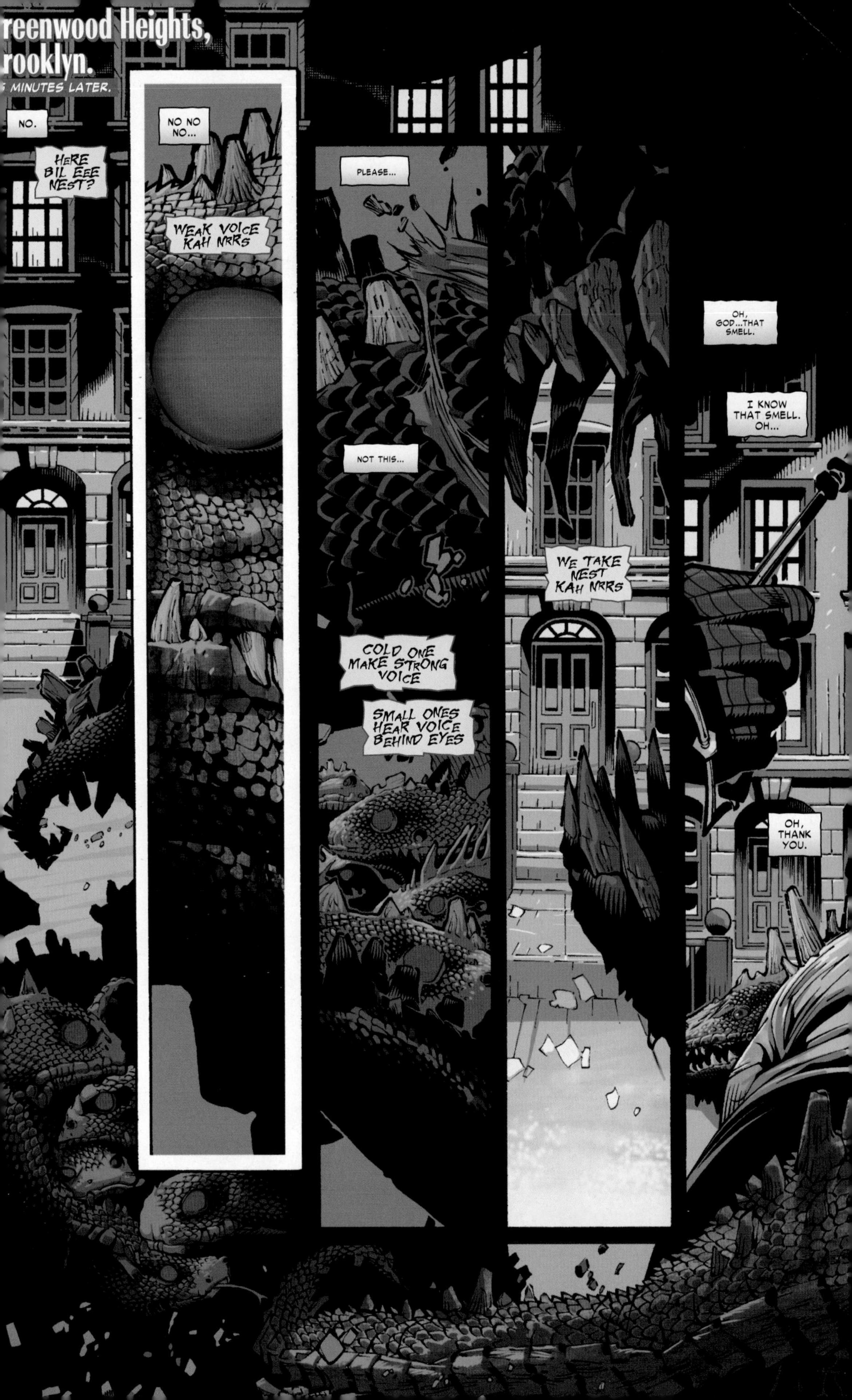
reenwood Heights,
rooklyn.
5 MINUTES LATER.
NO.
HERE BIL EEE NEST?
NO NO NO...
WEAK VOICE KAH NRRS
PLEASE...
NOT THIS...
COLD ONE MAKE STRONG VOICE
SMALL ONES HEAR VOICE BEHIND EYES
WE TAKE NEST KAH NRRS
OH, GOD...THAT SMELL.
I KNOW THAT SMELL. OH...
OH, THANK YOU.

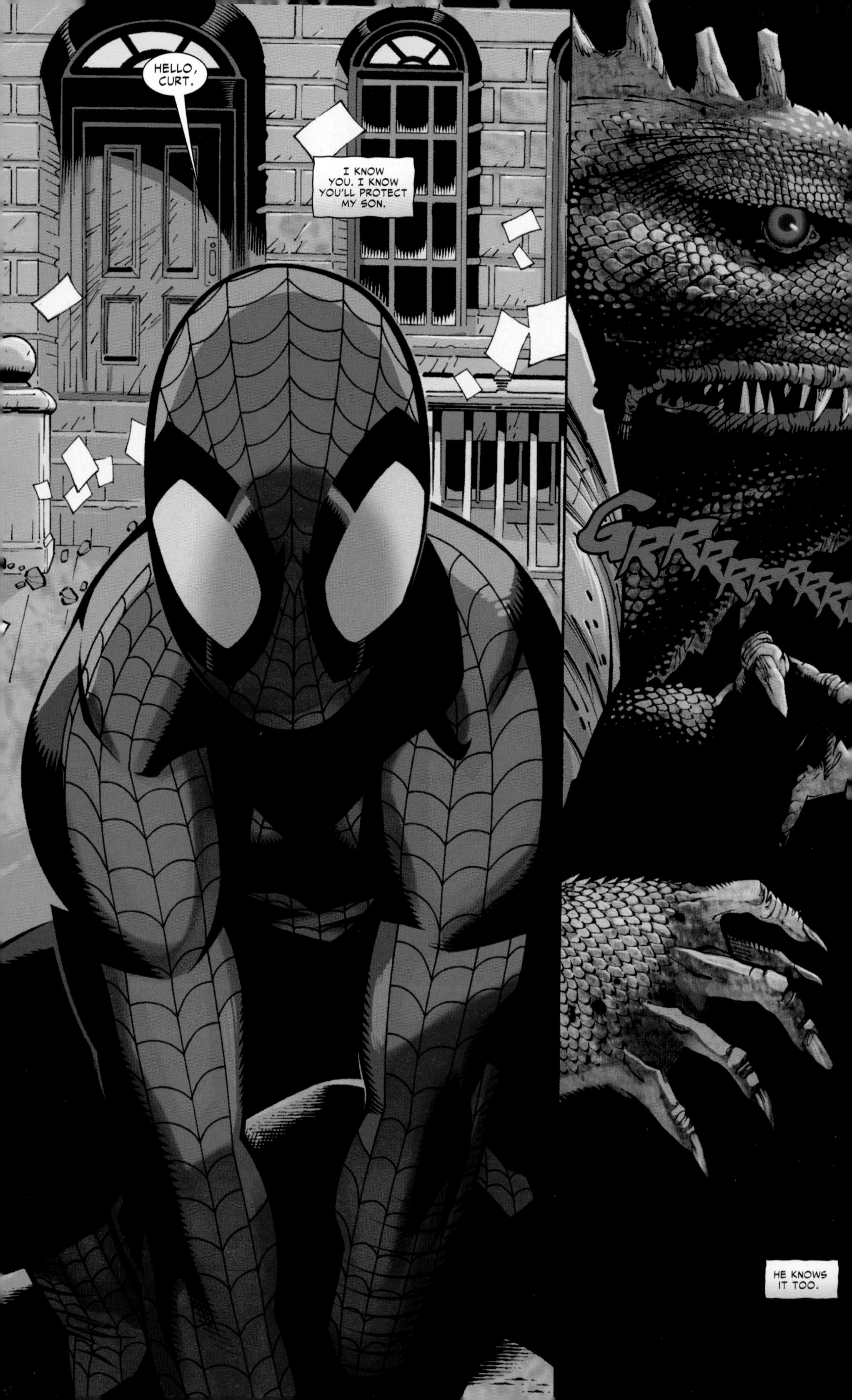
HELLO, CURT.
I KNOW YOU. I KNOW YOU'LL PROTECT MY SON.
GRRRRRRRR
HE KNOWS IT TOO.

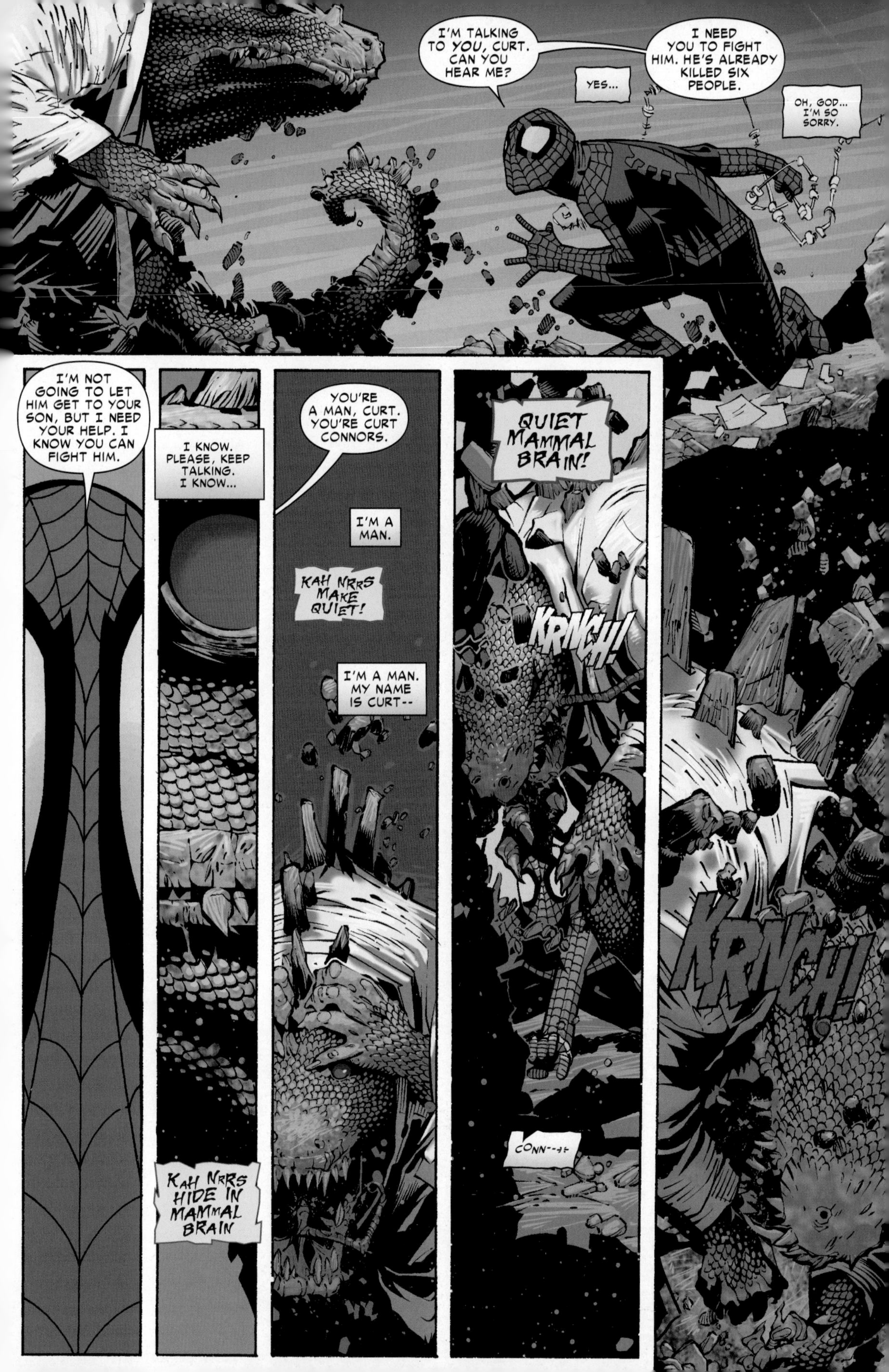
I'M TALKING TO YOU, CURT. CAN YOU HEAR ME?
YES...
I NEED YOU TO FIGHT HIM. HE'S ALREADY KILLED SIX PEOPLE.
OH, GOD... I'M SO SORRY.
I'M NOT GOING TO LET HIM GET TO YOUR SON, BUT I NEED YOUR HELP. I KNOW YOU CAN FIGHT HIM.
I KNOW. PLEASE, KEEP TALKING. I KNOW...
KAH NRRS HIDE IN MAMMAL BRAIN
YOU'RE A MAN, CURT. YOU'RE CURT CONNORS.
I'M A MAN.
KAH NRRS MAKE QUIET!
I'M A MAN. MY NAME IS CURT--
QUIET MAMMAL BRAIN!
KRNCH!
CONN--
KRNCH!

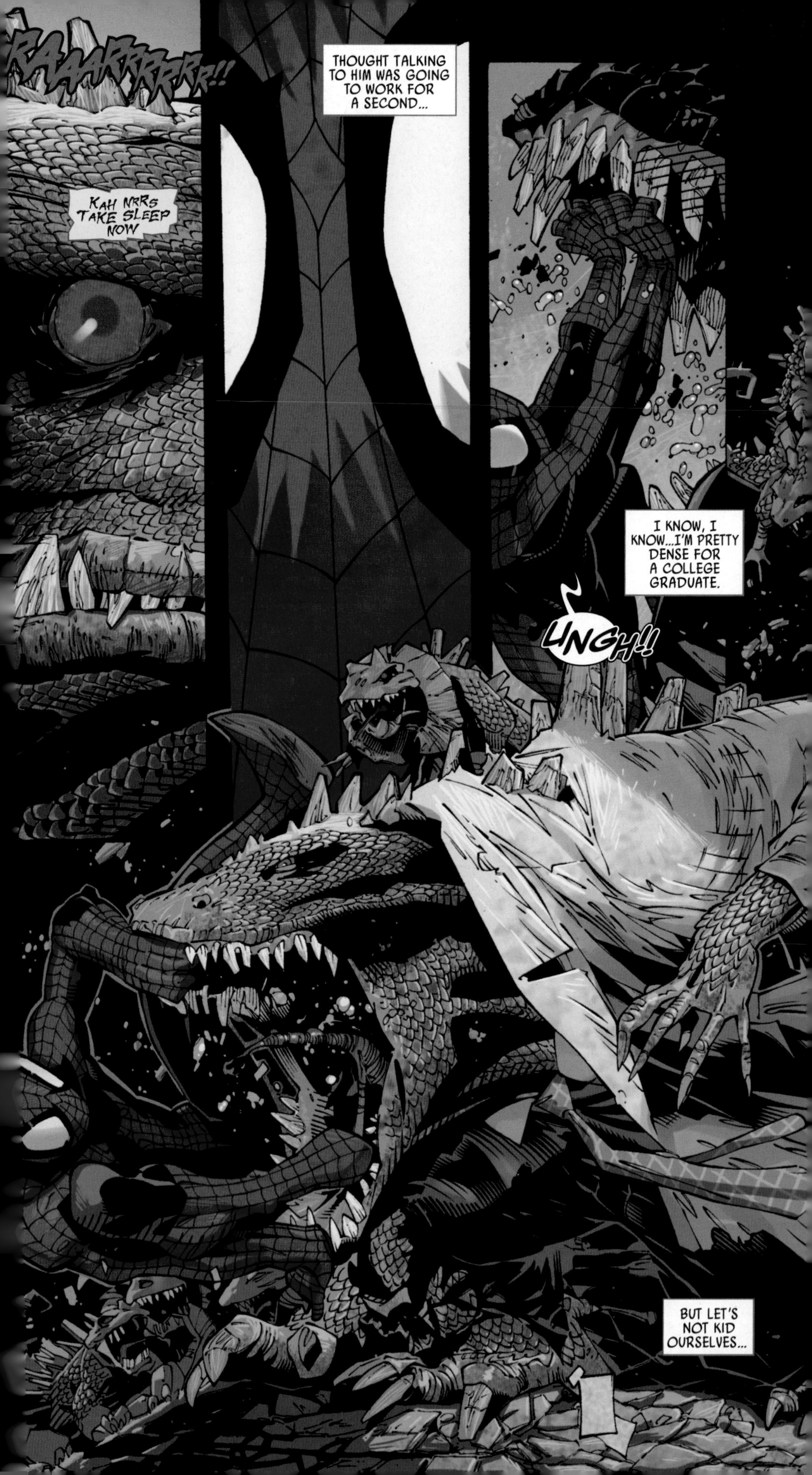
RAAARRRRRR!!
KAH NRRS TAKE SLEEP NOW
THOUGHT TALKING TO HIM WAS GOING TO WORK FOR A SECOND...
I KNOW, I KNOW...I'M PRETTY DENSE FOR A COLLEGE GRADUATE.
UNGH!!
BUT LET'S NOT KID OURSELVES...

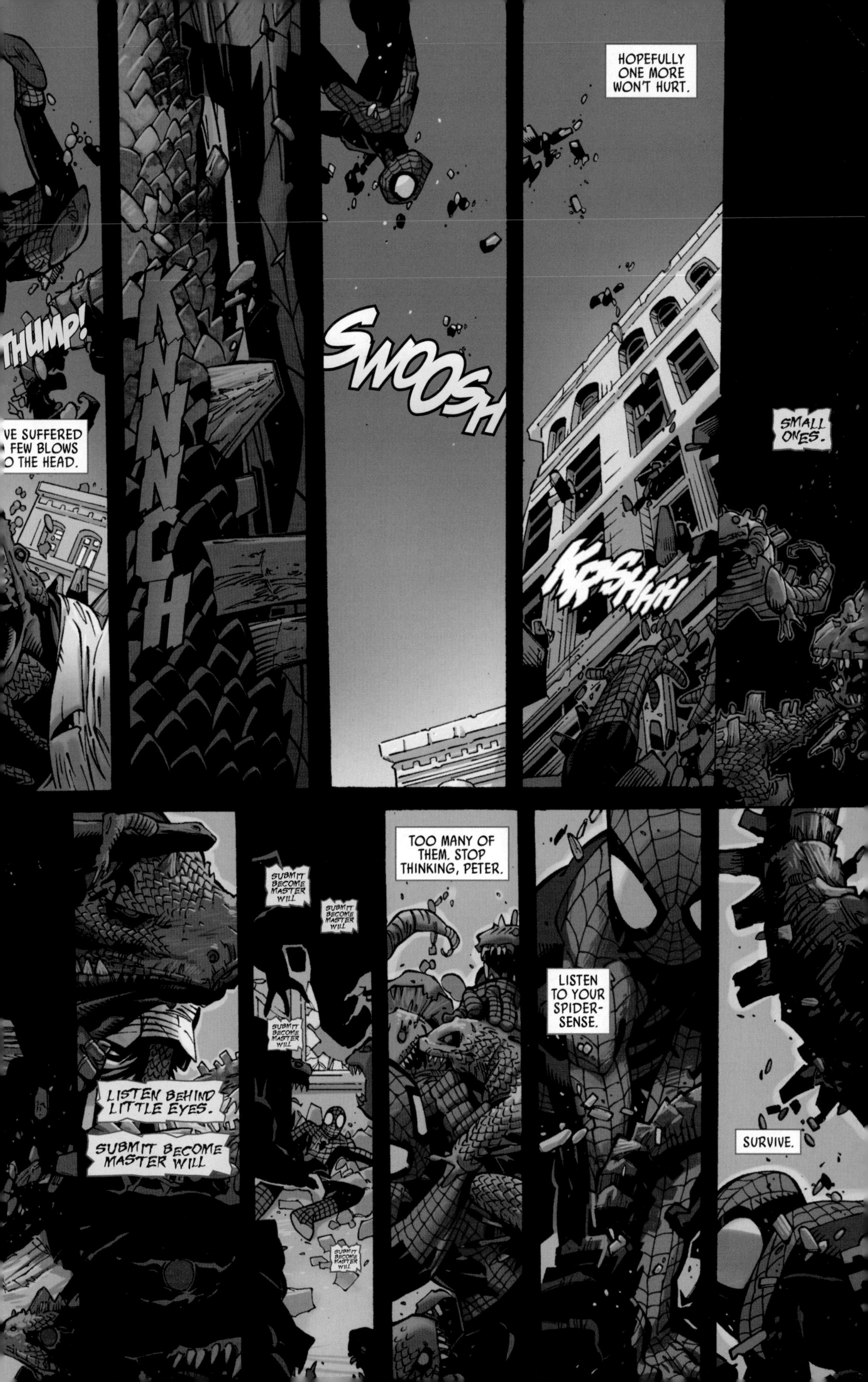
THUMP!
VE SUFFERED
FEW BLOWS
O THE HEAD.
KANNCH
SWOOSH
HOPEFULLY ONE MORE WON'T HURT.
KRSHHH
SMALL ONES.
LISTEN BEHIND LITTLE EYES.
SUBMIT BECOME MASTER WILL
SUBMIT BECOME MASTER WILL
SUBMIT BECOME MASTER WILL
SUBMIT BECOME MASTER WILL
SUBMIT BECOME MASTER WILL
TOO MANY OF THEM. STOP THINKING, PETER.
LISTEN TO YOUR SPIDER-SENSE.
SURVIVE.

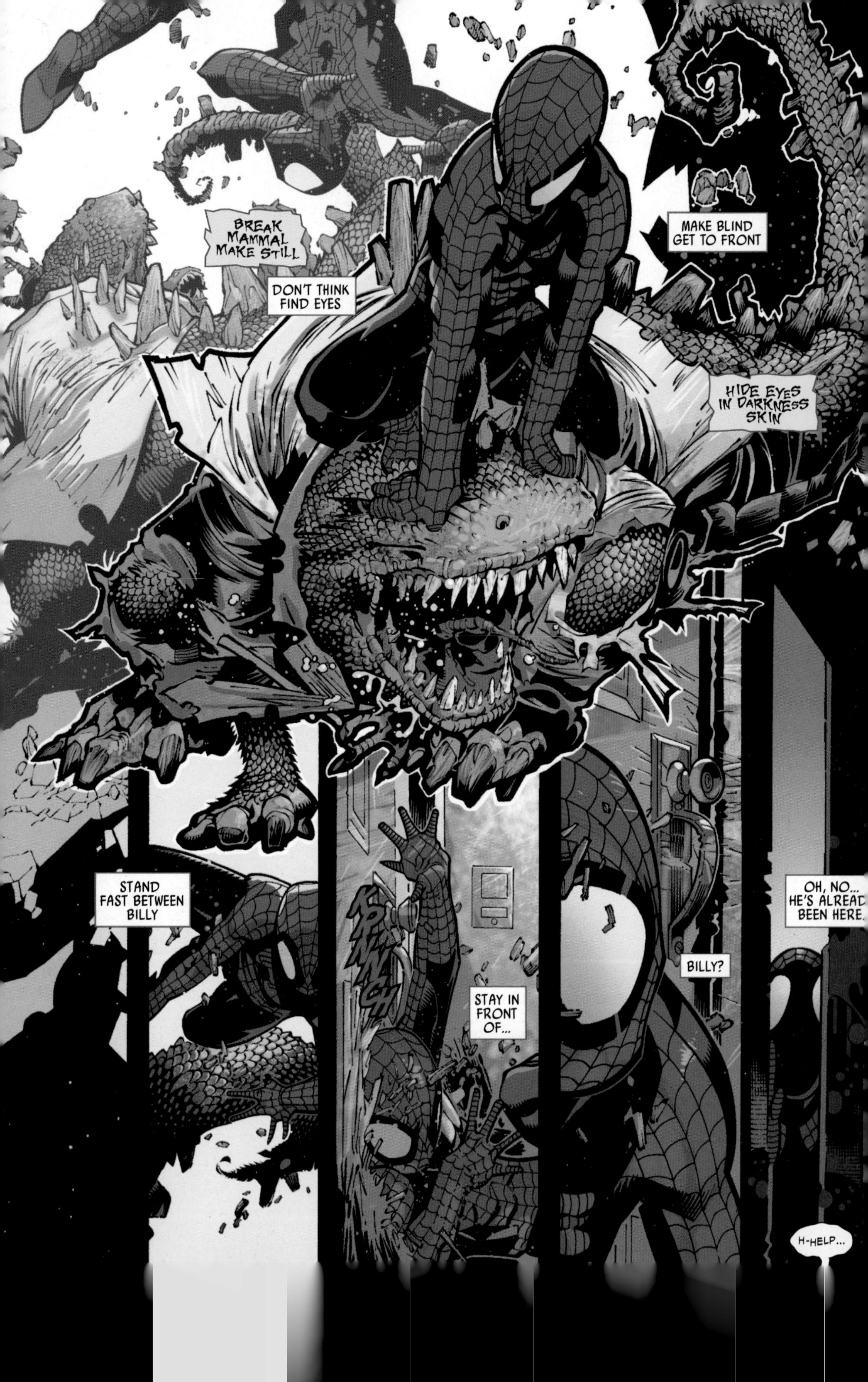
BREAK MAMMAL MAKE STILL
DON'T THINK FIND EYES
MAKE BLIND GET TO FRONT
HIDE EYES IN DARKNESS SKIN
STAND FAST BETWEEN BILLY
STAY IN FRONT OF...
BILLY?
OH, NO... HE'S ALREAD BEEN HERE.
H-HELP...

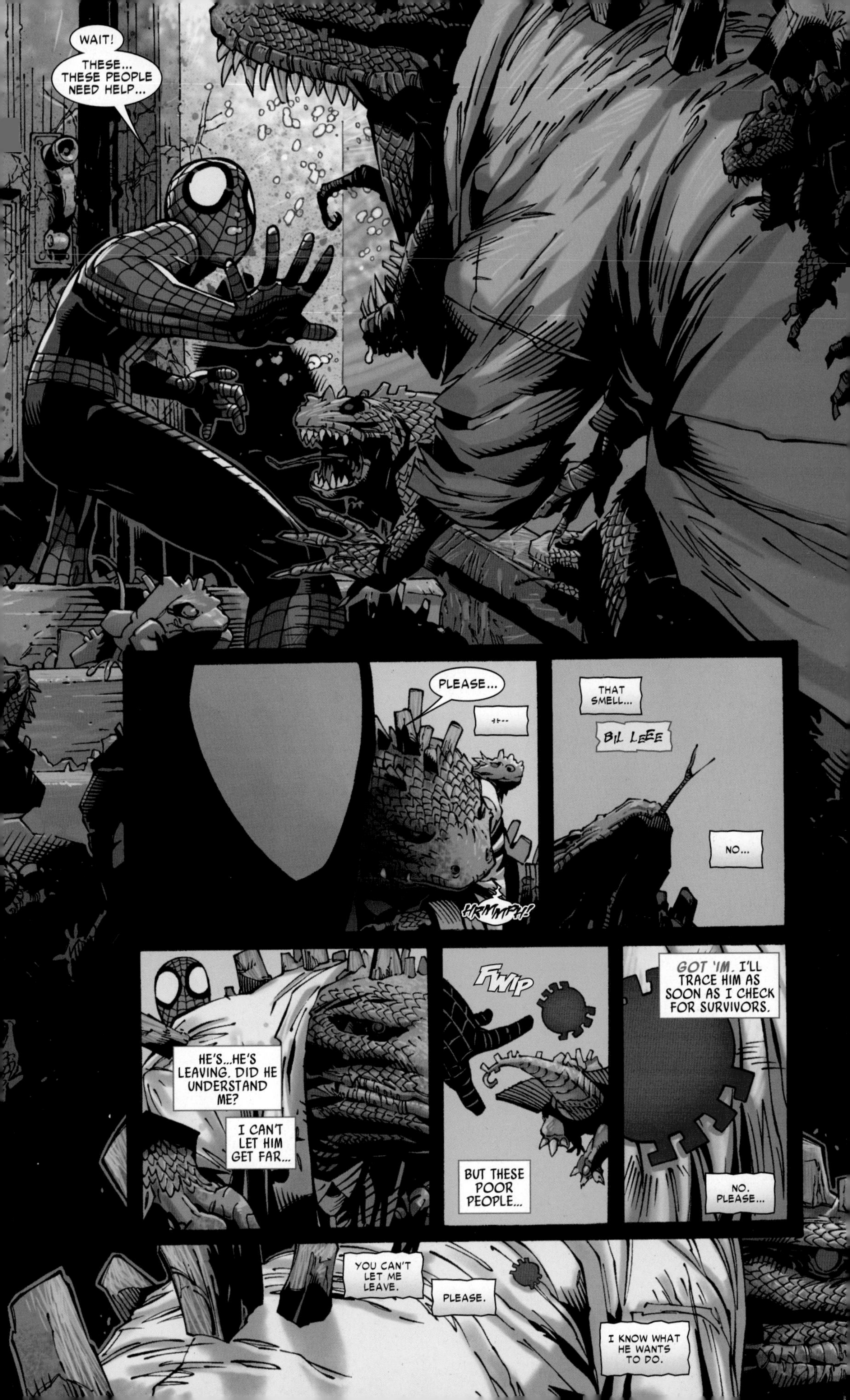

WAIT!
THESE... THESE PEOPLE NEED HELP...
PLEASE...
THAT SMELL...
NO...
HRMMPH!
HE'S...HE'S LEAVING. DID HE UNDERSTAND ME?
I CAN'T LET HIM GET FAR...
FWIP
BUT THESE POOR PEOPLE...
GOT 'IM. I'LL TRACE HIM AS SOON AS I CHECK FOR SURVIVORS.
NO. PLEASE...
YOU CAN'T LET ME LEAVE.
PLEASE.
I KNOW WHAT HE WANTS TO DO.

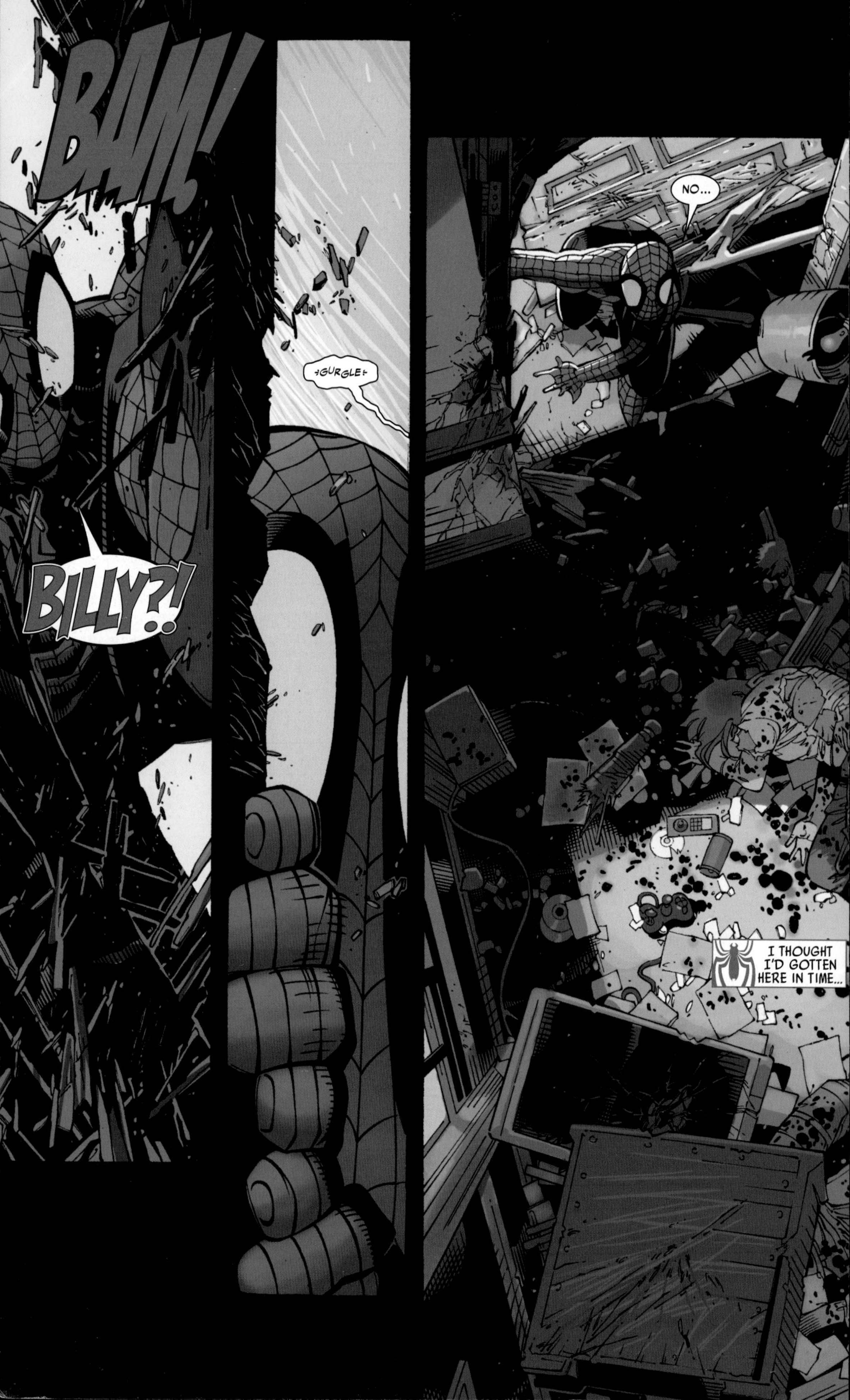
BAM!
BILLY?!
GURGLE
NO...
I THOUGHT I'D GOTTEN HERE IN TIME...

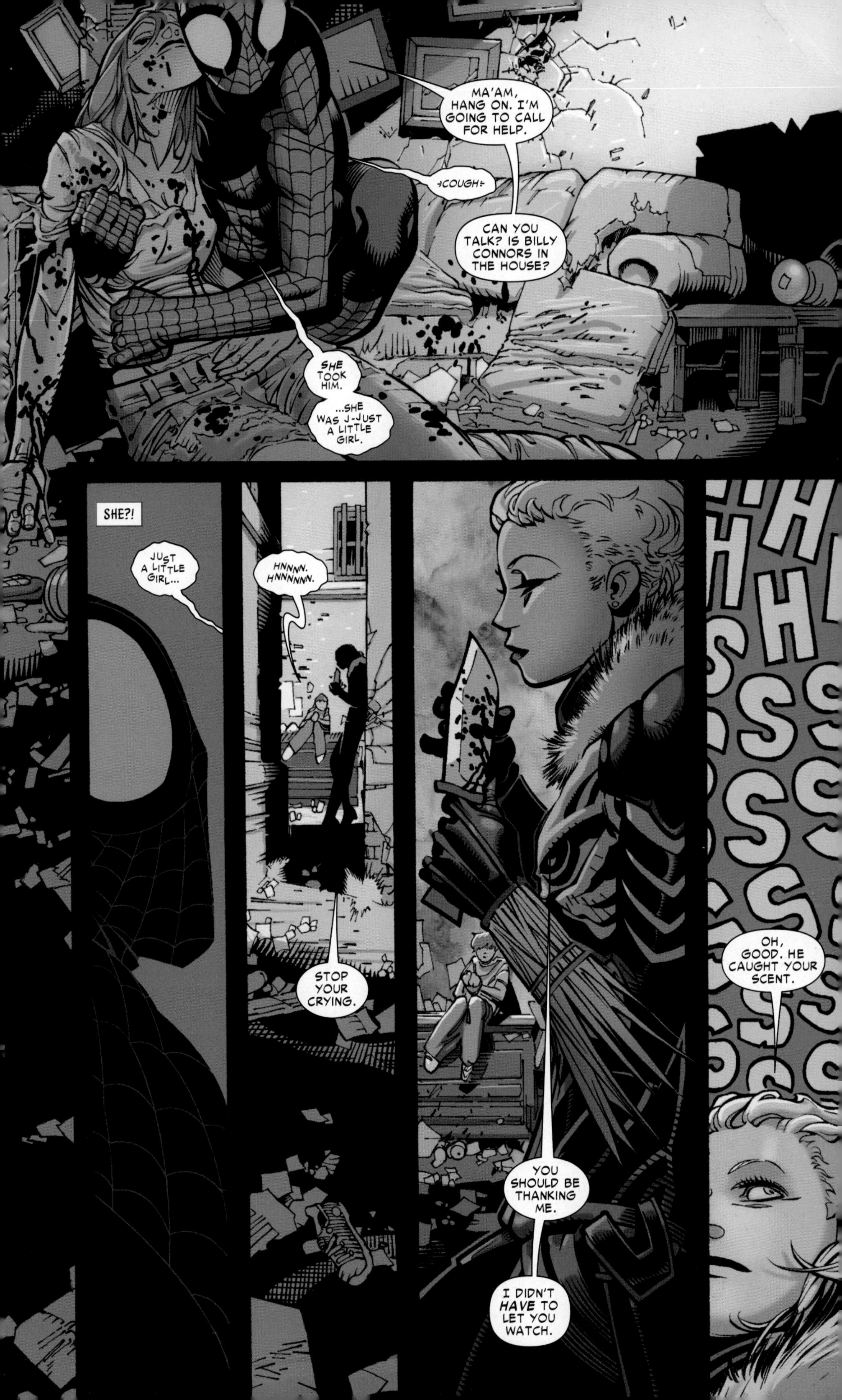

MA'AM, HANG ON. I'M GOING TO CALL FOR HELP.
«COUGH»
CAN YOU TALK? IS BILLY CONNORS IN THE HOUSE?
SHE TOOK HIM.
...SHE WAS J-JUST A LITTLE GIRL.
SHE?!
JUST A LITTLE GIRL...
HNNNN. HNNNNNN.
STOP YOUR CRYING.
YOU SHOULD BE THANKING ME.
I DIDN'T HAVE TO LET YOU WATCH.
HHHHSSSSSSSS
OH, GOOD. HE CAUGHT YOUR SCENT.

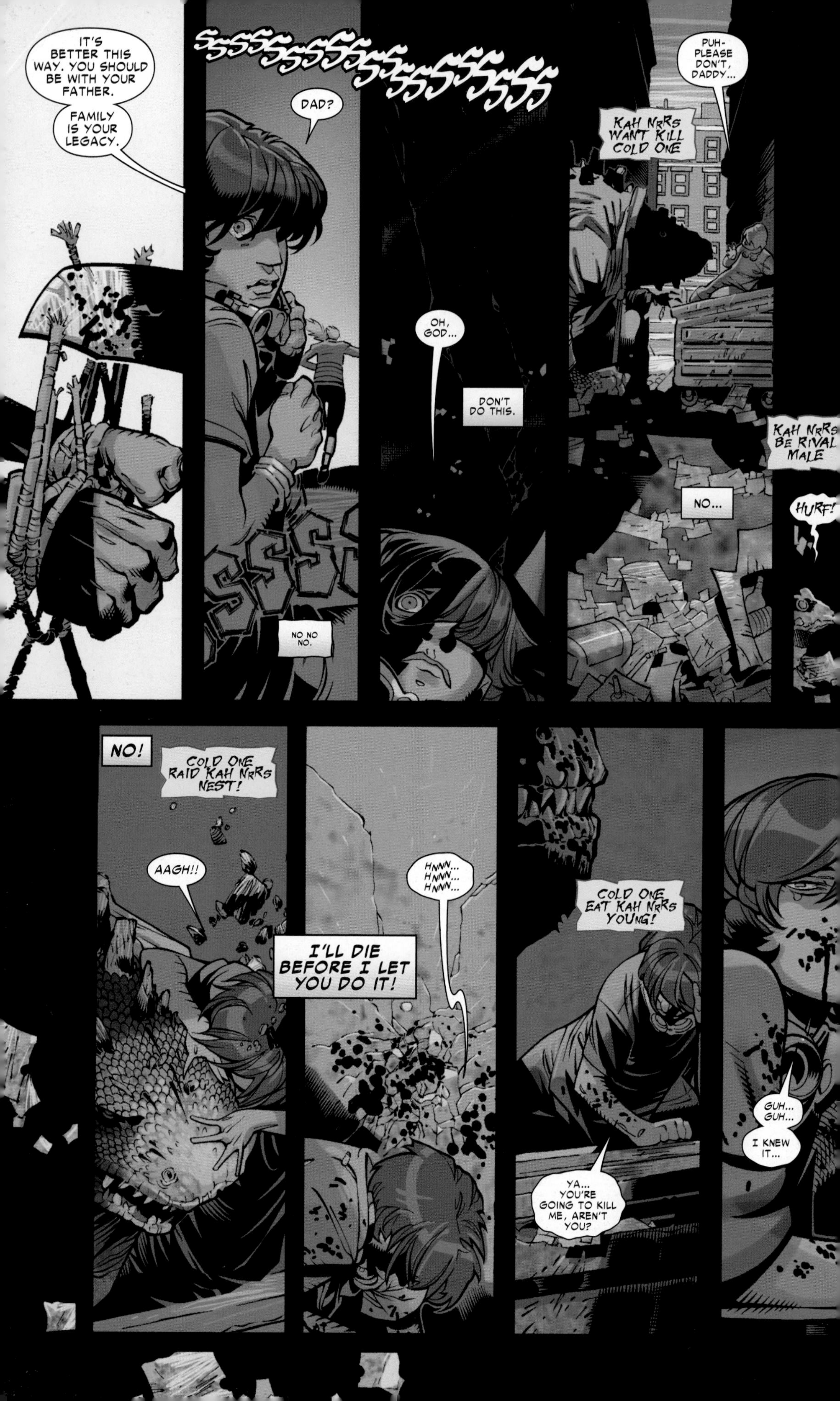

IT'S BETTER THIS WAY. YOU SHOULD BE WITH YOUR FATHER.
FAMILY IS YOUR LEGACY.
SSSSSSSSSSSSSSSSSSSSS
DAD?
NO NO NO.
OH, GOD...
DON'T DO THIS.
KAH NRRS WANT KILL COLD ONE
PUH-PLEASE DON'T, DADDY...
NO...
KAH NRRS BE RIVAL MALE
HURF!
NO!
COLD ONE RAID KAH NRRS NEST!
AAGH!!
I'LL DIE BEFORE I LET YOU DO IT!
HNNN... HNNN... HNNN...
COLD ONE EAT KAH NRRS YOUNG!
YA... YOU'RE GOING TO KILL ME, AREN'T YOU?
GUH... GUH...
I KNEW IT...

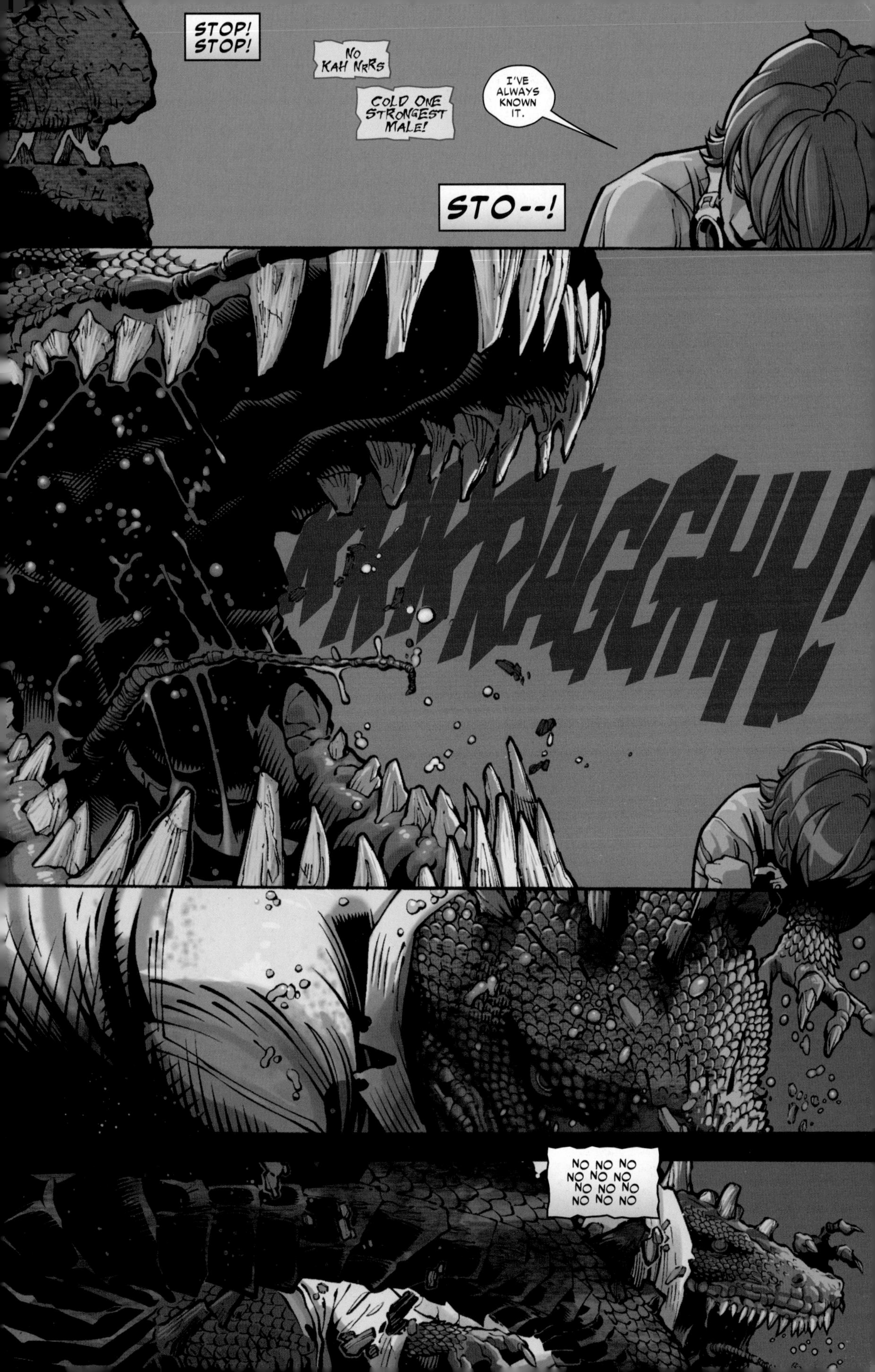
STOP! STOP!
NO KAH NRRS
COLD ONE STRONGEST MALE!
I'VE ALWAYS KNOWN IT.
STO--!
NO NO NO NO NO NO NO NO NO NO NO NO

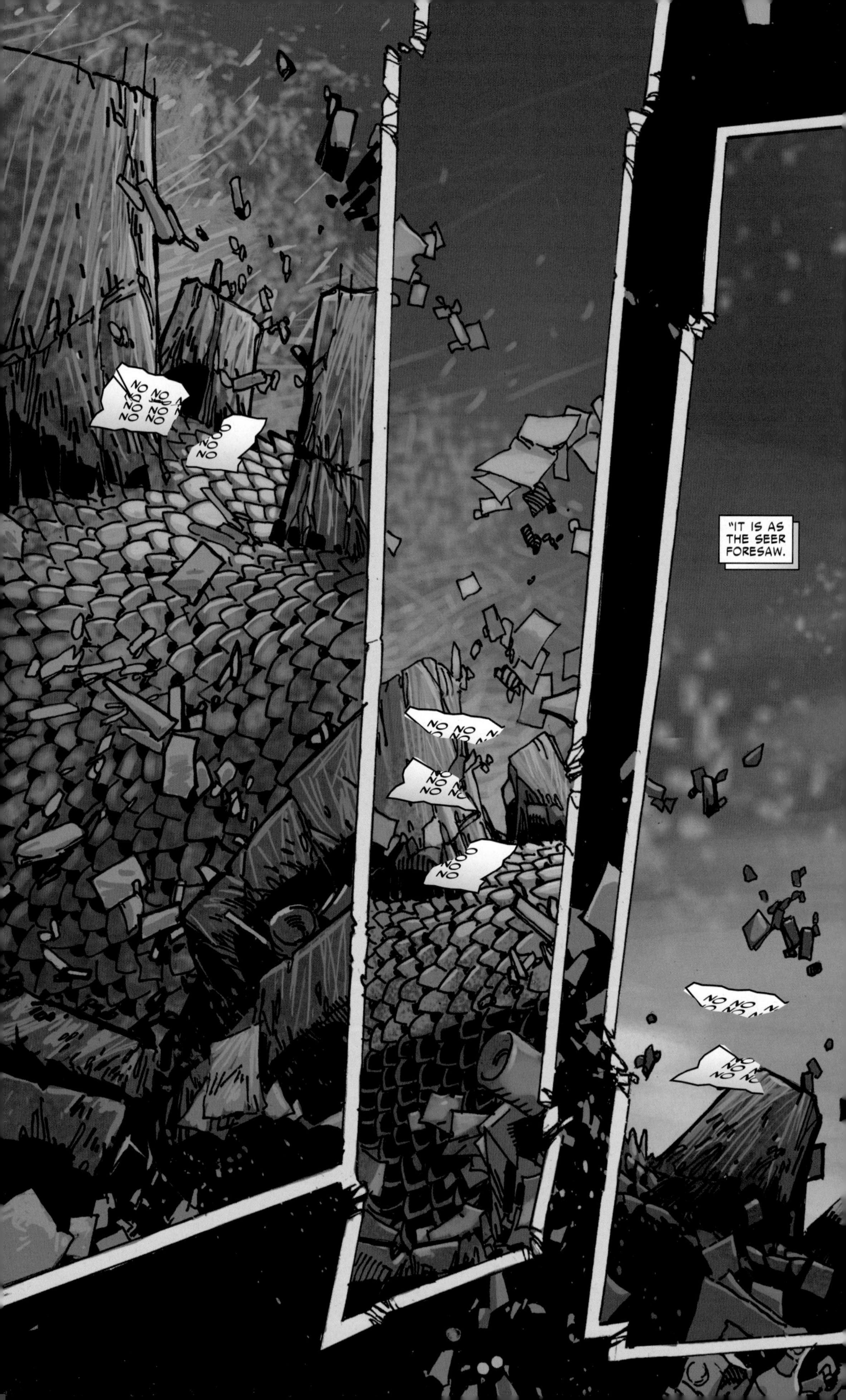
NO NO
NO NO
NO NO
NO
NO
NO
NO NO
NO NO
NO NO
NO
NO
NO
"IT IS AS THE SEER FORESAW.
NO NO
NO NO
NO NO

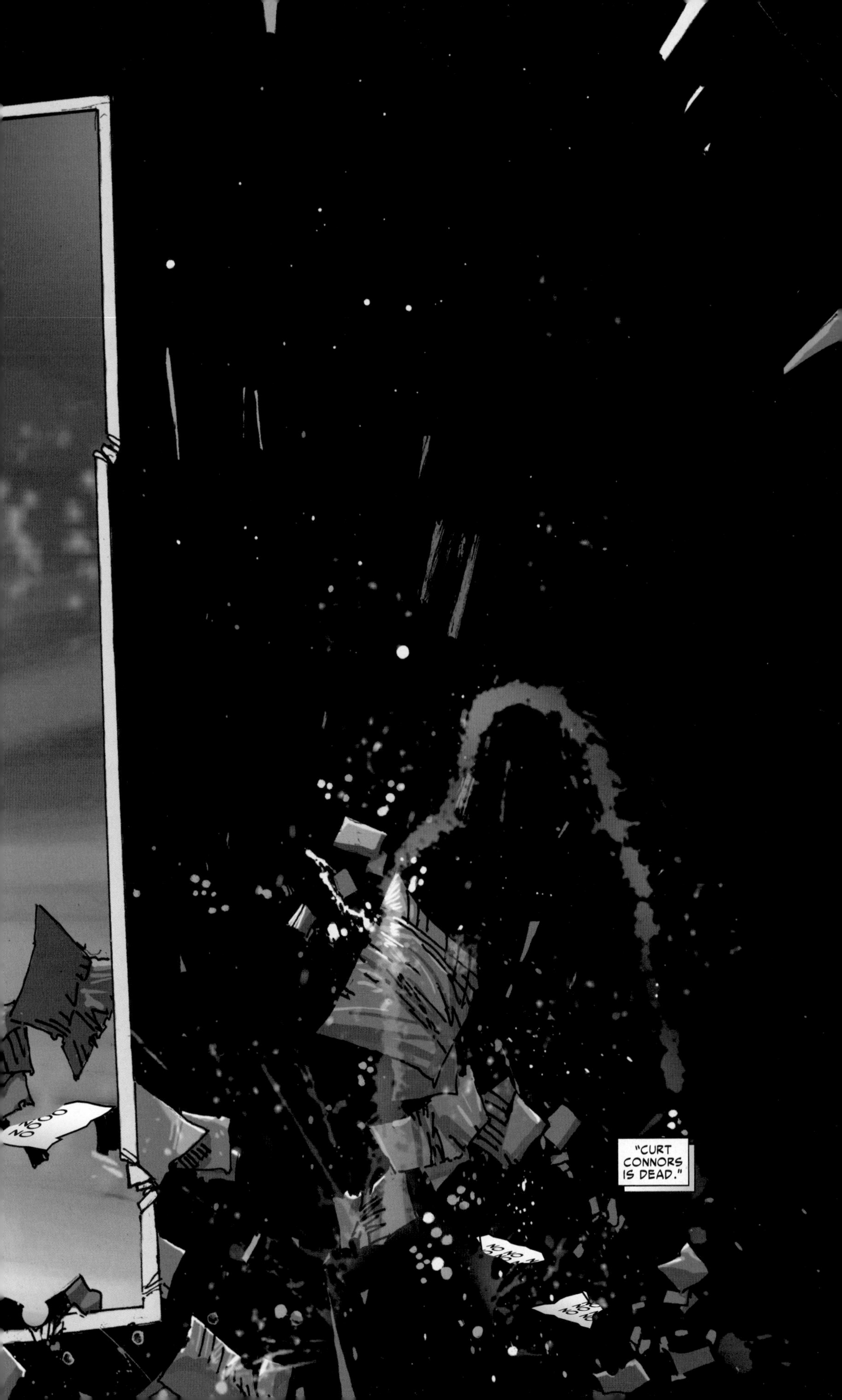
"CURT CONNORS IS DEAD."

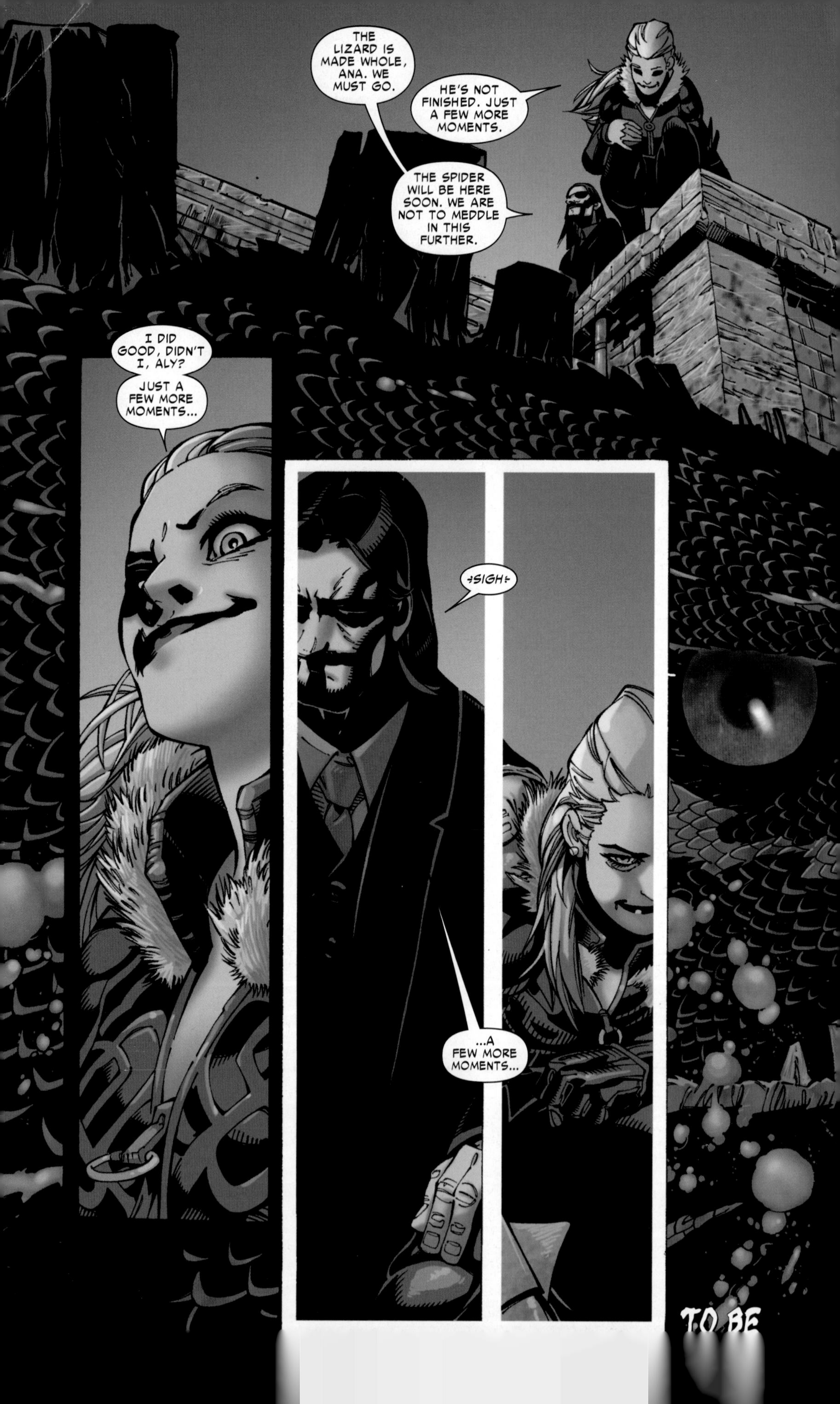
THE LIZARD IS MADE WHOLE, ANA. WE MUST GO.
HE'S NOT FINISHED. JUST A FEW MORE MOMENTS.
THE SPIDER WILL BE HERE SOON. WE ARE NOT TO MEDDLE IN THIS FURTHER.
I DID GOOD, DIDN'T I, ALY?
JUST A FEW MORE MOMENTS...
SIGH
...A FEW MORE MOMENTS...
TO BE

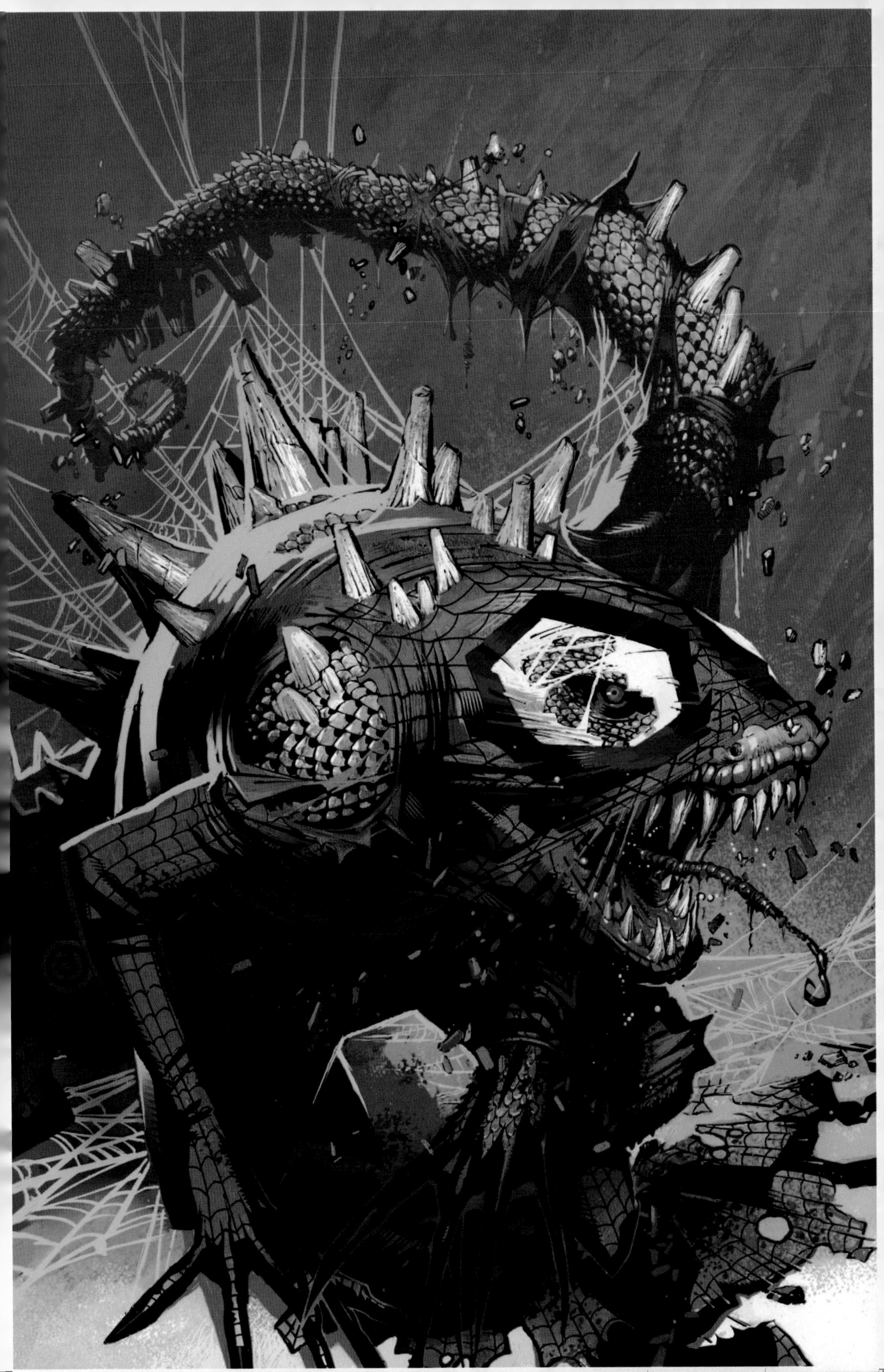

SPIDER-MAN #632
O & TIM TOWNSEND

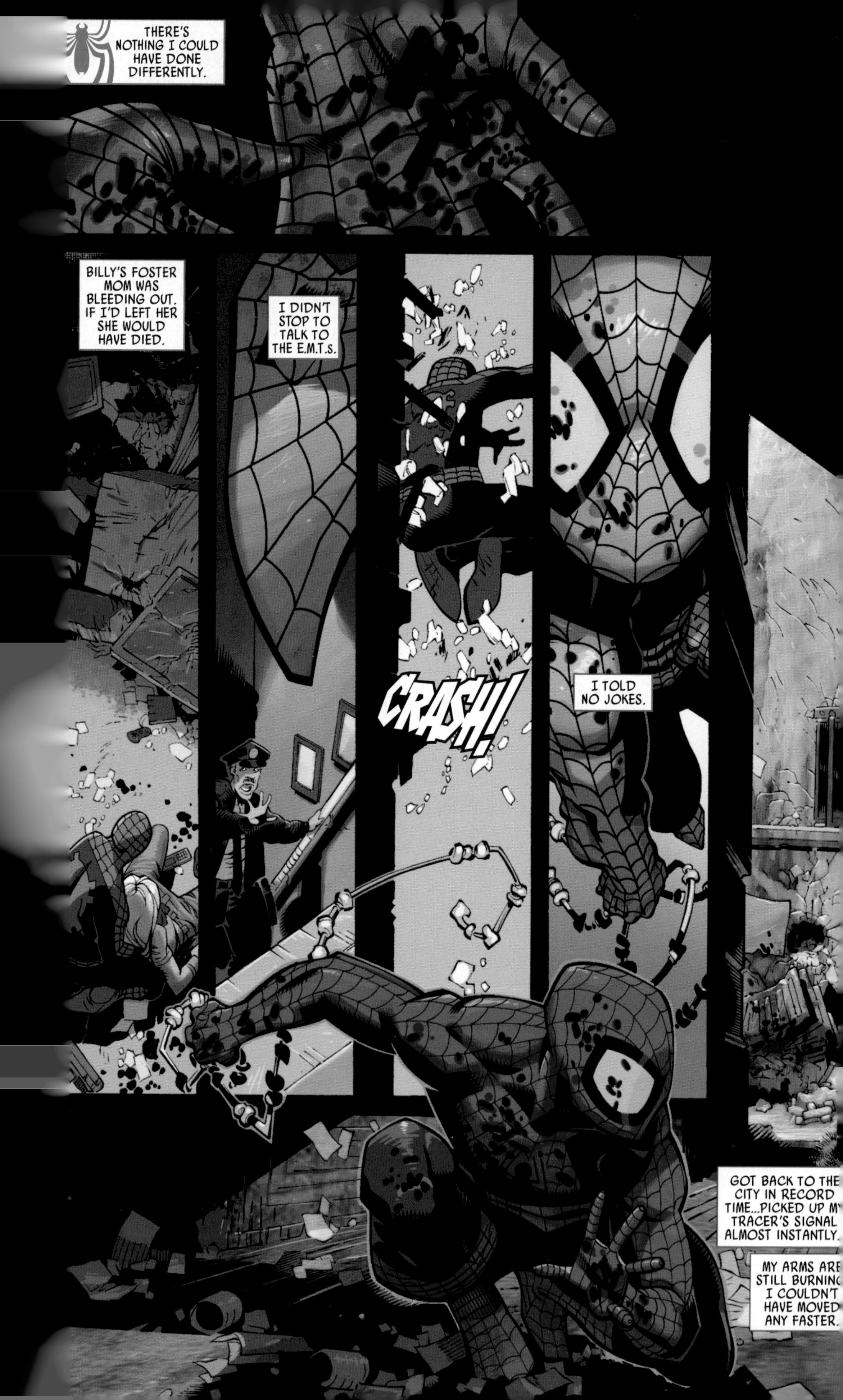

THERE'S NOTHING I COULD HAVE DONE DIFFERENTLY.
BILLY'S FOSTER MOM WAS BLEEDING OUT. IF I'D LEFT HER SHE WOULD HAVE DIED.
I DIDN'T STOP TO TALK TO THE E.M.T.S.
CRASH!
I TOLD NO JOKES.
GOT BACK TO THE CITY IN RECORD TIME...PICKED UP MY TRACER'S SIGNAL ALMOST INSTANTLY.
MY ARMS ARE STILL BURNING. I COULDN'T HAVE MOVED ANY FASTER.

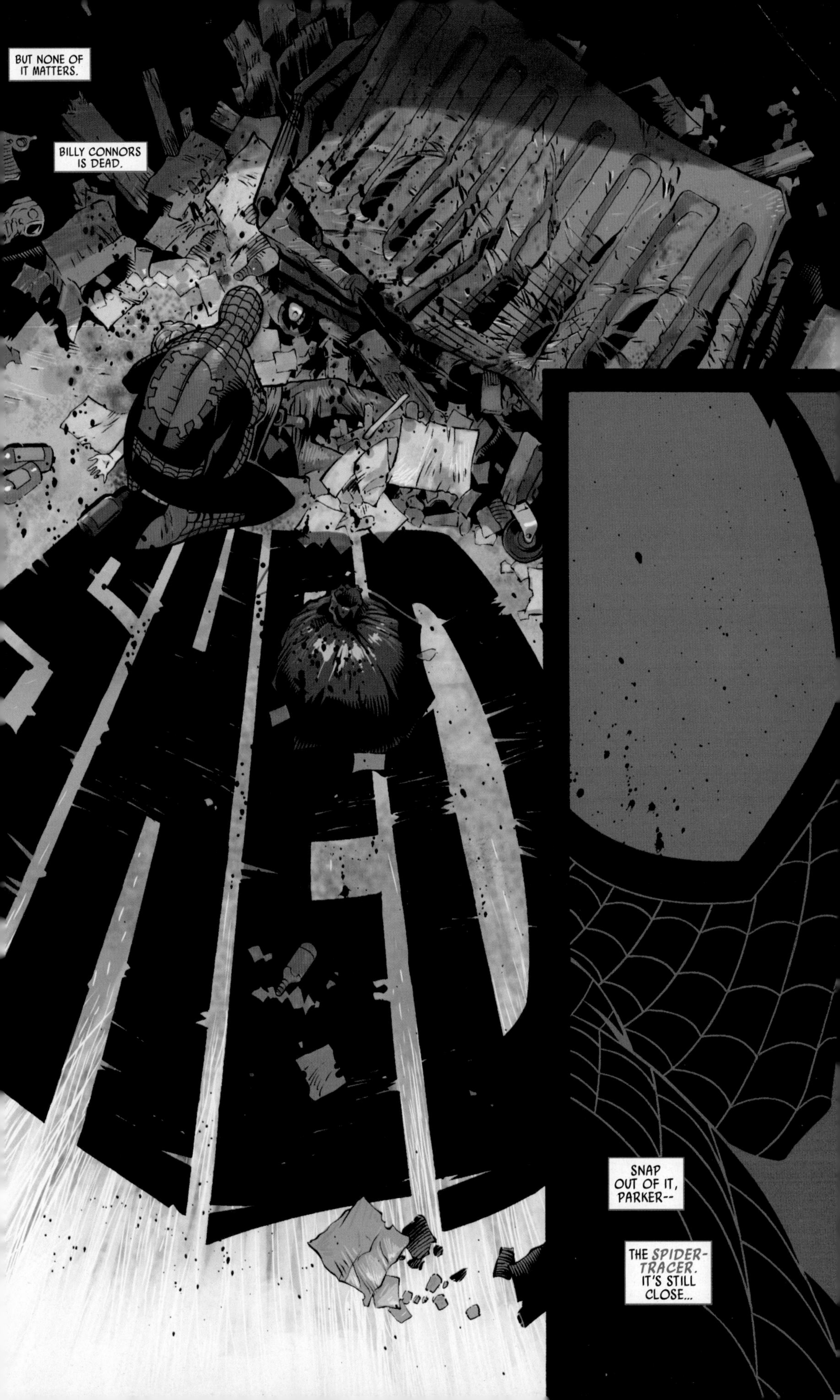
BUT NONE OF IT MATTERS.
BILLY CONNORS IS DEAD.
SNAP OUT OF IT, PARKER--
THE SPIDER-TRACER. IT'S STILL CLOSE...

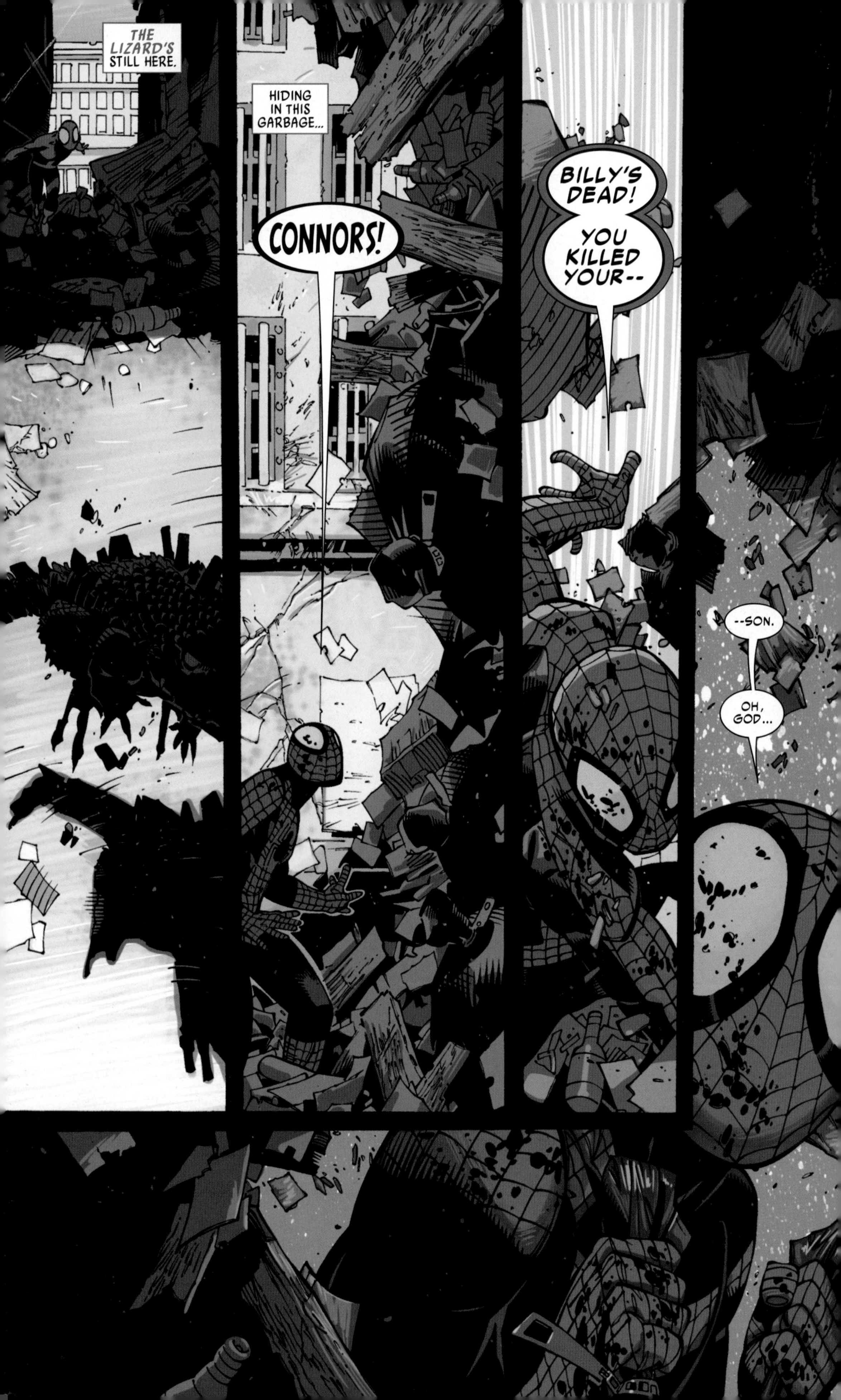
THE LIZARD'S STILL HERE.
HIDING IN THIS GARBAGE...
CONNORS!
BILLY'S DEAD!
YOU KILLED YOUR--
--SON.
OH, GOD...

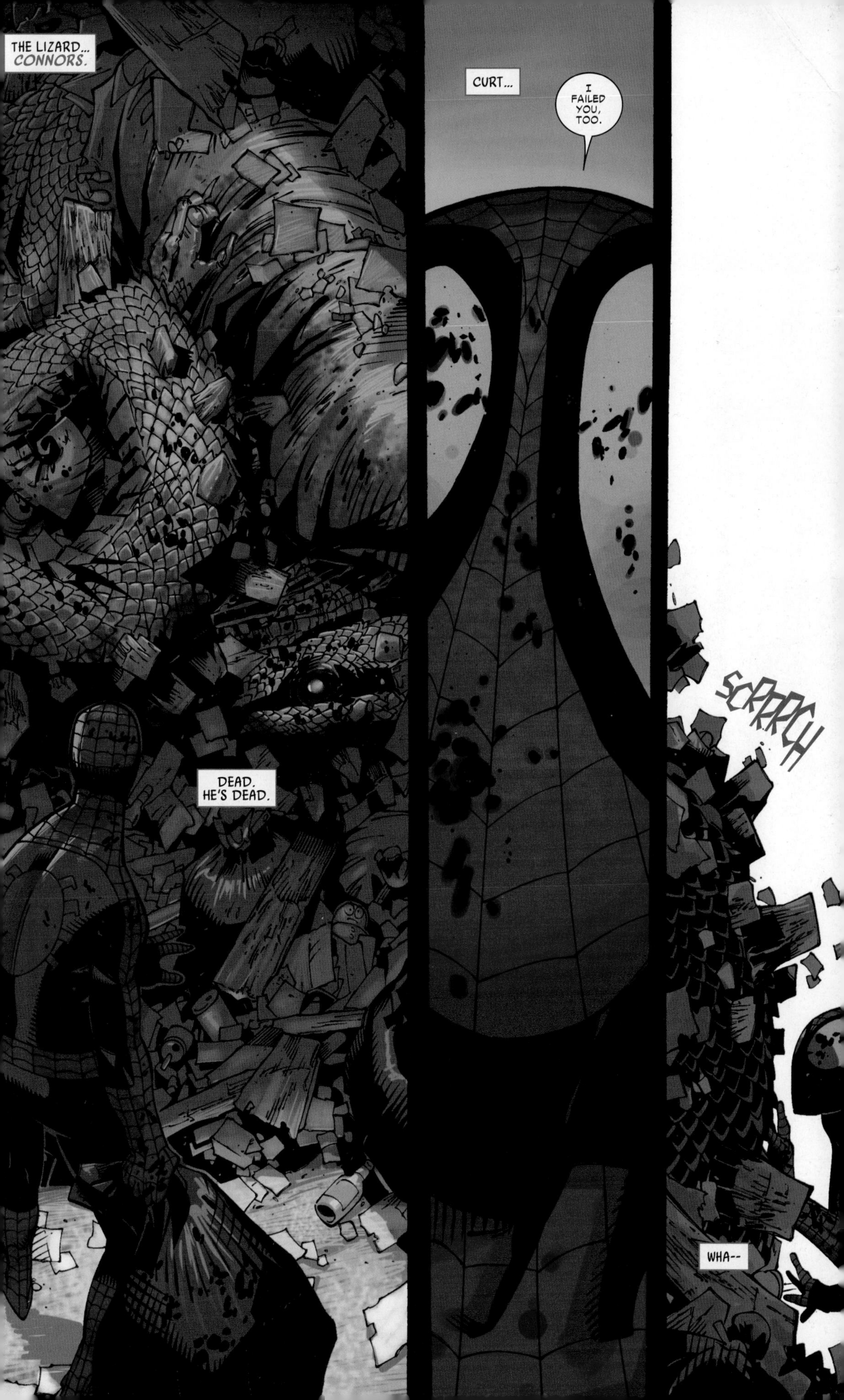
THE LIZARD... CONNORS.
DEAD. HE'S DEAD.
CURT...
I FAILED YOU, TOO.
SCRRRCH
WHA--

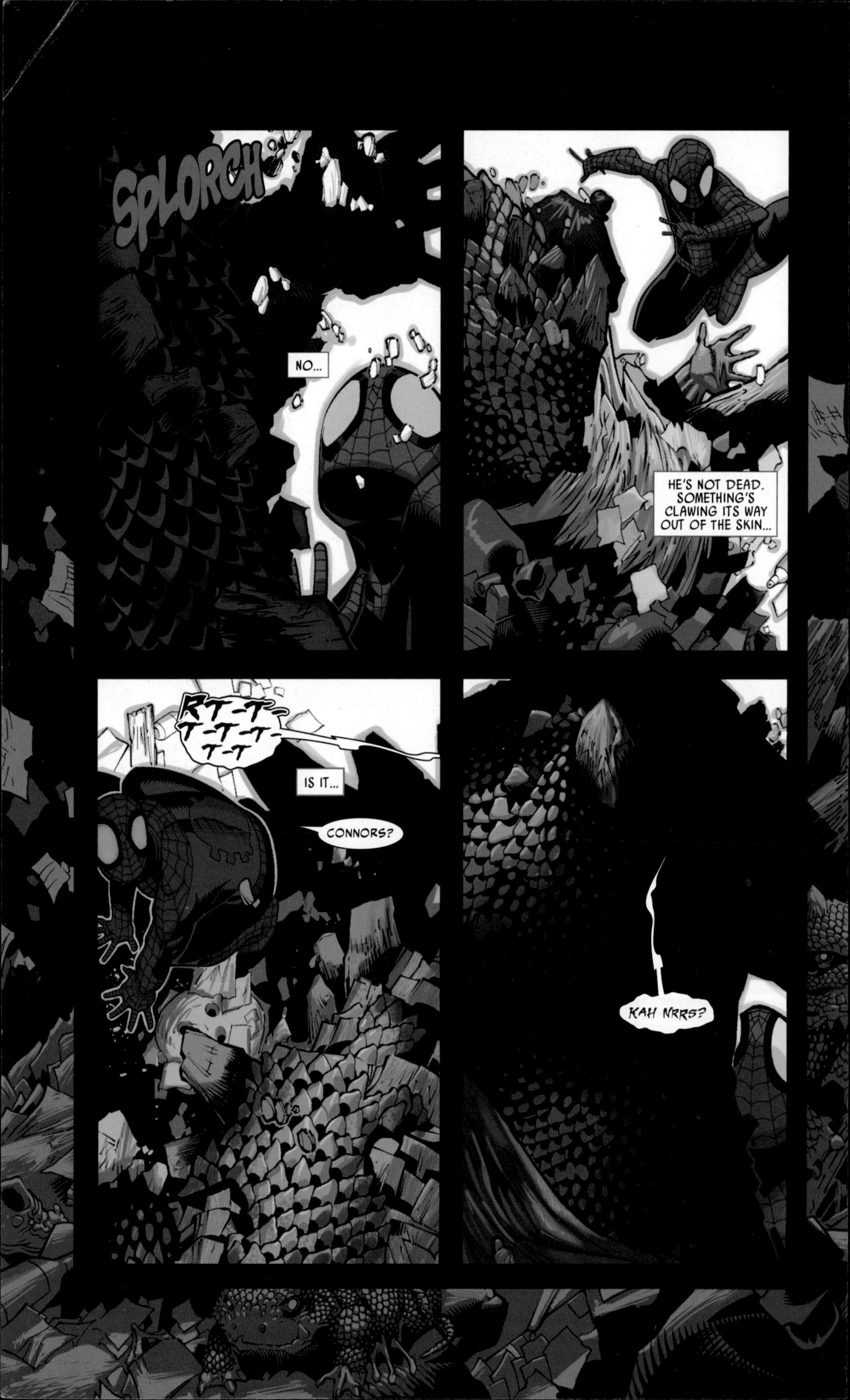
SPLORCH
NO...
HE'S NOT DEAD. SOMETHING'S CLAWING ITS WAY OUT OF THE SKIN...
RT-T-T-T-T-T-T
IS IT...
CONNORS?
KAH NRRS?

KAHN RRS... IS SHED.

IT...IT'S THE LIZARD BUT...

CURT, LISTEN TO ME...

MONKEY BRAIN IS LIZARD HOME NOW. NO MORE KAH NRRS...

KAHNARS...

CAHNNURS...

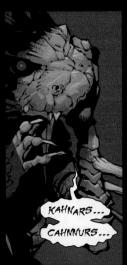

CONNORS.

YOU...YOU'RE TALKING...

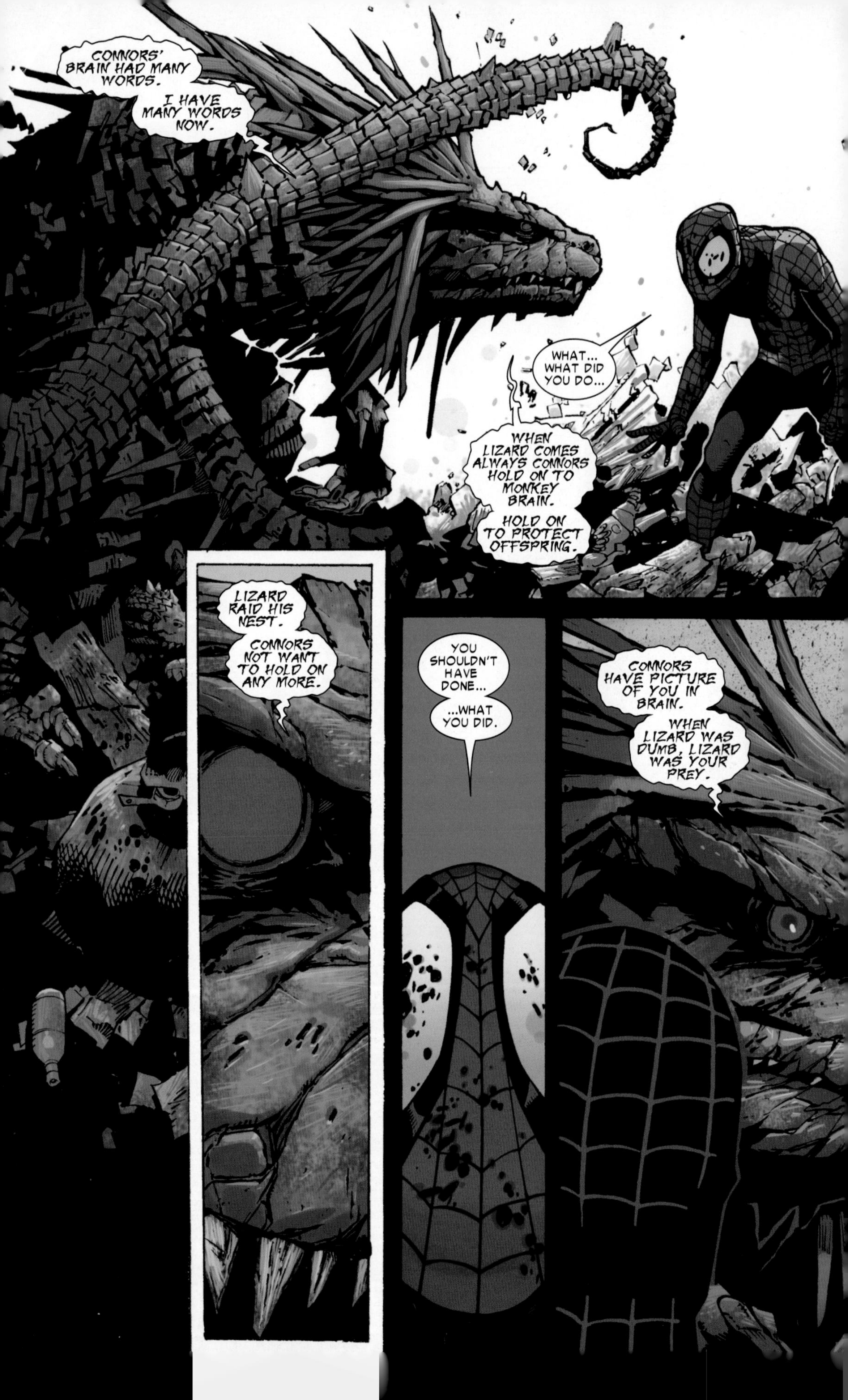
CONNORS' BRAIN HAD MANY WORDS.
I HAVE MANY WORDS NOW.
WHAT... WHAT DID YOU DO...
WHEN LIZARD COMES ALWAYS CONNORS HOLD ON TO MONKEY BRAIN.
HOLD ON TO PROTECT OFFSPRING.
LIZARD RAID HIS NEST.
CONNORS NOT WANT TO HOLD ON ANY MORE.
YOU SHOULDN'T HAVE DONE...
...WHAT YOU DID.
CONNORS HAVE PICTURE OF YOU IN BRAIN.
WHEN LIZARD WAS DUMB, LIZARD WAS YOUR PREY.

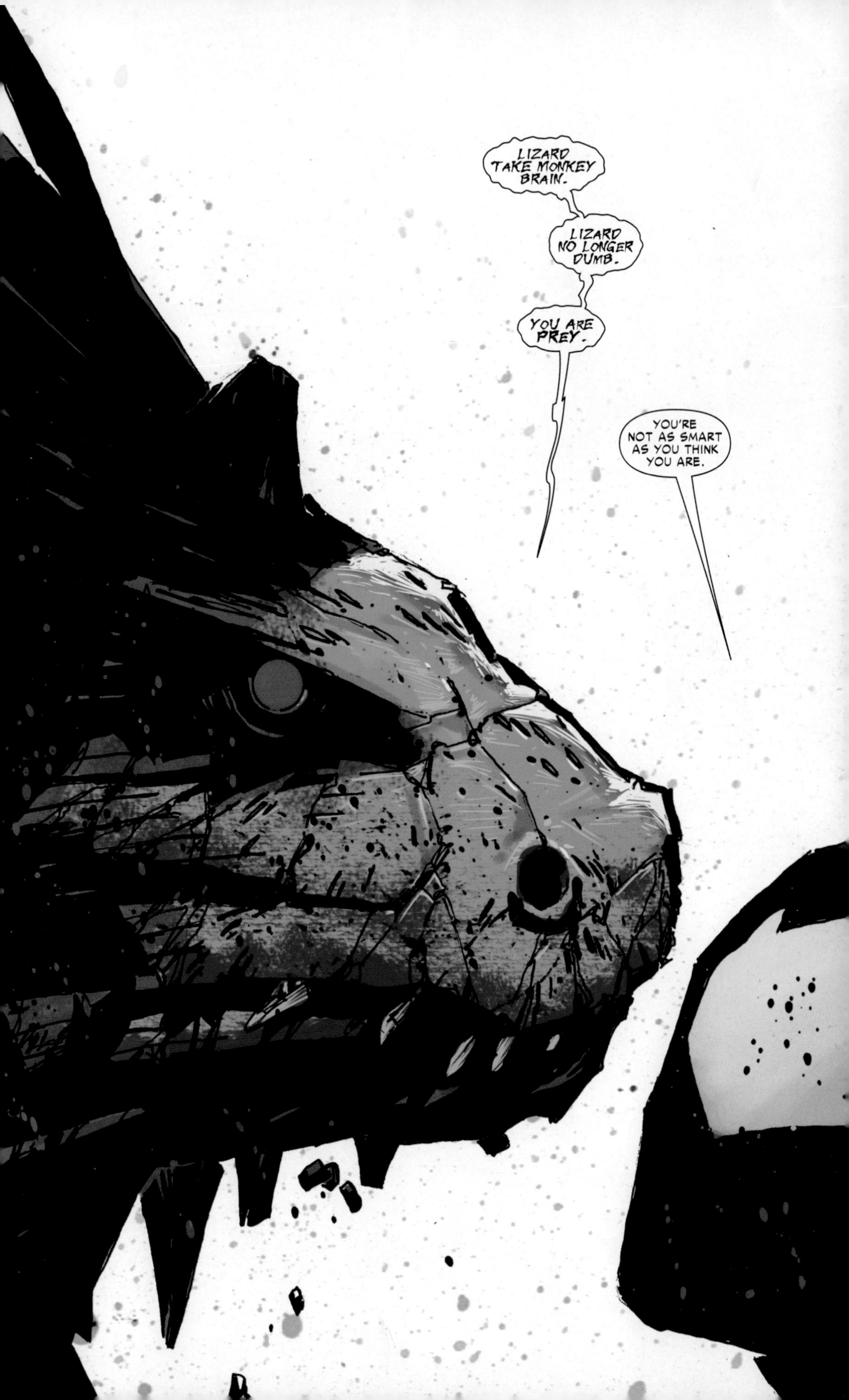
LIZARD TAKE MONKEY BRAIN.
LIZARD NO LONGER DUMB.
YOU ARE PREY.
YOU'RE NOT AS SMART AS YOU THINK YOU ARE.

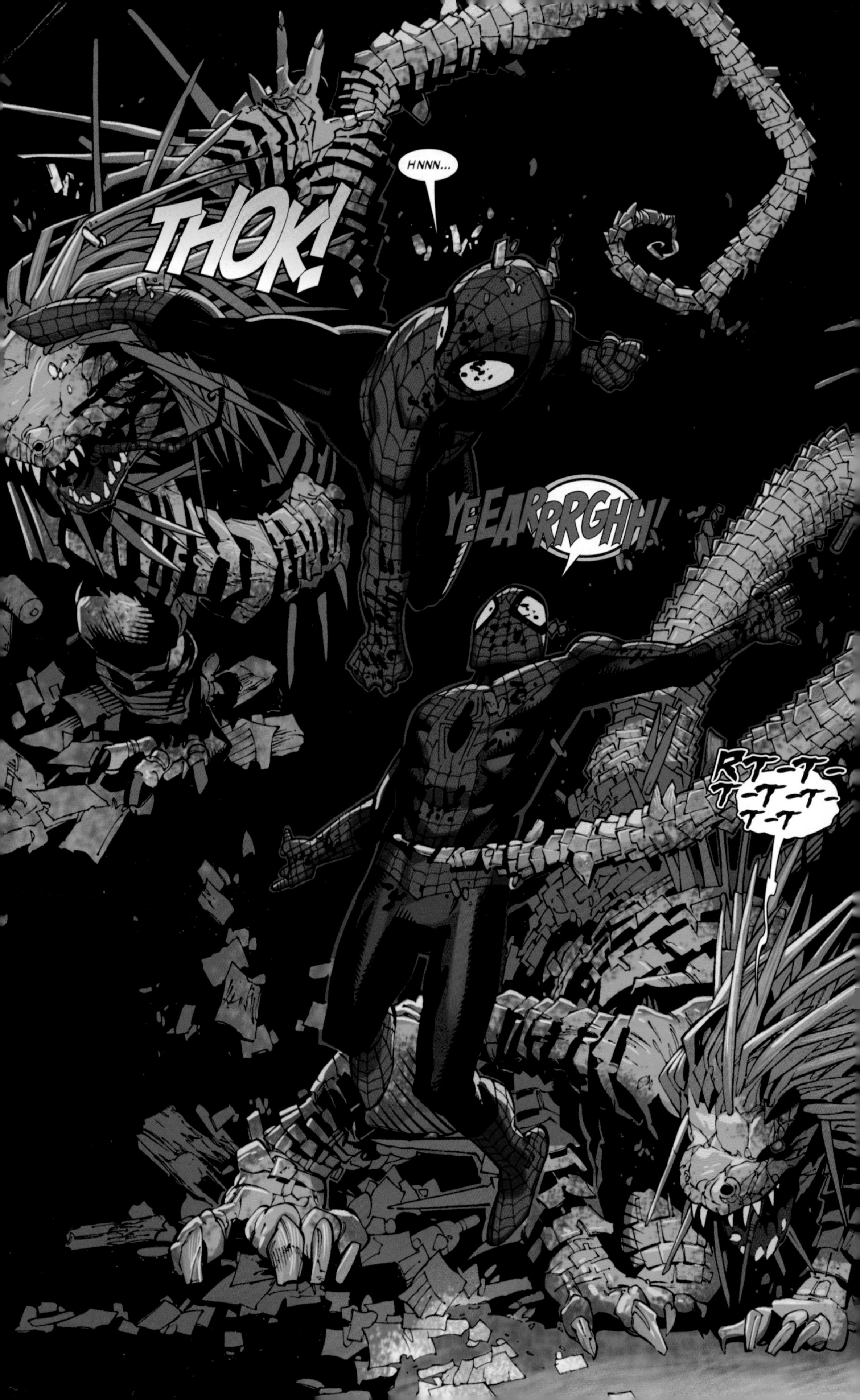
THOK!
HNNN...
YEEARRRGHH!
RT-T-T-T-T-T-T

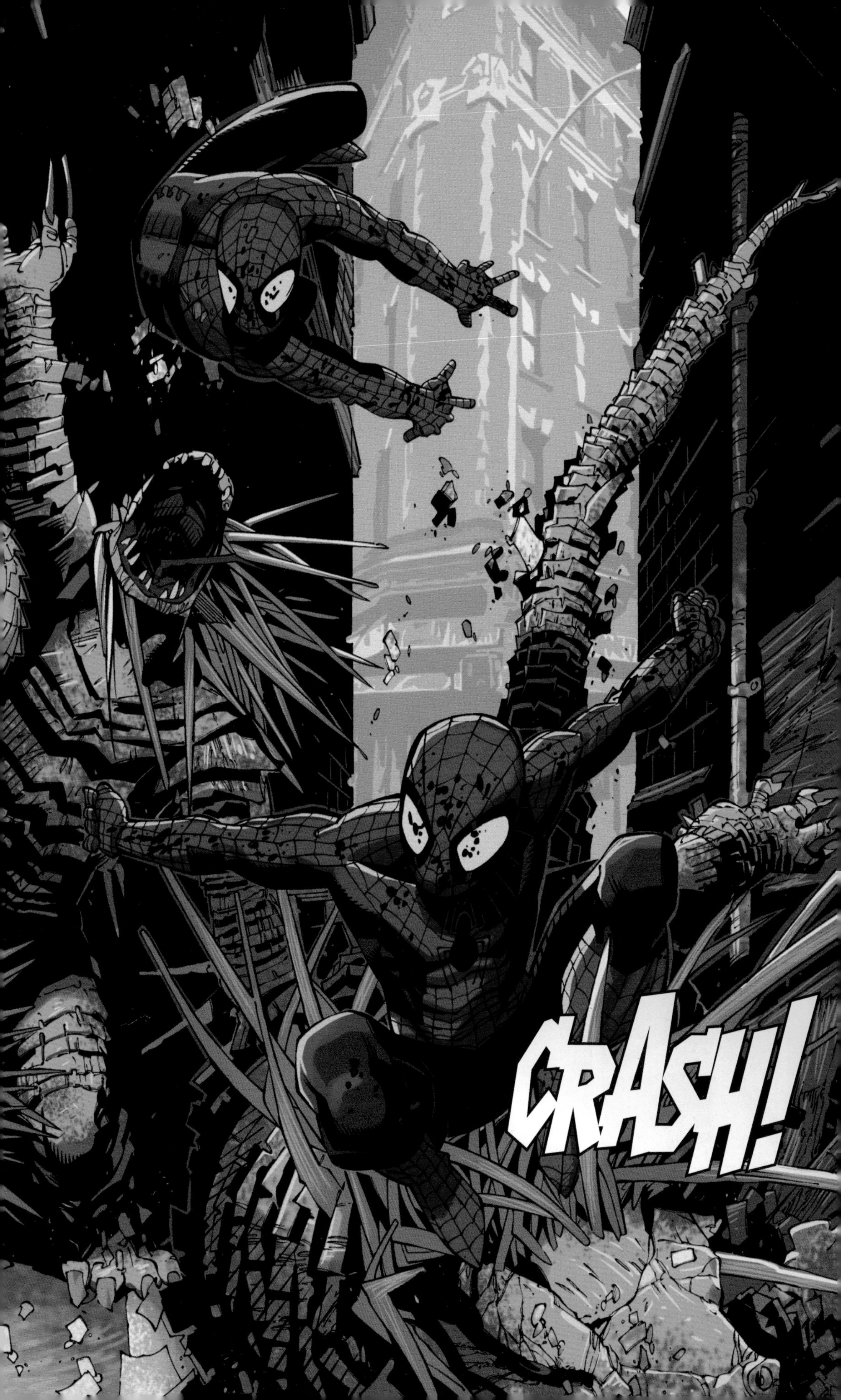
CRASH!

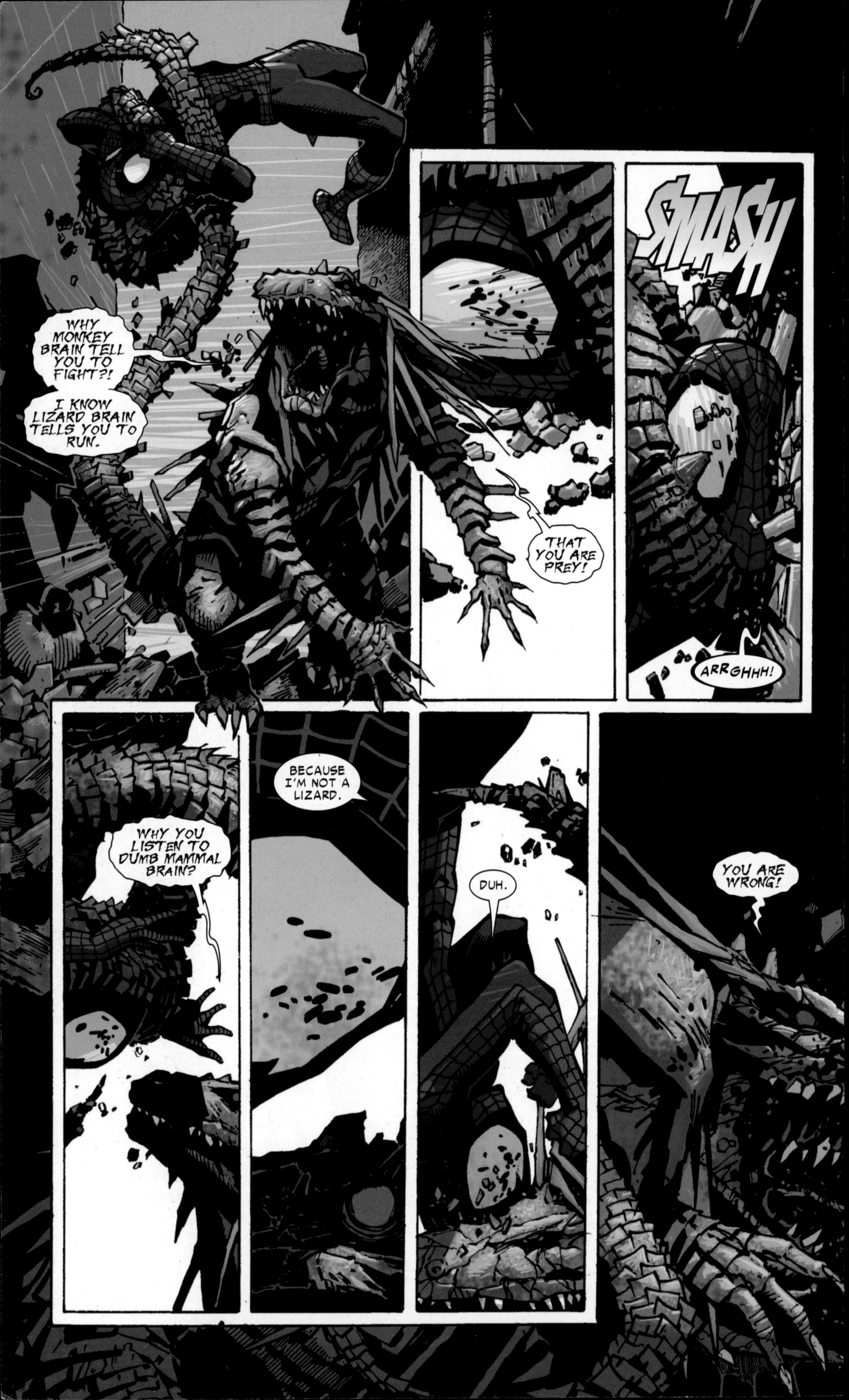
WHY MONKEY BRAIN TELL YOU TO FIGHT?!
I KNOW LIZARD BRAIN TELLS YOU TO RUN.
THAT YOU ARE PREY!
SMASH
ARRGHHH!
WHY YOU LISTEN TO DUMB MAMMAL BRAIN?
BECAUSE I'M NOT A LIZARD.
DUH.
YOU ARE WRONG!

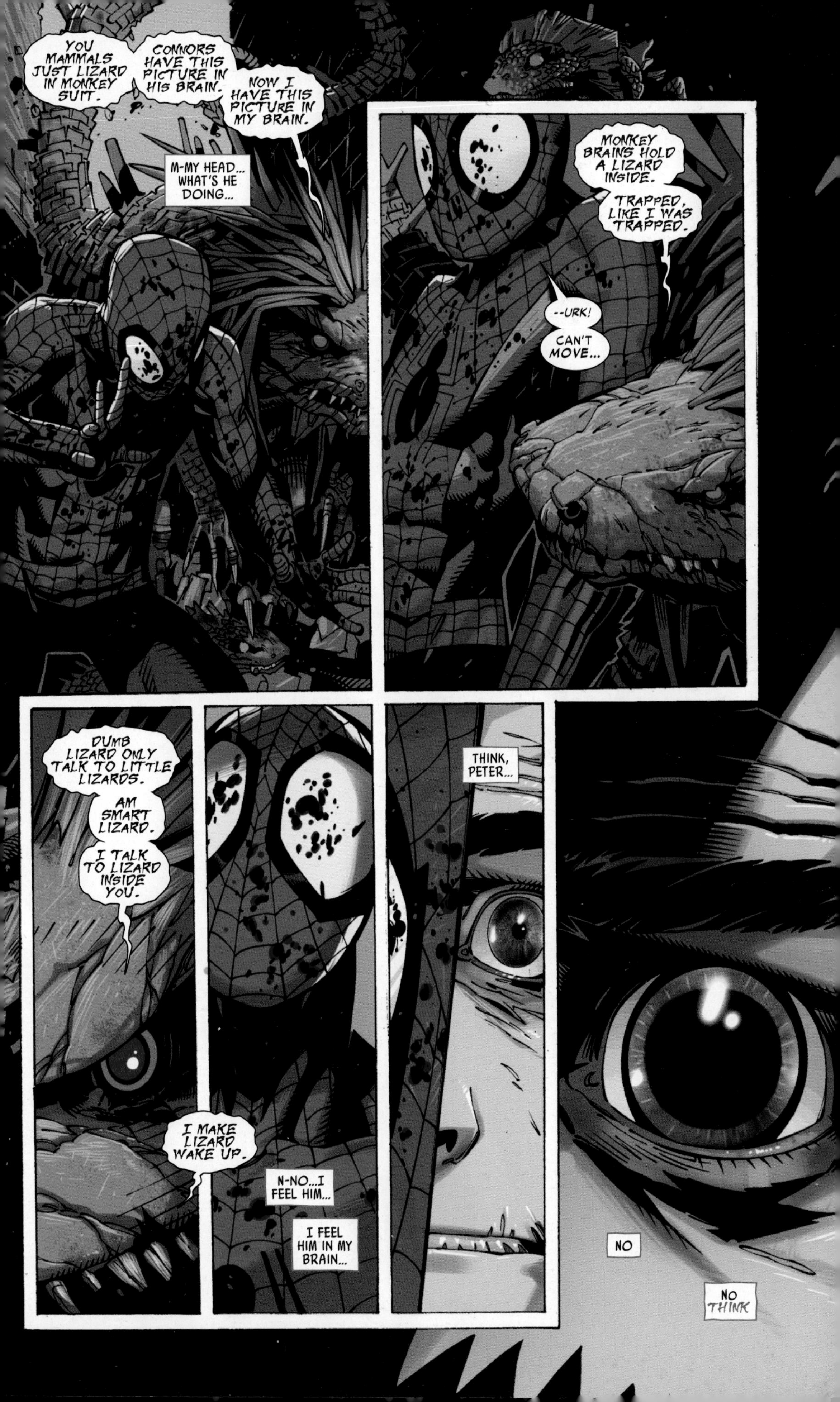
YOU MAMMALS JUST LIZARD IN MONKEY SUIT.
CONNORS HAVE THIS PICTURE IN HIS BRAIN.
NOW I HAVE THIS PICTURE IN MY BRAIN.
M-MY HEAD... WHAT'S HE DOING...
MONKEY BRAINS HOLD A LIZARD INSIDE.
TRAPPED, LIKE I WAS TRAPPED.
--URK!
CAN'T MOVE...
DUMB LIZARD ONLY TALK TO LITTLE LIZARDS.
AM SMART LIZARD.
I TALK TO LIZARD INSIDE YOU.
I MAKE LIZARD WAKE UP.
N-NO...I FEEL HIM...
I FEEL HIM IN MY BRAIN...
THINK, PETER...
NO
NO THINK

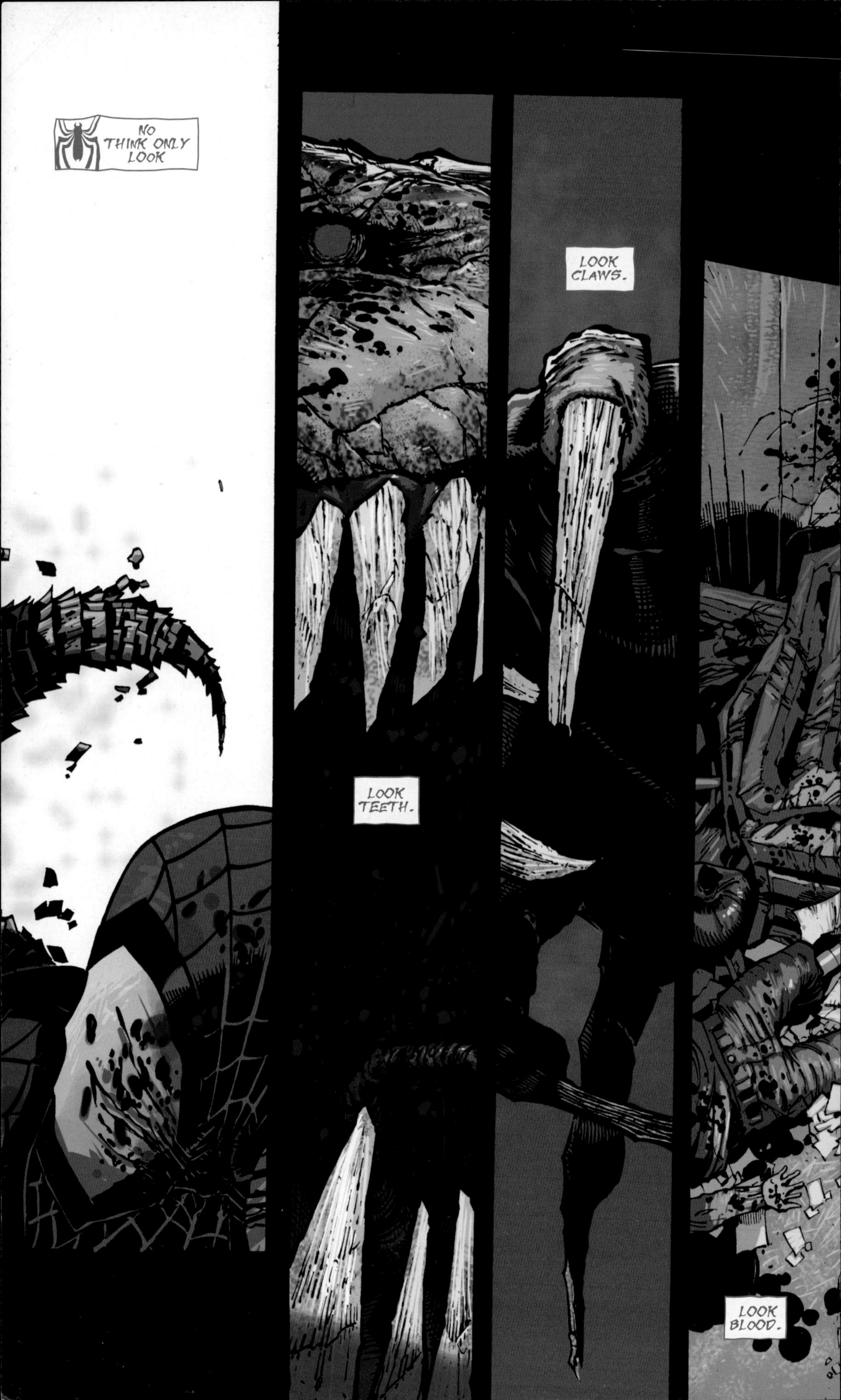
NO THINK ONLY LOOK
LOOK TEETH.
LOOK CLAWS.
LOOK BLOOD.

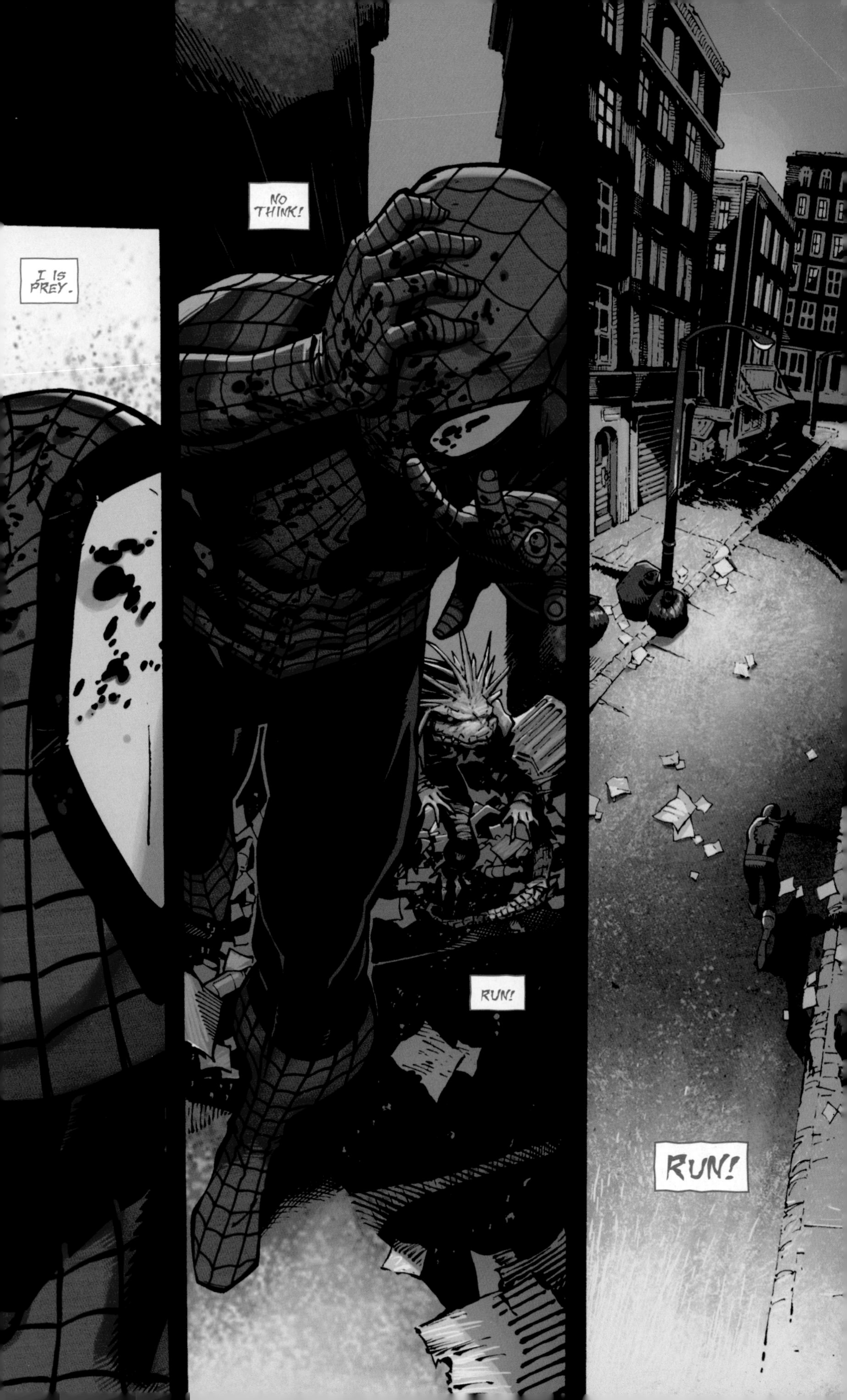
I IS PREY.
NO THINK!
RUN!
RUN!

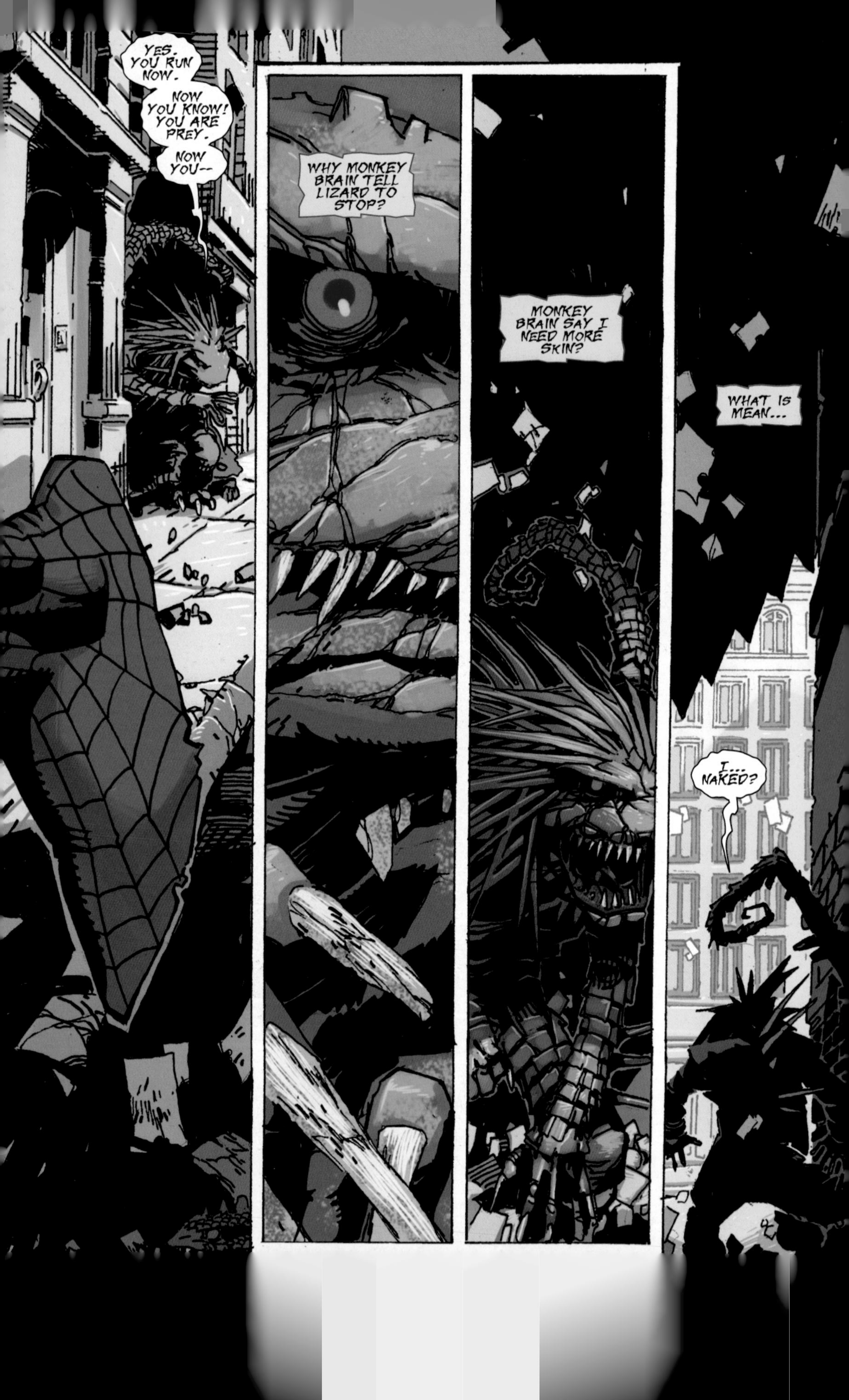
YES. YOU RUN NOW.
NOW YOU KNOW! YOU ARE PREY.
NOW YOU--
WHY MONKEY BRAIN TELL LIZARD TO STOP?
MONKEY BRAIN SAY I NEED MORE SKIN?
WHAT IS MEAN...
I... NAKED?

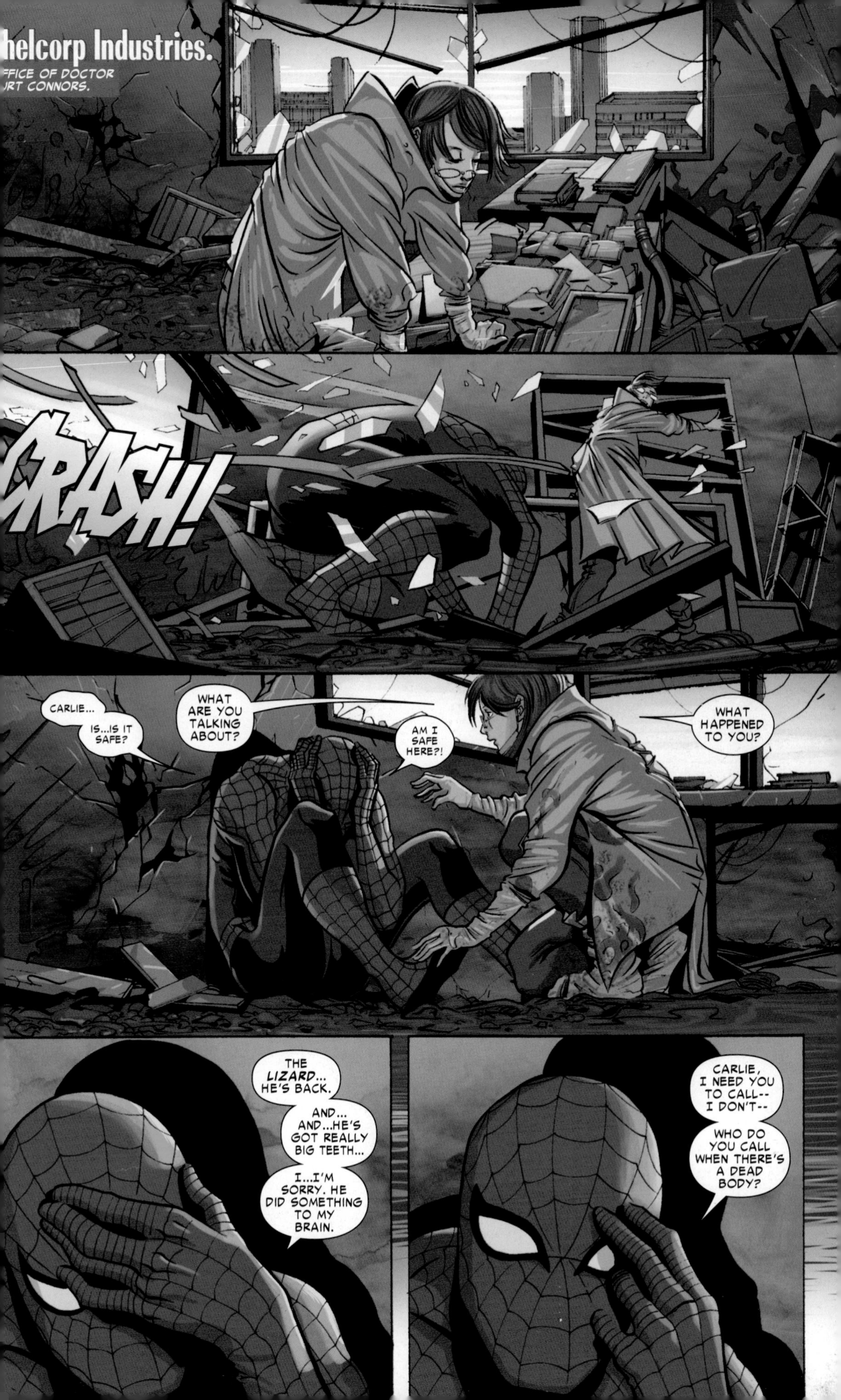

helcorp Industries.
FFICE OF DOCTOR
JRT CONNORS.
RASH!
CARLIE... IS...IS IT SAFE?
WHAT ARE YOU TALKING ABOUT?
AM I SAFE HERE?!
WHAT HAPPENED TO YOU?
THE LIZARD... HE'S BACK.
AND... AND...HE'S GOT REALLY BIG TEETH...
I...I'M SORRY. HE DID SOMETHING TO MY BRAIN.
CARLIE, I NEED YOU TO CALL-- I DON'T--
WHO DO YOU CALL WHEN THERE'S A DEAD BODY?

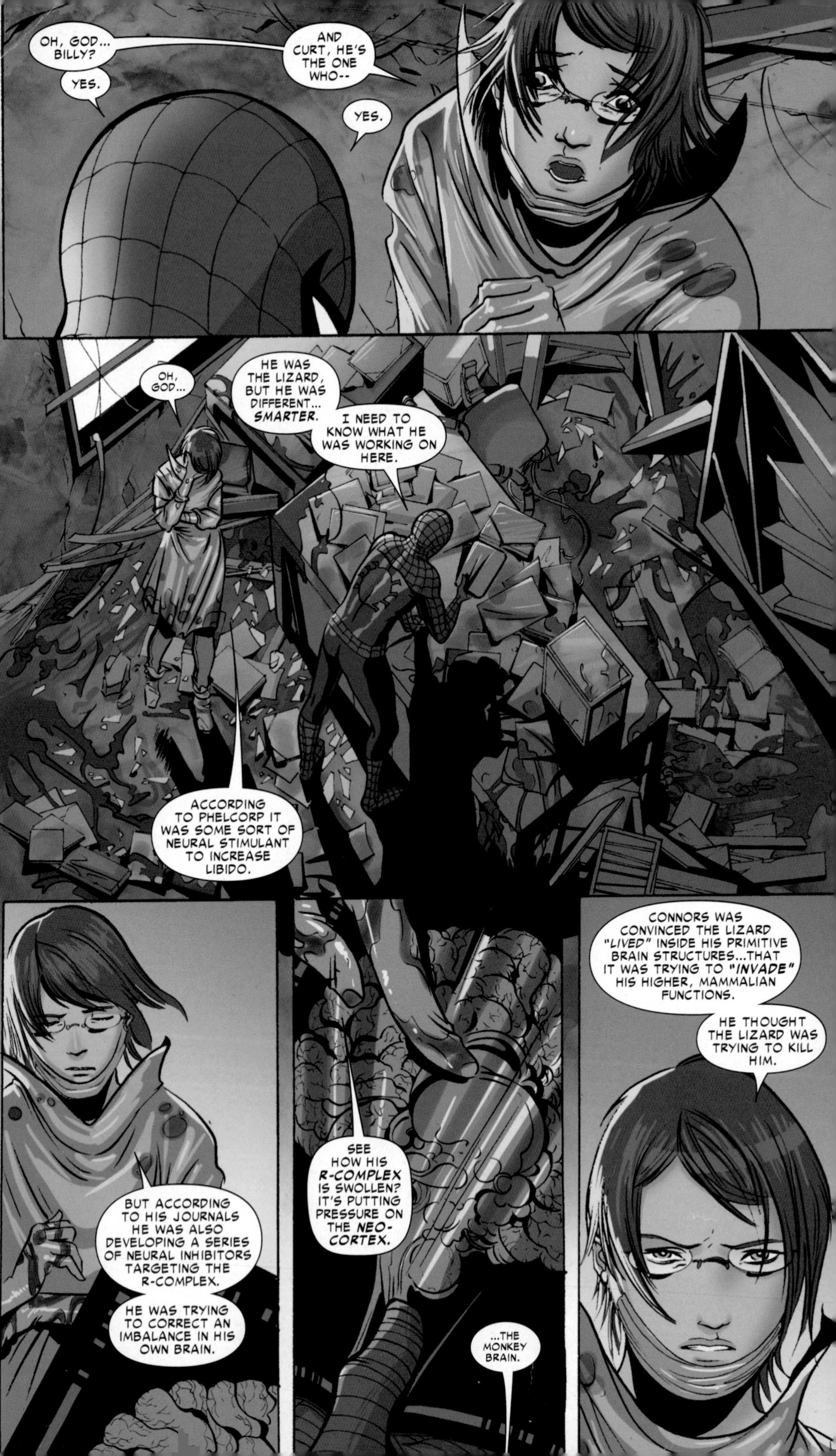
OH, GOD... BILLY?
YES.
AND CURT, HE'S THE ONE WHO--
YES.
OH, GOD...
HE WAS THE LIZARD, BUT HE WAS DIFFERENT... SMARTER.
I NEED TO KNOW WHAT HE WAS WORKING ON HERE.
ACCORDING TO PHELCORP IT WAS SOME SORT OF NEURAL STIMULANT TO INCREASE LIBIDO.
BUT ACCORDING TO HIS JOURNALS HE WAS ALSO DEVELOPING A SERIES OF NEURAL INHIBITORS TARGETING THE R-COMPLEX.
HE WAS TRYING TO CORRECT AN IMBALANCE IN HIS OWN BRAIN.
SEE HOW HIS R-COMPLEX IS SWOLLEN? IT'S PUTTING PRESSURE ON THE NEO-CORTEX.
...THE MONKEY BRAIN.
CONNORS WAS CONVINCED THE LIZARD "LIVED" INSIDE HIS PRIMITIVE BRAIN STRUCTURES...THAT IT WAS TRYING TO "INVADE" HIS HIGHER, MAMMALIAN FUNCTIONS.
HE THOUGHT THE LIZARD WAS TRYING TO KILL HIM.

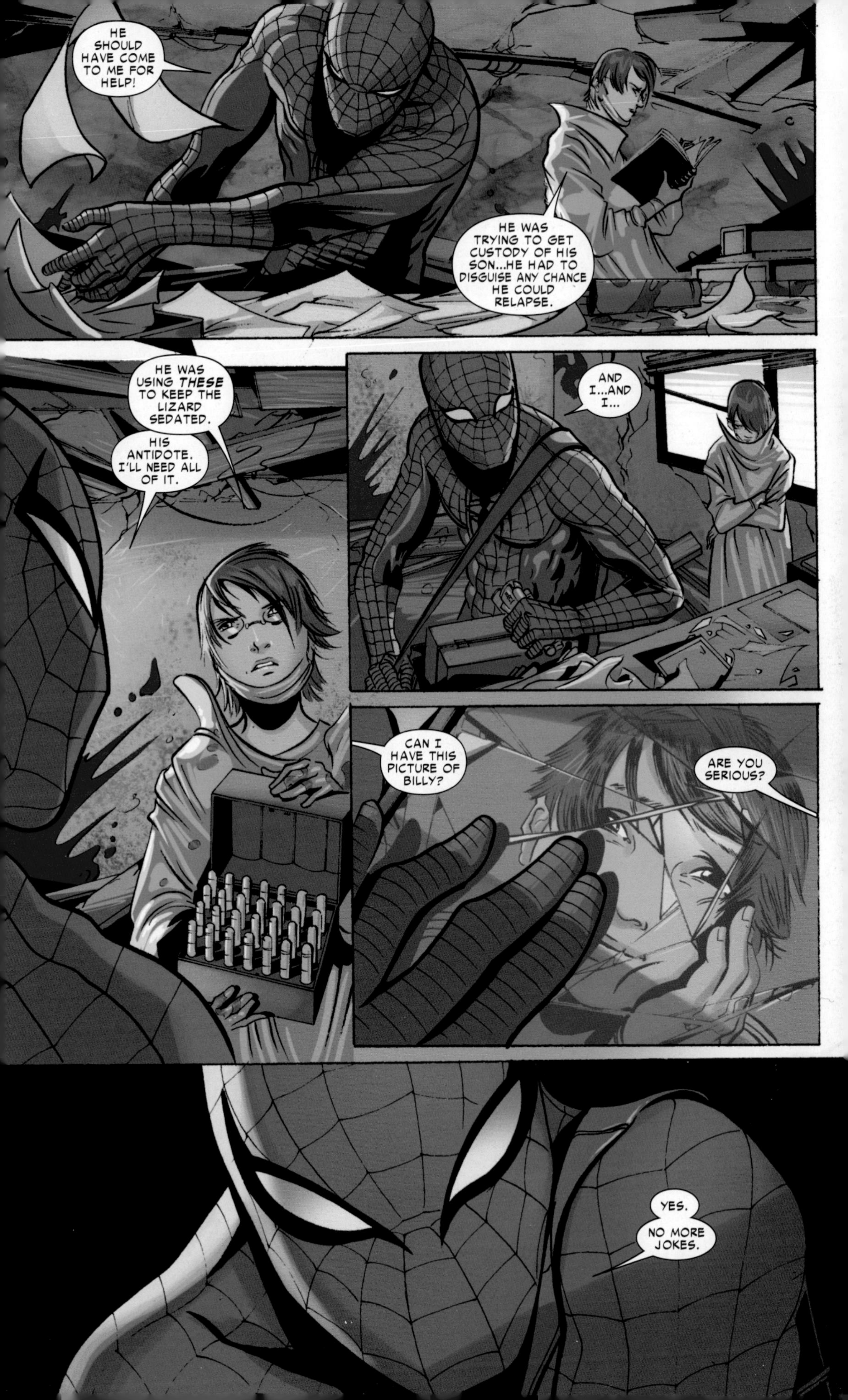
HE SHOULD HAVE COME TO ME FOR HELP!
HE WAS TRYING TO GET CUSTODY OF HIS SON...HE HAD TO DISGUISE ANY CHANCE HE COULD RELAPSE.
HE WAS USING *THESE* TO KEEP THE LIZARD SEDATED.
HIS ANTIDOTE. I'LL NEED ALL OF IT.
AND I...AND I...
CAN I HAVE THIS PICTURE OF BILLY?
ARE YOU SERIOUS?
YES.
NO MORE JOKES.

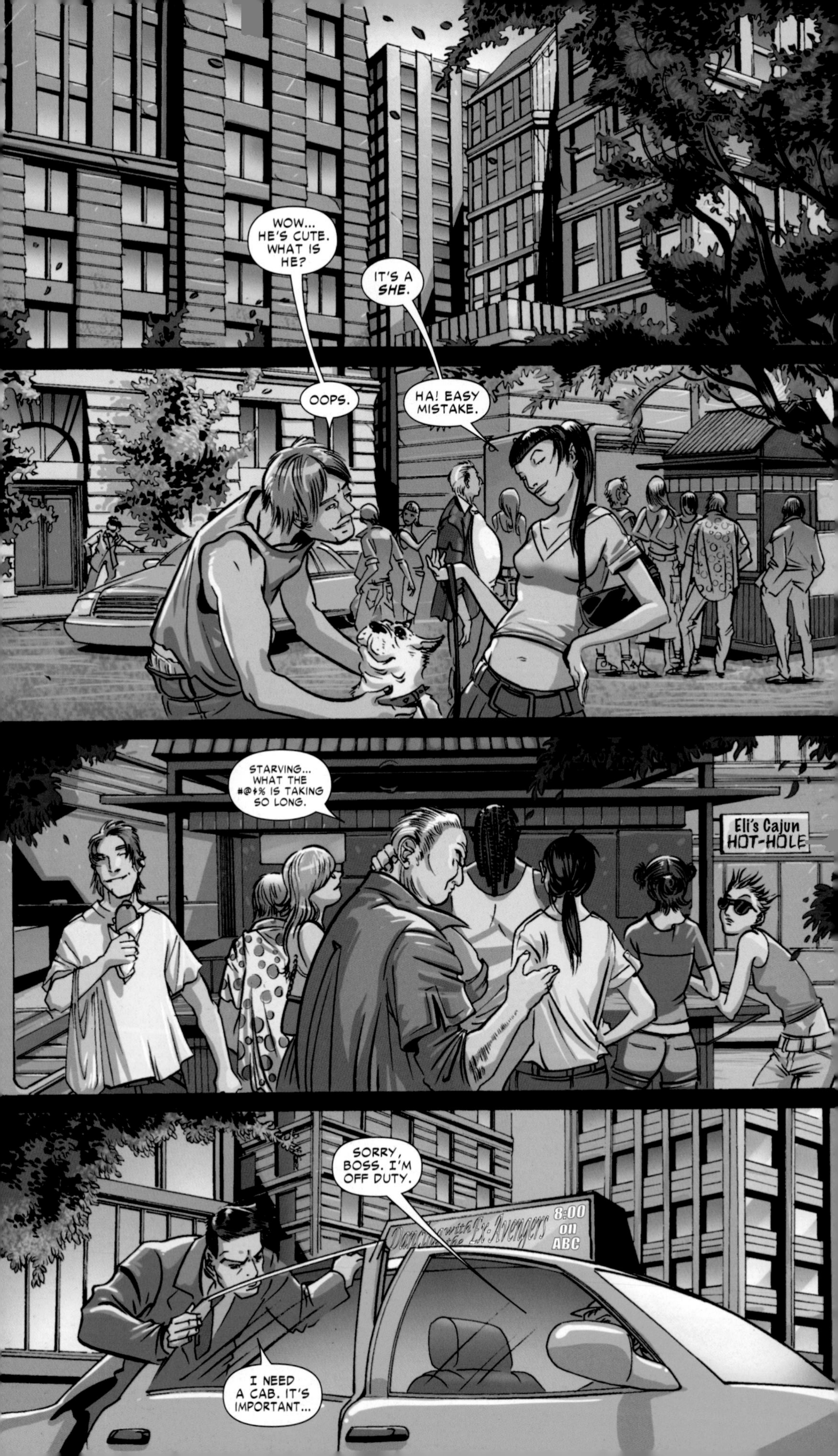
WOW... HE'S CUTE. WHAT IS HE?
IT'S A SHE.
OOPS.
HA! EASY MISTAKE.
STARVING... WHAT THE #@$% IS TAKING SO LONG.
Eli's Cajun HOT-HOLE
SORRY, BOSS. I'M OFF DUTY.
8:00 on ABC
I NEED A CAB. IT'S IMPORTANT...

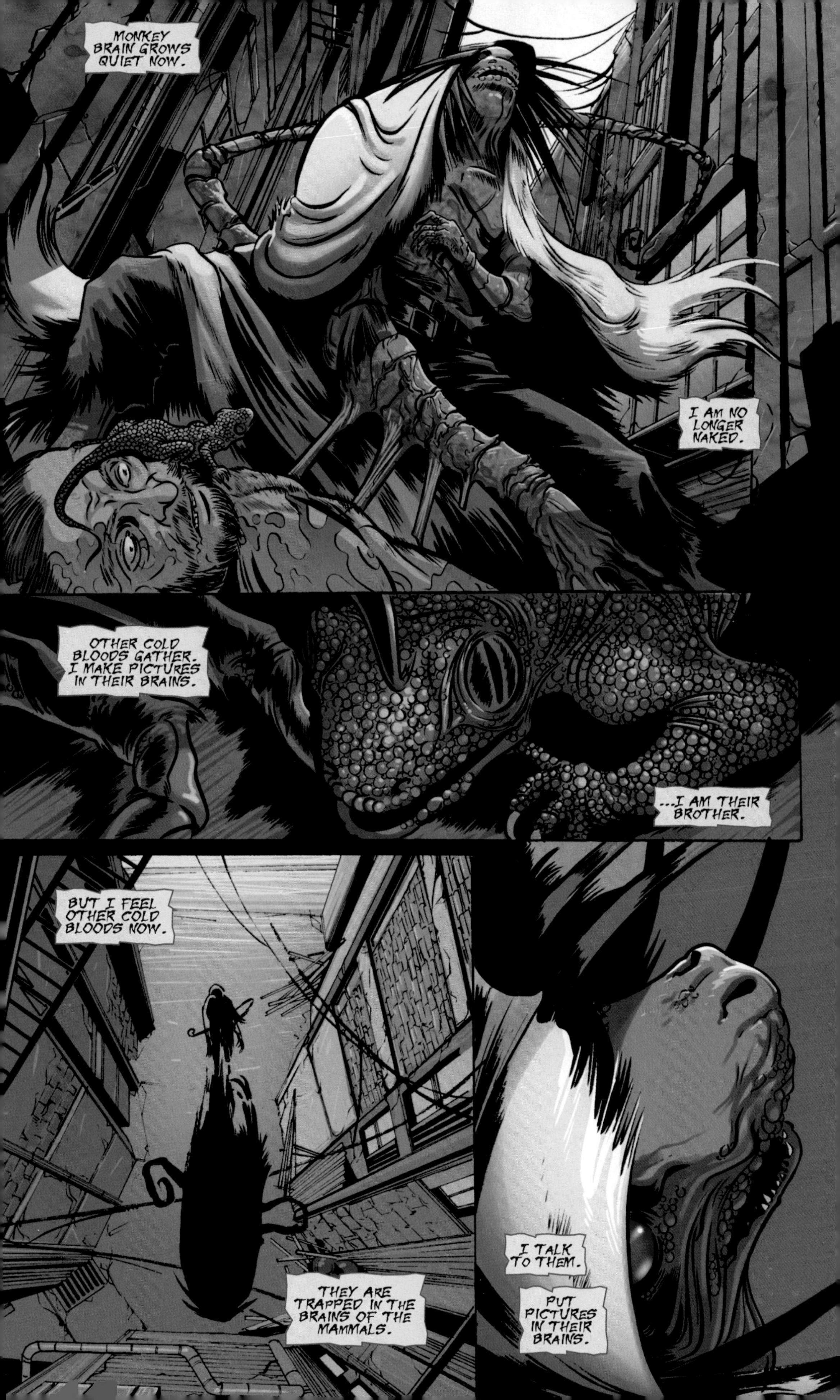
MONKEY BRAIN GROWS QUIET NOW.
I AM NO LONGER NAKED.
OTHER COLD BLOODS GATHER. I MAKE PICTURES IN THEIR BRAINS.
...I AM THEIR BROTHER.
BUT I FEEL OTHER COLD BLOODS NOW.
THEY ARE TRAPPED IN THE BRAINS OF THE MAMMALS.
I TALK TO THEM.
PUT PICTURES IN THEIR BRAINS.

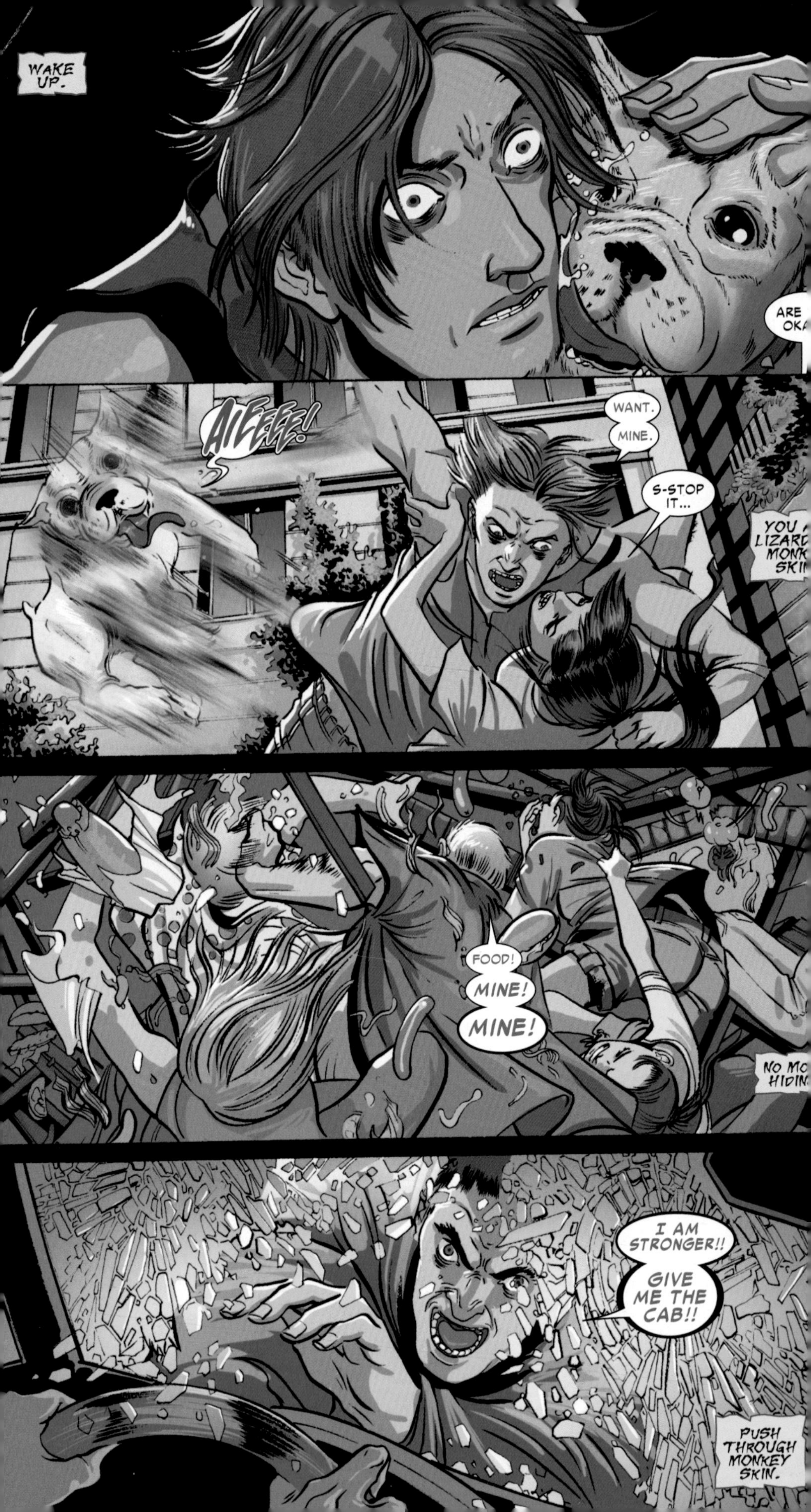
WAKE UP.
ARE OKA
AIEEEE!
WANT.
MINE.
S-STOP IT...
YOU LIZARD MONK SKI
FOOD!
MINE!
MINE!
NO MO HIDIN
I AM STRONGER!!
GIVE ME THE CAB!!
PUSH THROUGH MONKEY SKIN.

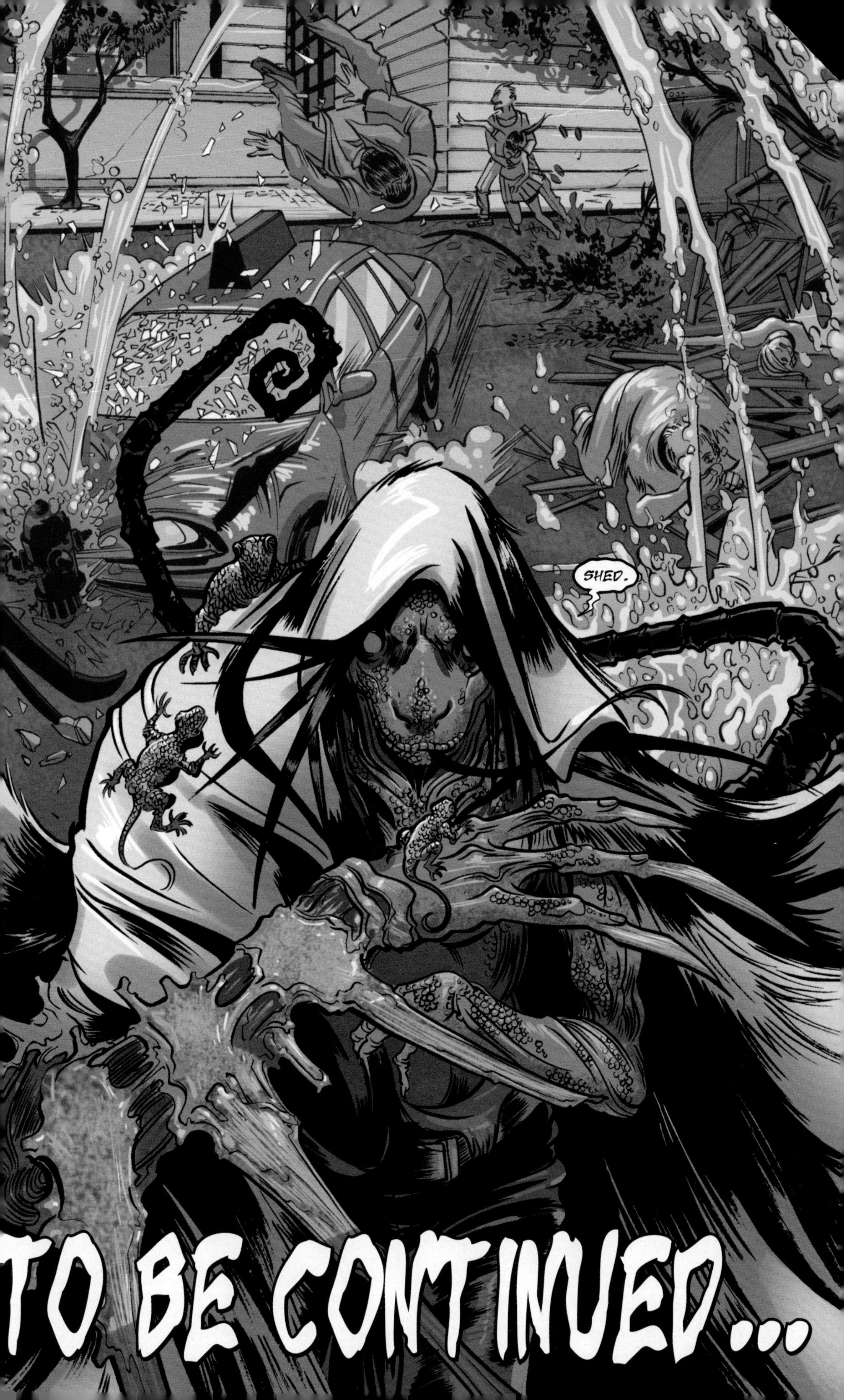
SHED.
TO BE CONTINUED...

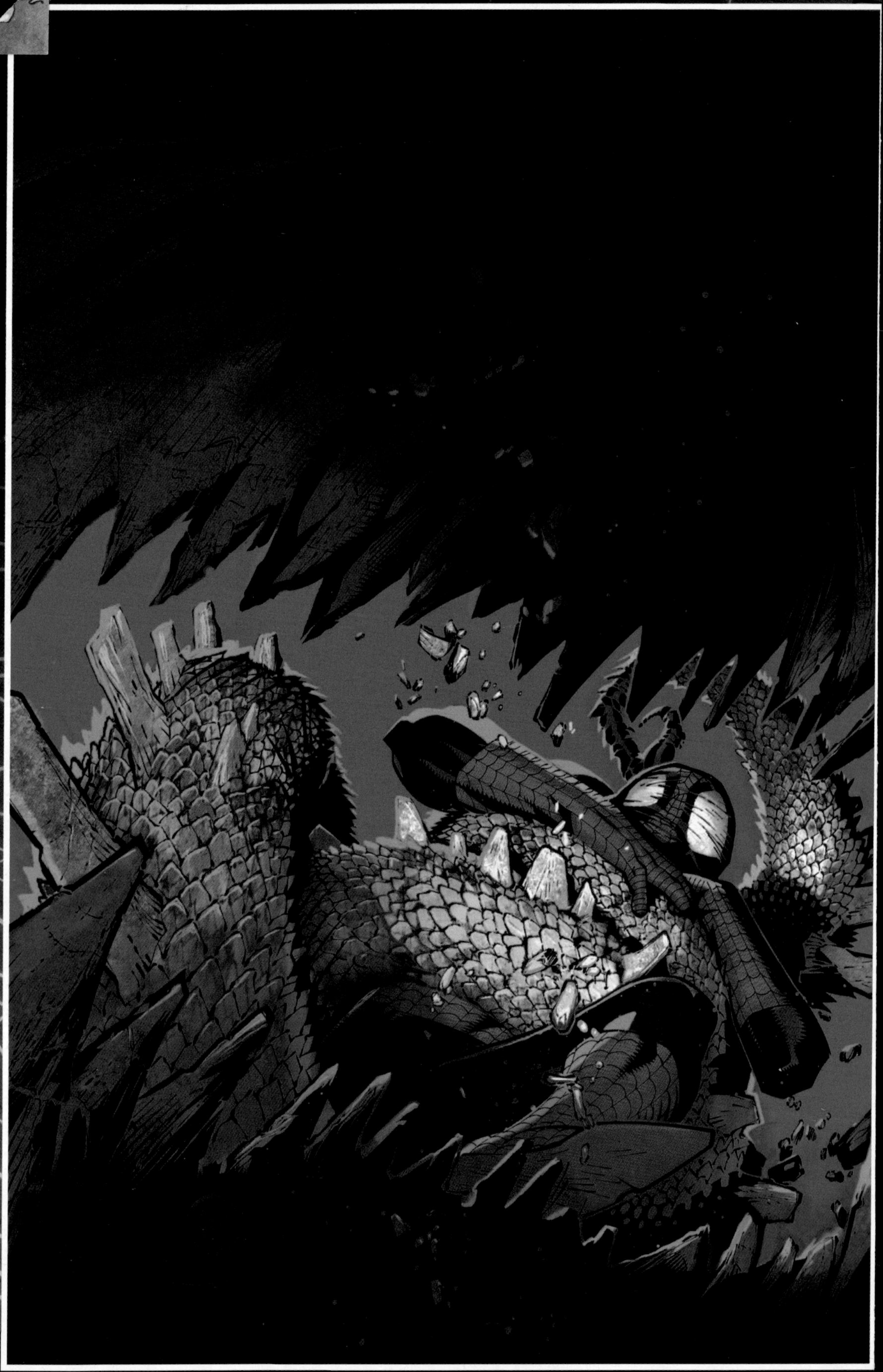

AMAZING SPIDER-MAN #633
COVER BY CHRIS BACHALO & TIM TOWNSEND

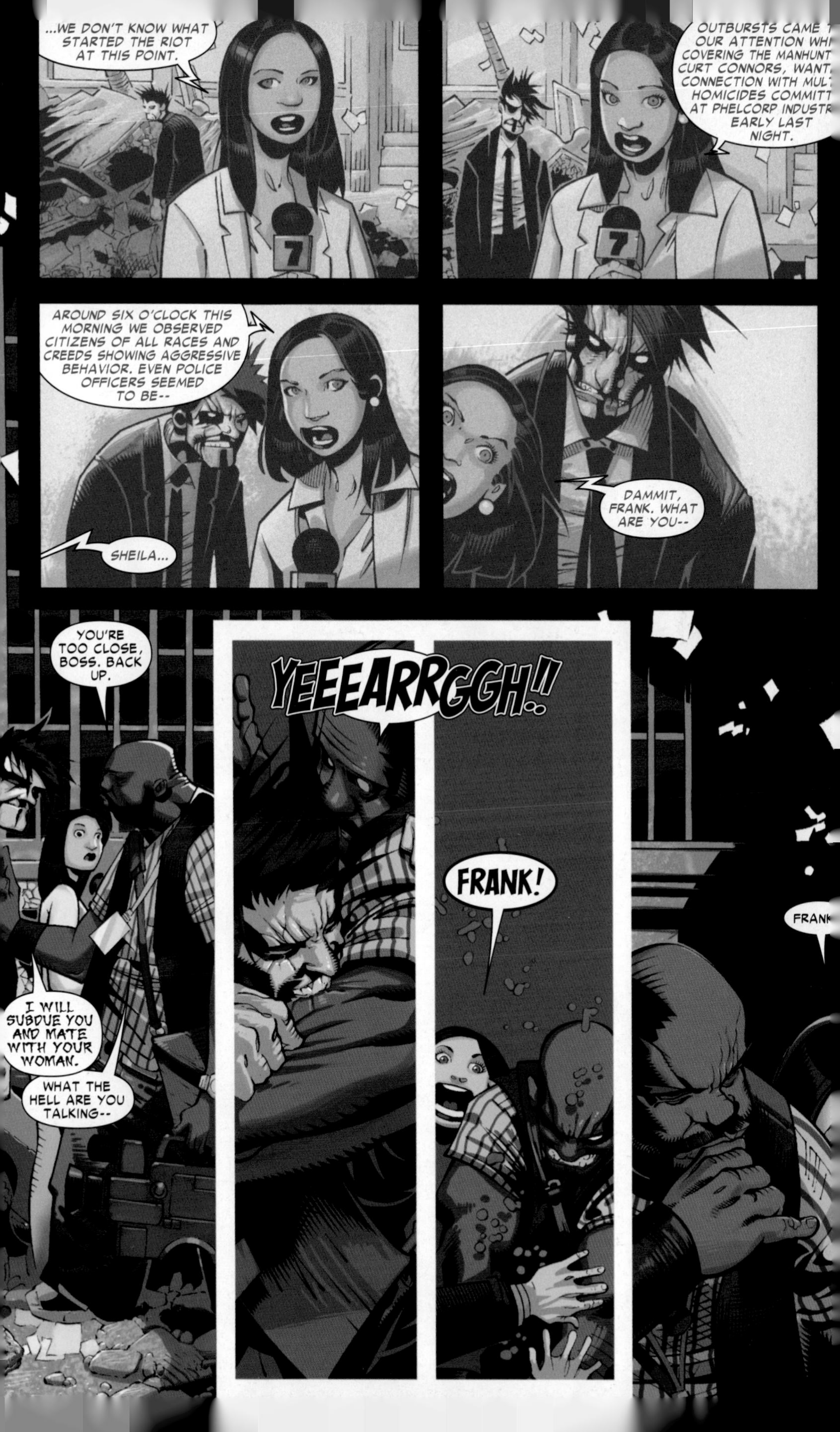
...WE DON'T KNOW WHAT STARTED THE RIOT AT THIS POINT.
OUTBURSTS CAME T OUR ATTENTION WHI COVERING THE MANHUNT CURT CONNORS, WANT CONNECTION WITH MULT HOMICIDES COMMITT AT PHELCORP INDUSTR EARLY LAST NIGHT.
AROUND SIX O'CLOCK THIS MORNING WE OBSERVED CITIZENS OF ALL RACES AND CREEDS SHOWING AGGRESSIVE BEHAVIOR. EVEN POLICE OFFICERS SEEMED TO BE--
SHEILA...
DAMMIT, FRANK. WHAT ARE YOU--
YOU'RE TOO CLOSE, BOSS. BACK UP.
I WILL SUBDUE YOU AND MATE WITH YOUR WOMAN.
WHAT THE HELL ARE YOU TALKING--
YEEEARRGGH!!
FRANK!
FRANK

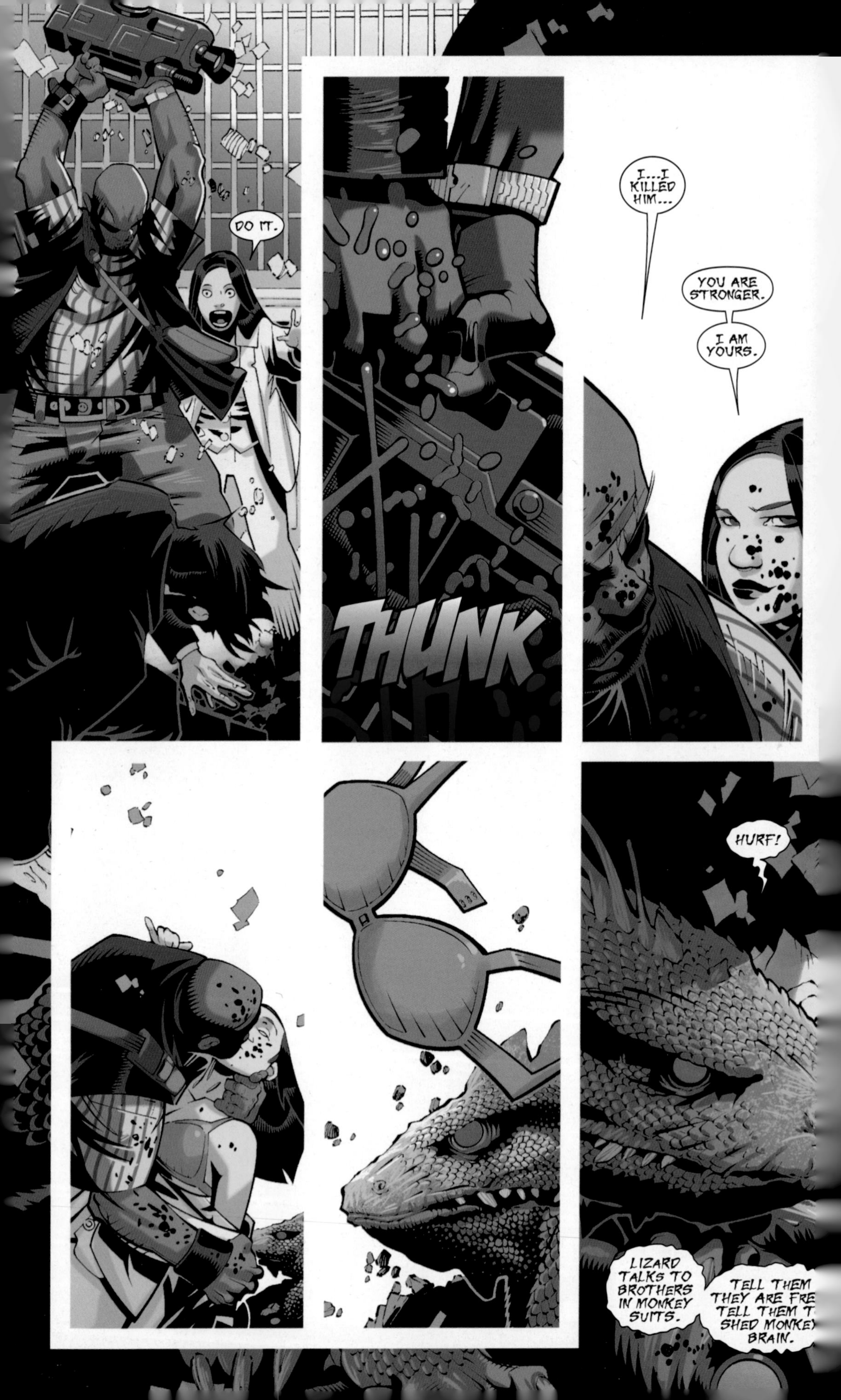
DO IT.
THUNK
I...I KILLED HIM...
YOU ARE STRONGER.
I AM YOURS.
HURF!
LIZARD TALKS TO BROTHERS IN MONKEY SUITS.
TELL THEM THEY ARE FRE
TELL THEM T
SHED MONKEY
BRAIN.

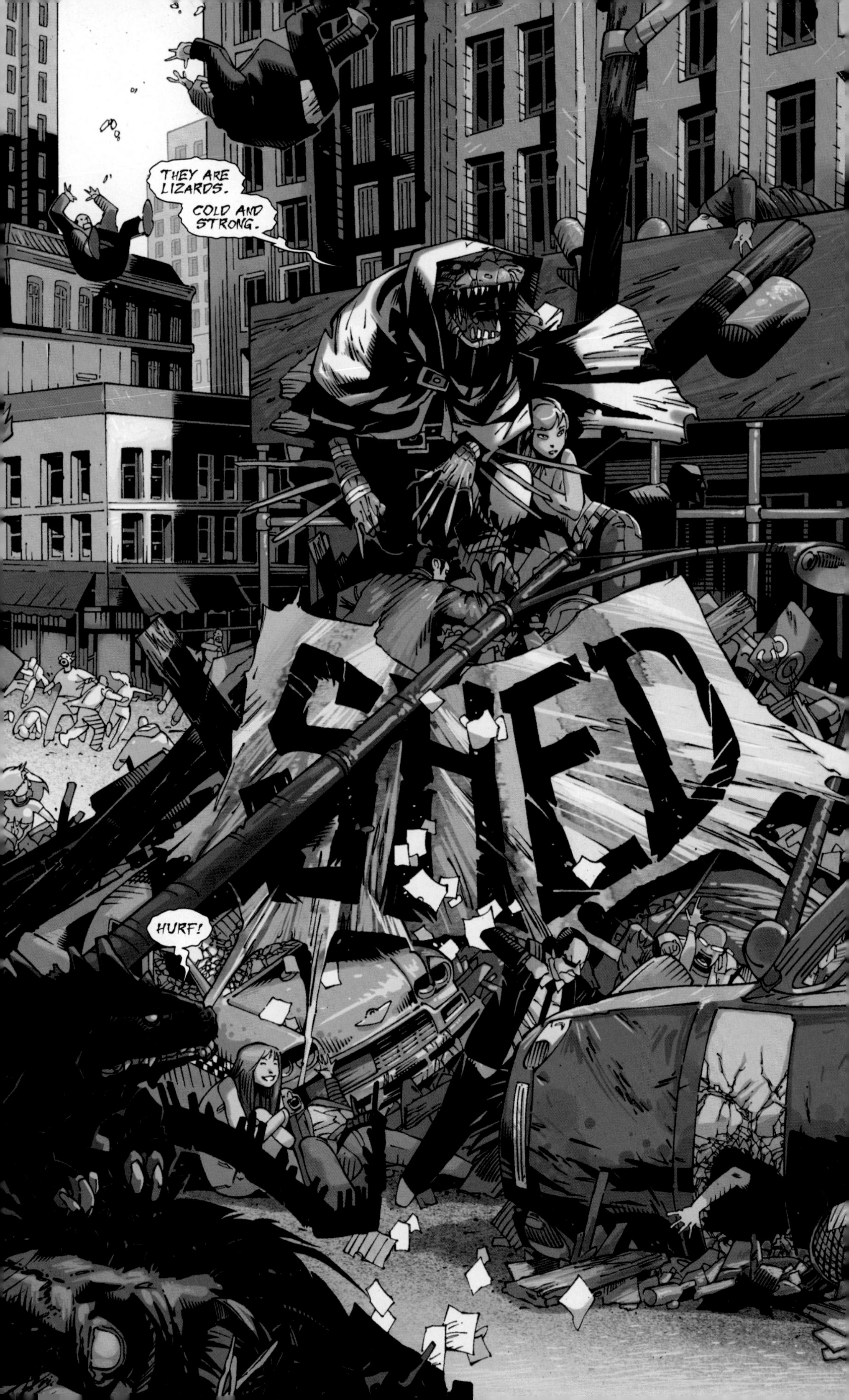
THEY ARE LIZARDS.
COLD AND STRONG.
HURF!

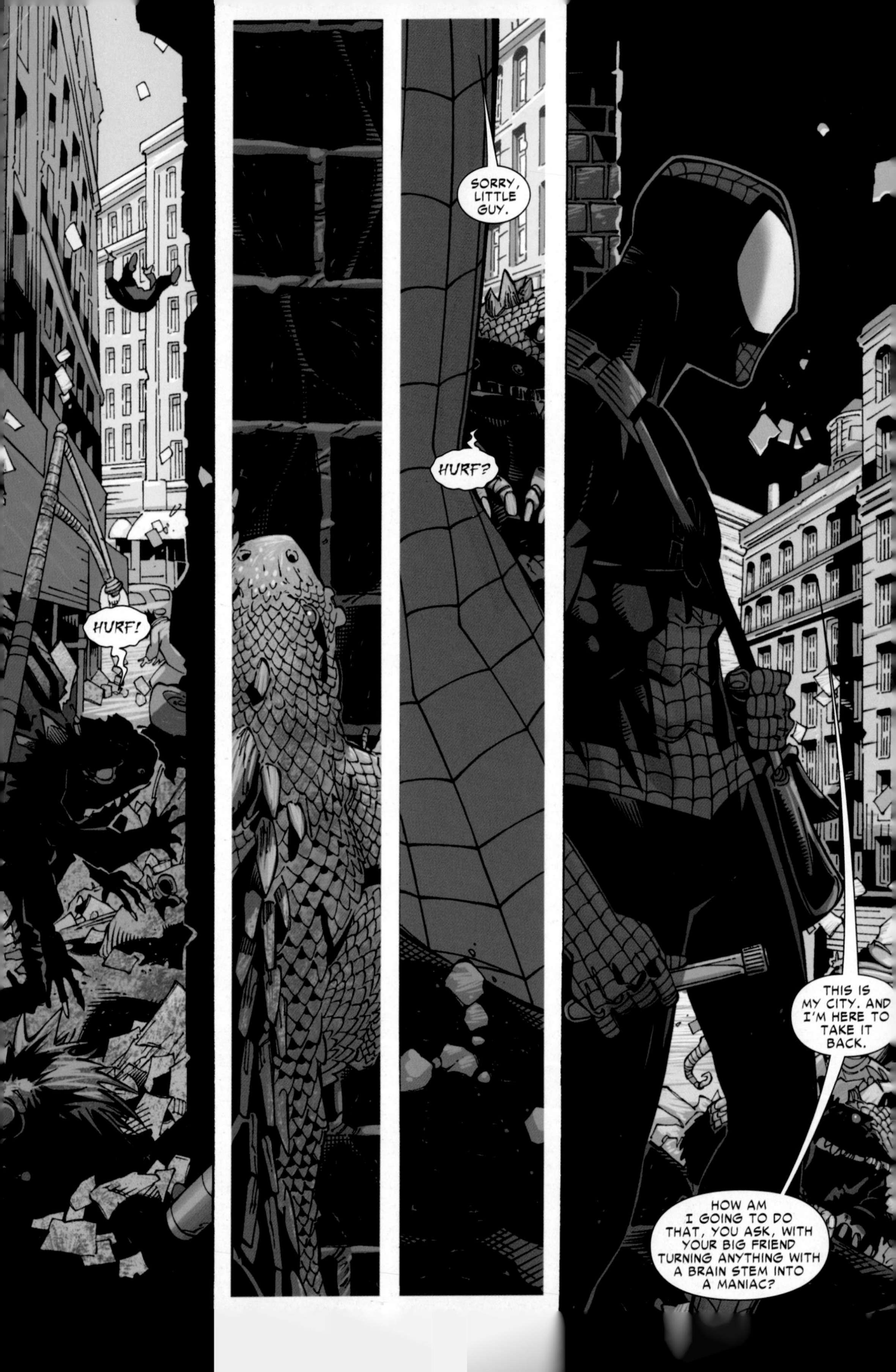
HURF!
SORRY, LITTLE GUY.
HURF?
THIS IS MY CITY. AND I'M HERE TO TAKE IT BACK.
HOW AM I GOING TO DO THAT, YOU ASK, WITH YOUR BIG FRIEND TURNING ANYTHING WITH A BRAIN STEM INTO A MANIAC?

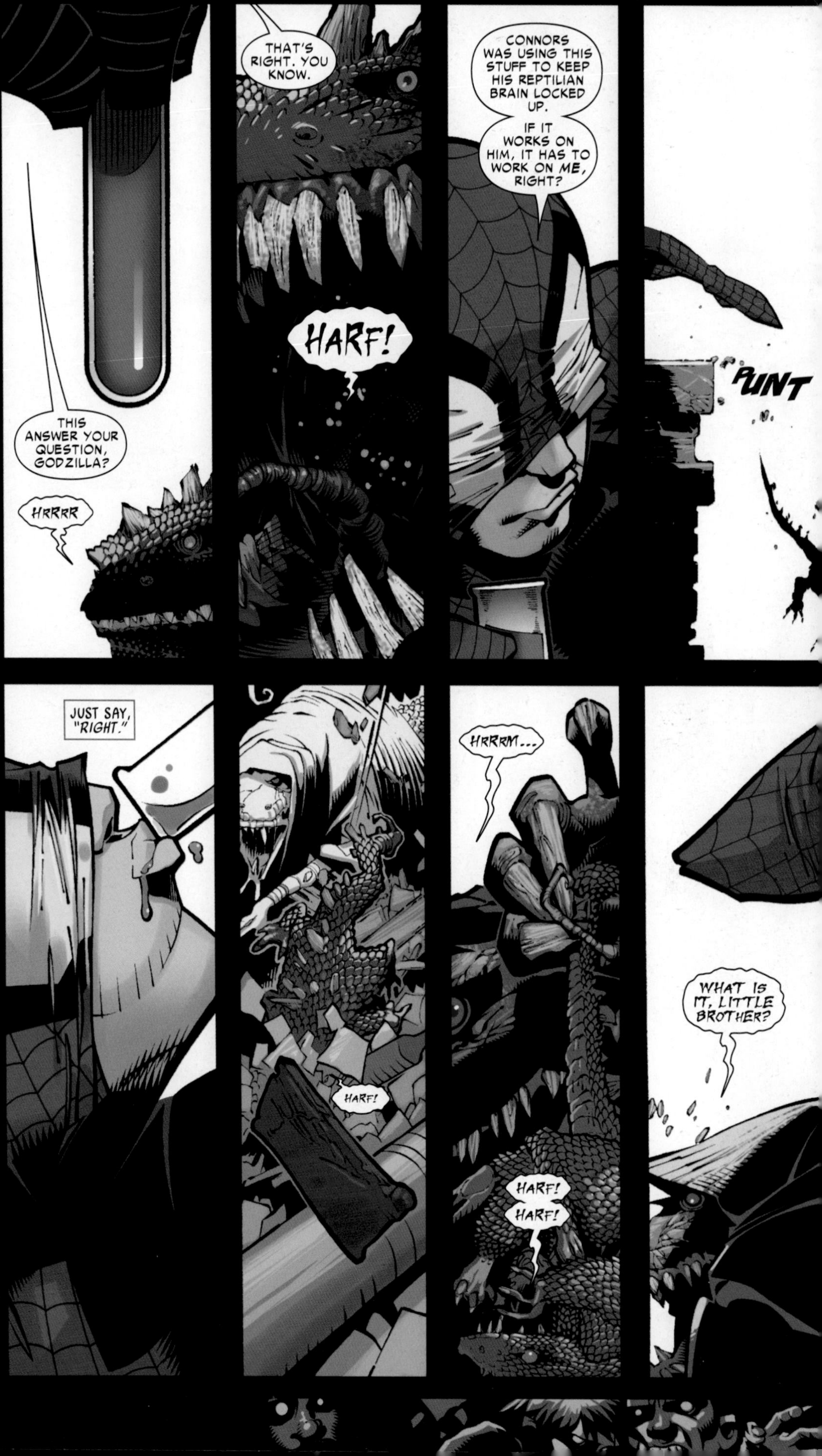
THIS ANSWER YOUR QUESTION, GODZILLA?
HRRRR
THAT'S RIGHT. YOU KNOW.
HARF!
CONNORS WAS USING THIS STUFF TO KEEP HIS REPTILIAN BRAIN LOCKED UP.
IF IT WORKS ON HIM, IT HAS TO WORK ON ME, RIGHT?
PUNT
JUST SAY, "RIGHT."
HARF!
HRRRM...
HARF! HARF!
WHAT IS IT, LITTLE BROTHER?

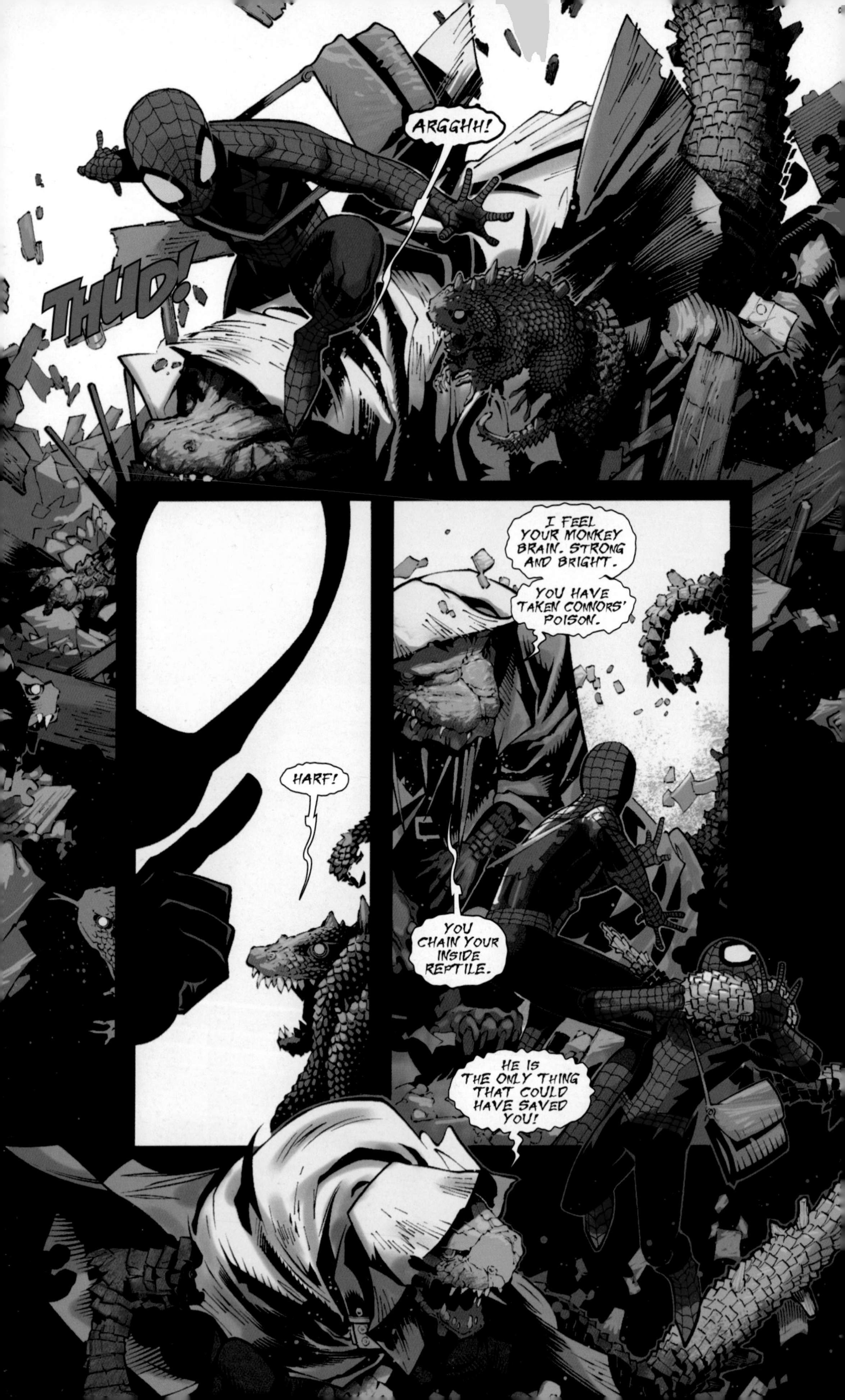
ARGGHH!
THUD!
HARF!
I FEEL YOUR MONKEY BRAIN. STRONG AND BRIGHT.
YOU HAVE TAKEN CONNORS' POISON.
YOU CHAIN YOUR INSIDE REPTILE.
HE IS THE ONLY THING THAT COULD HAVE SAVED YOU!

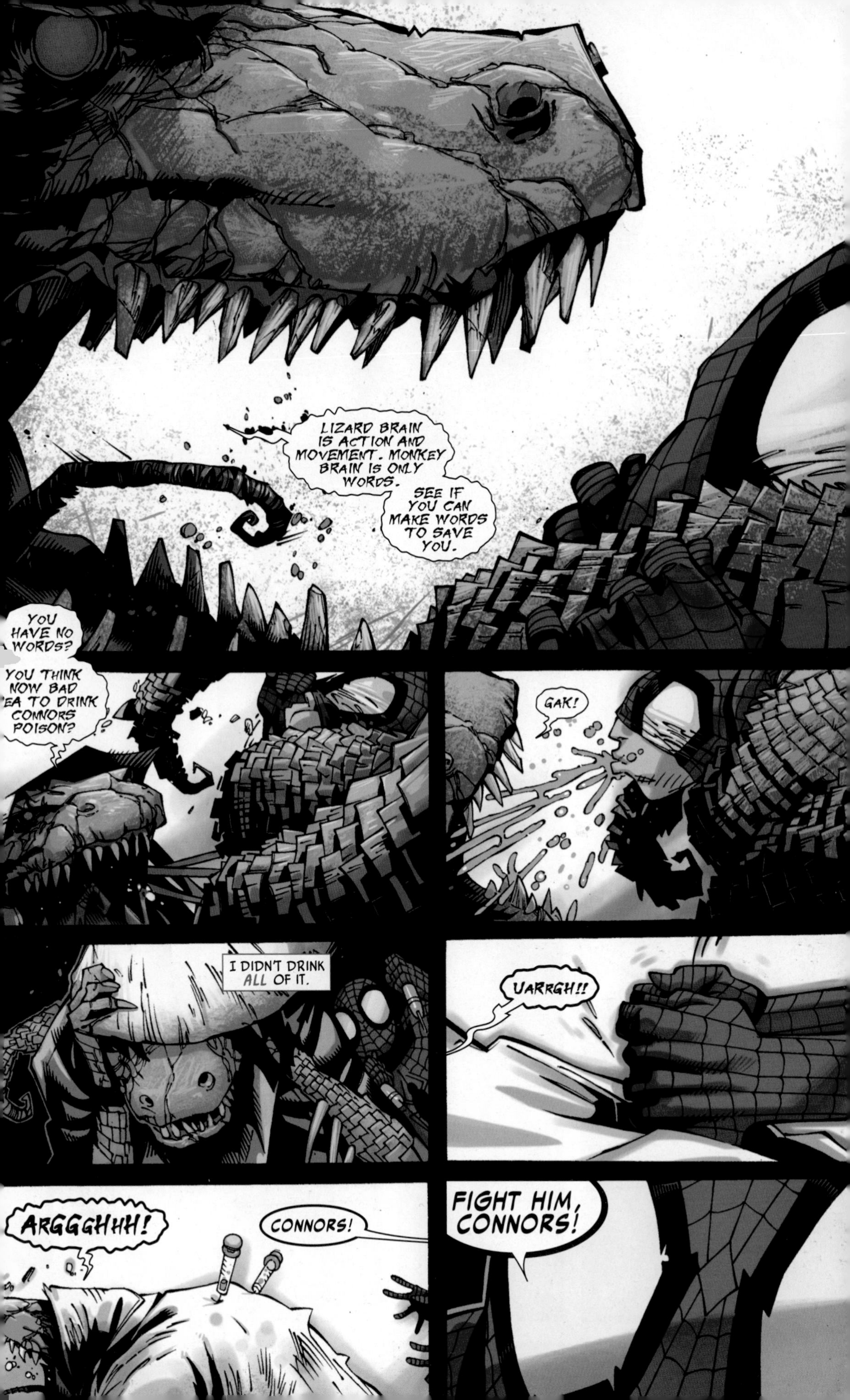
LIZARD BRAIN IS ACTION AND MOVEMENT. MONKEY BRAIN IS ONLY WORDS.
SEE IF YOU CAN MAKE WORDS TO SAVE YOU.
YOU HAVE NO WORDS?
YOU THINK NOW BAD EA TO DRINK CONNORS POISON?
GAK!
I DIDN'T DRINK ALL OF IT.
UARRGH!!
ARGGGHHH!
CONNORS!
FIGHT HIM, CONNORS!

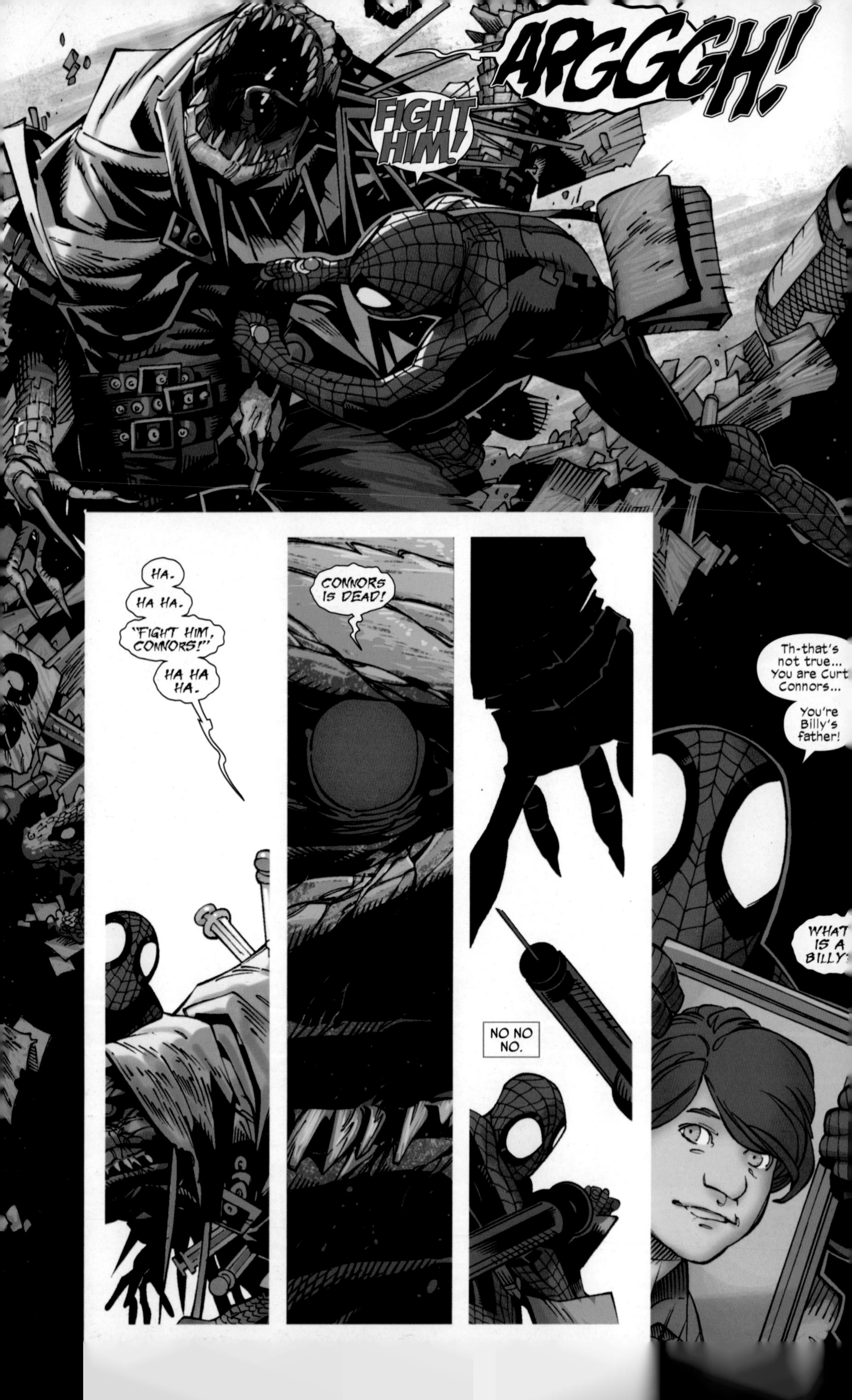
ARGGGH!
FIGHT HIM!
HA.
HA HA.
"FIGHT HIM, CONNORS!"
HA HA HA.
CONNORS IS DEAD!
NO NO NO.
Th-that's not true... You are Curt Connors...
You're Billy's father!
WHAT IS A BILLY?

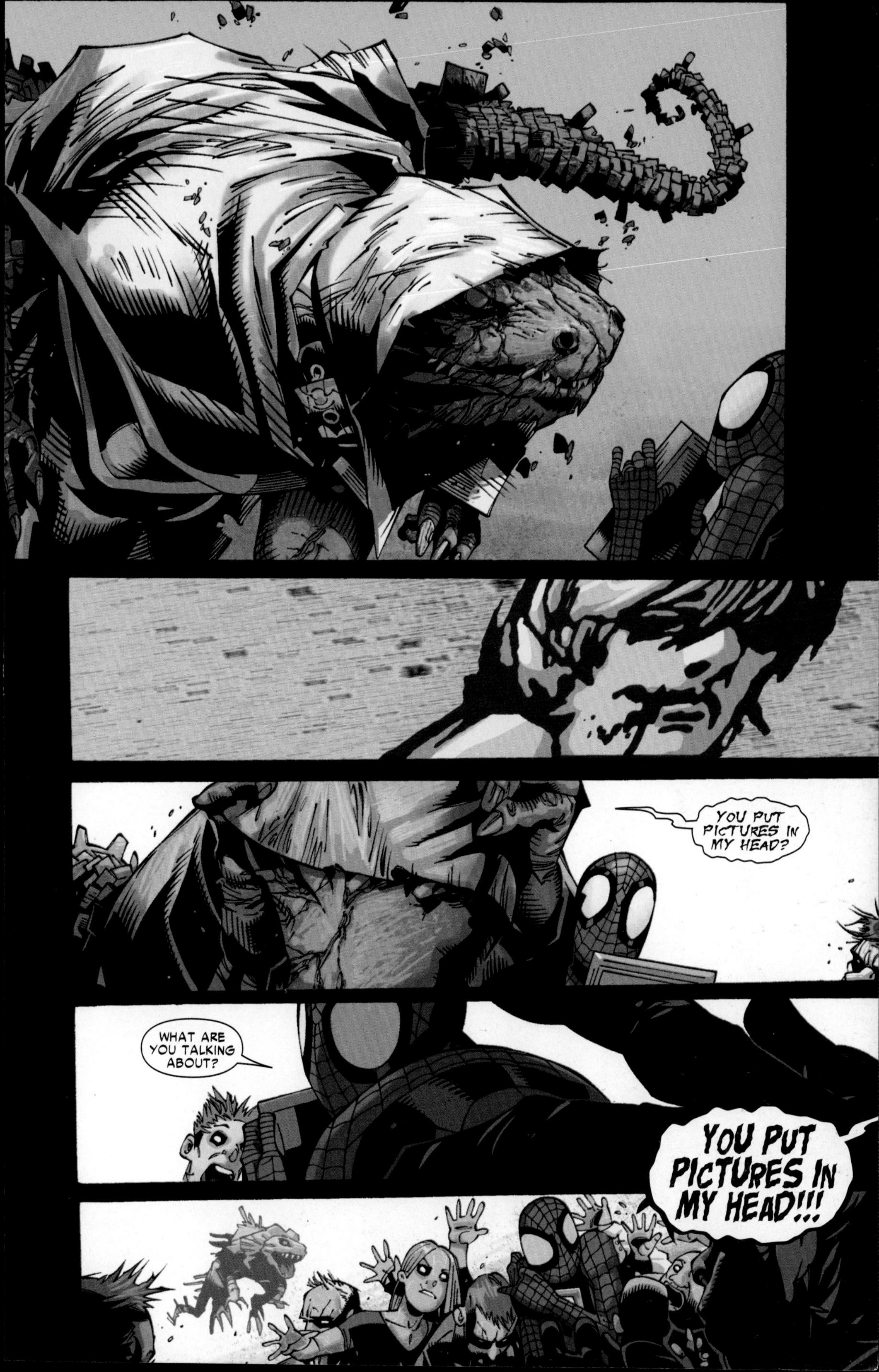
YOU PUT PICTURES IN MY HEAD?
WHAT ARE YOU TALKING ABOUT?
YOU PUT PICTURES IN MY HEAD!!!

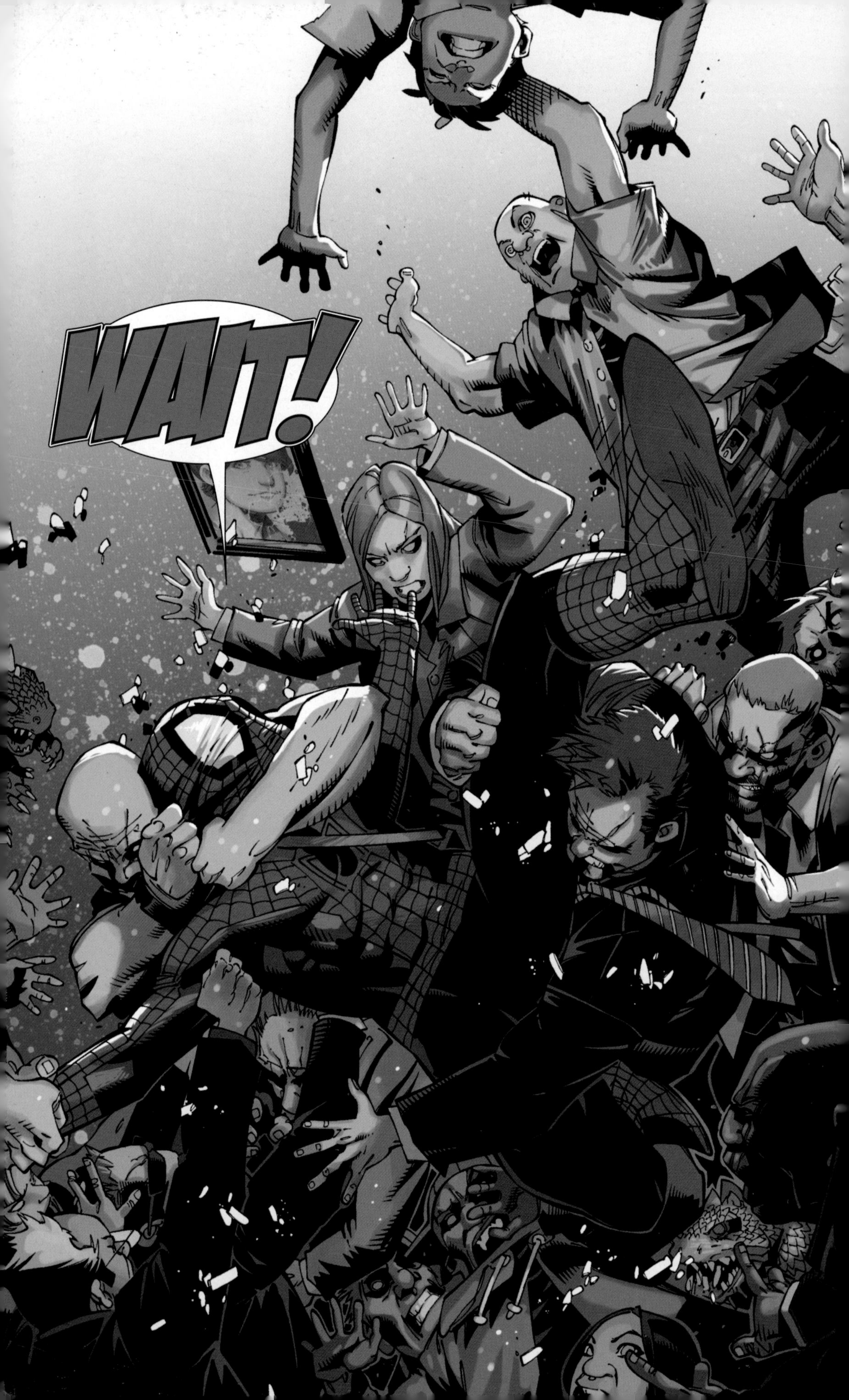
WAIT!

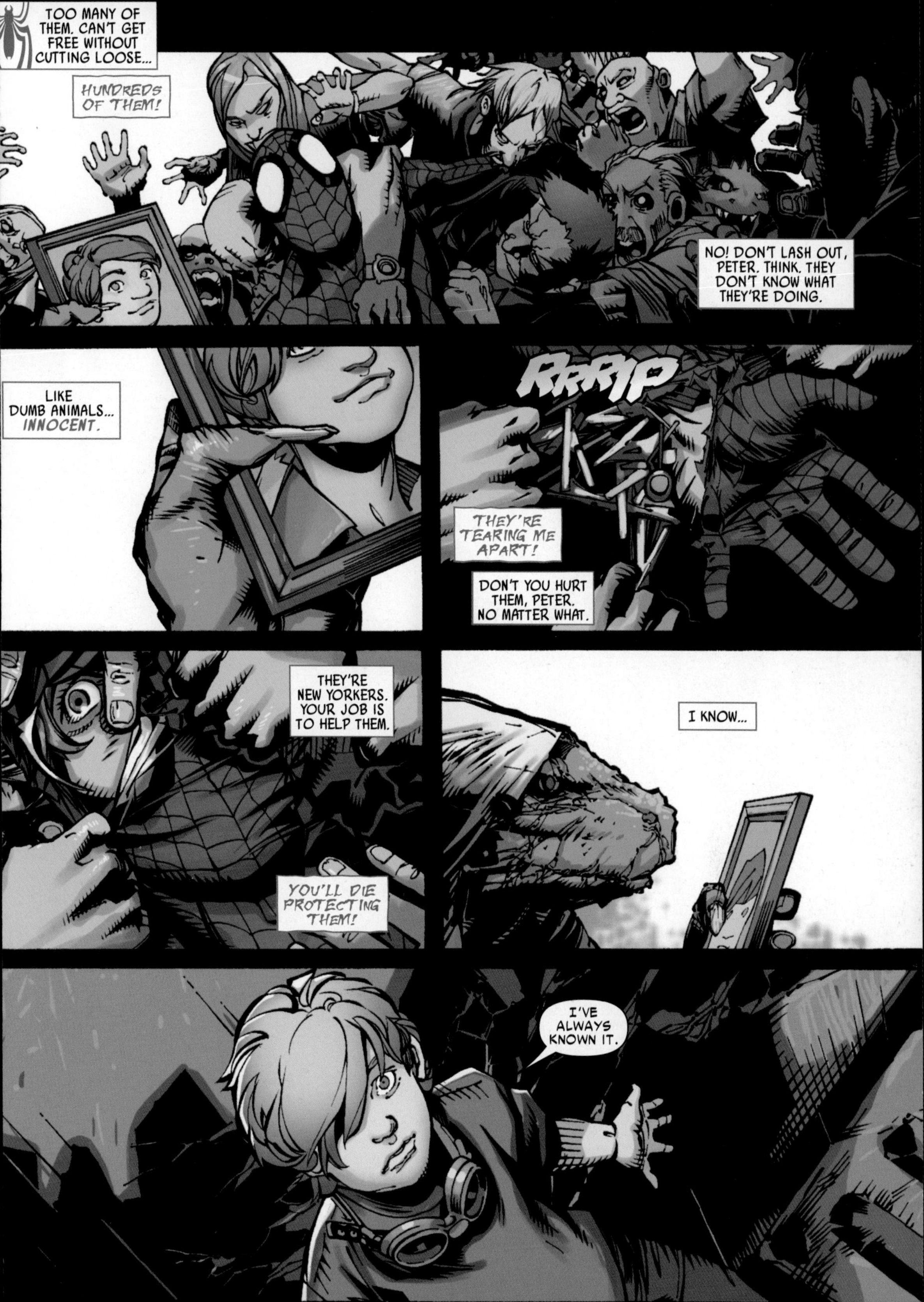
TOO MANY OF THEM. CAN'T GET FREE WITHOUT CUTTING LOOSE...
HUNDREDS OF THEM!
NO! DON'T LASH OUT, PETER. THINK. THEY DON'T KNOW WHAT THEY'RE DOING.
LIKE DUMB ANIMALS... INNOCENT.
RRRIP
THEY'RE TEARING ME APART!
DON'T YOU HURT THEM, PETER. NO MATTER WHAT.
THEY'RE NEW YORKERS. YOUR JOB IS TO HELP THEM.
YOU'LL DIE PROTECTING THEM!
I KNOW...
I'VE ALWAYS KNOWN IT.

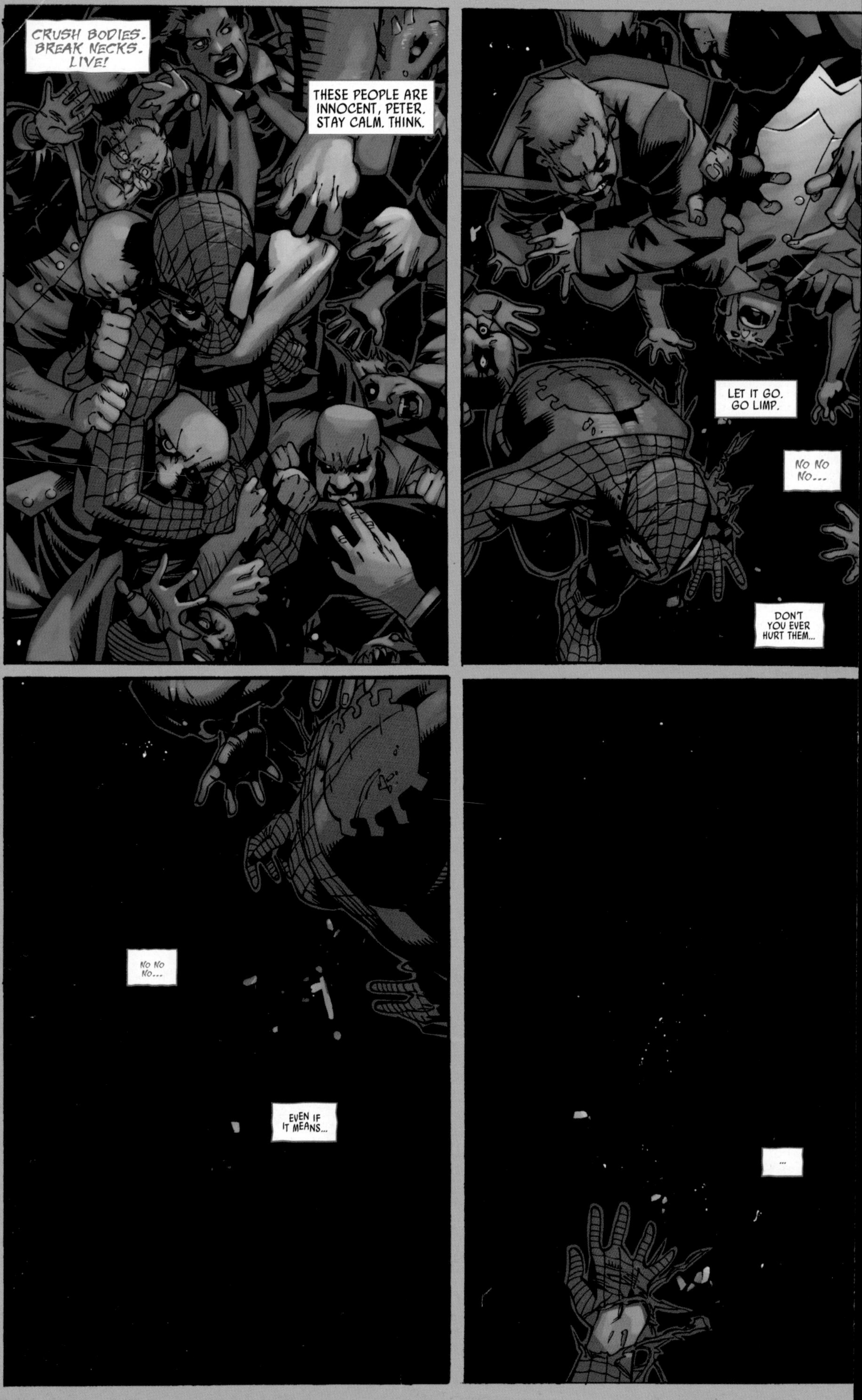
CRUSH BODIES. BREAK NECKS. LIVE!
THESE PEOPLE ARE INNOCENT, PETER. STAY CALM. THINK.
LET IT GO. GO LIMP.
NO NO NO...
DON'T YOU EVER HURT THEM...
NO NO NO...
EVEN IF IT MEANS...
...

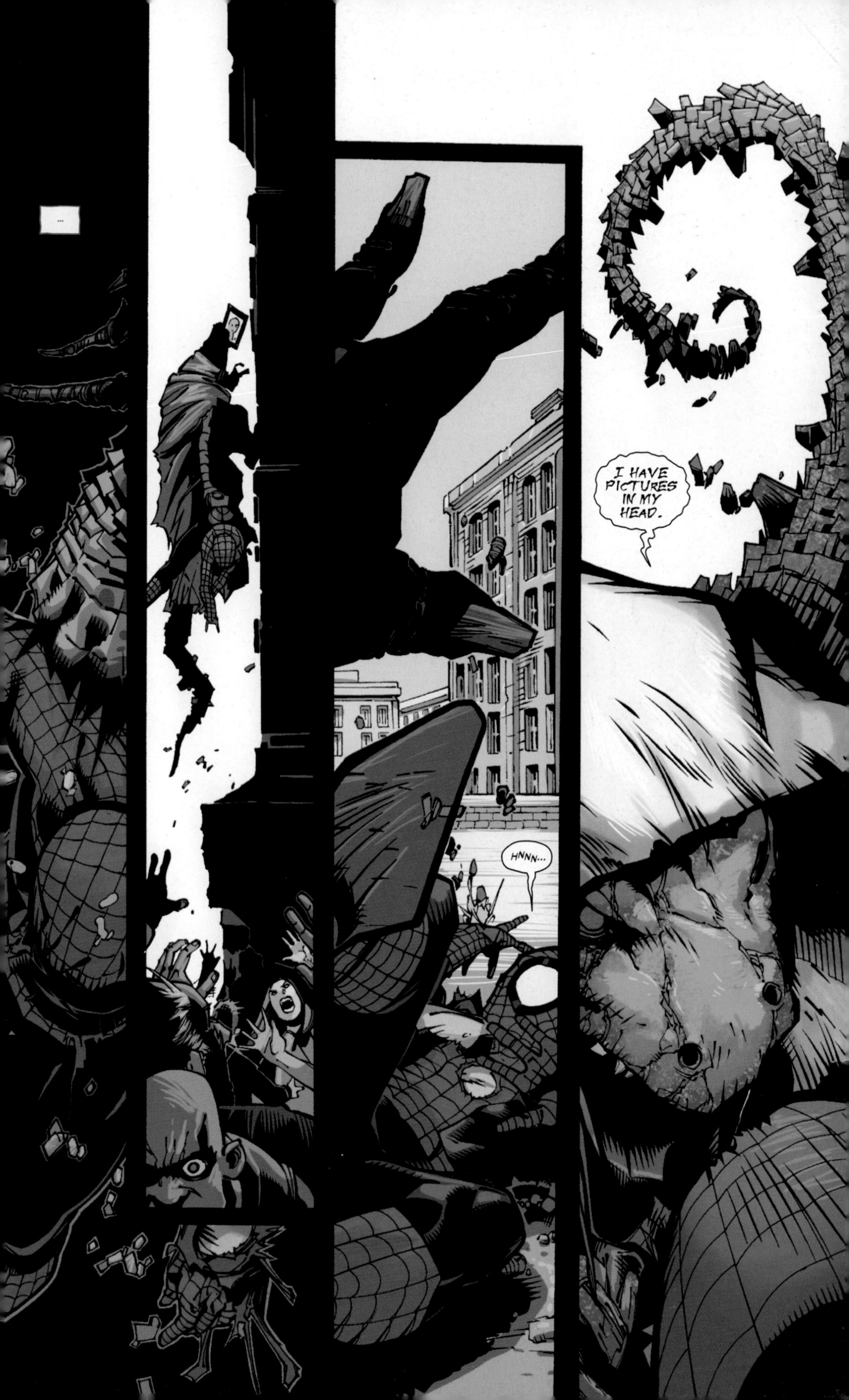
...
I HAVE PICTURES IN MY HEAD.
HNNN...

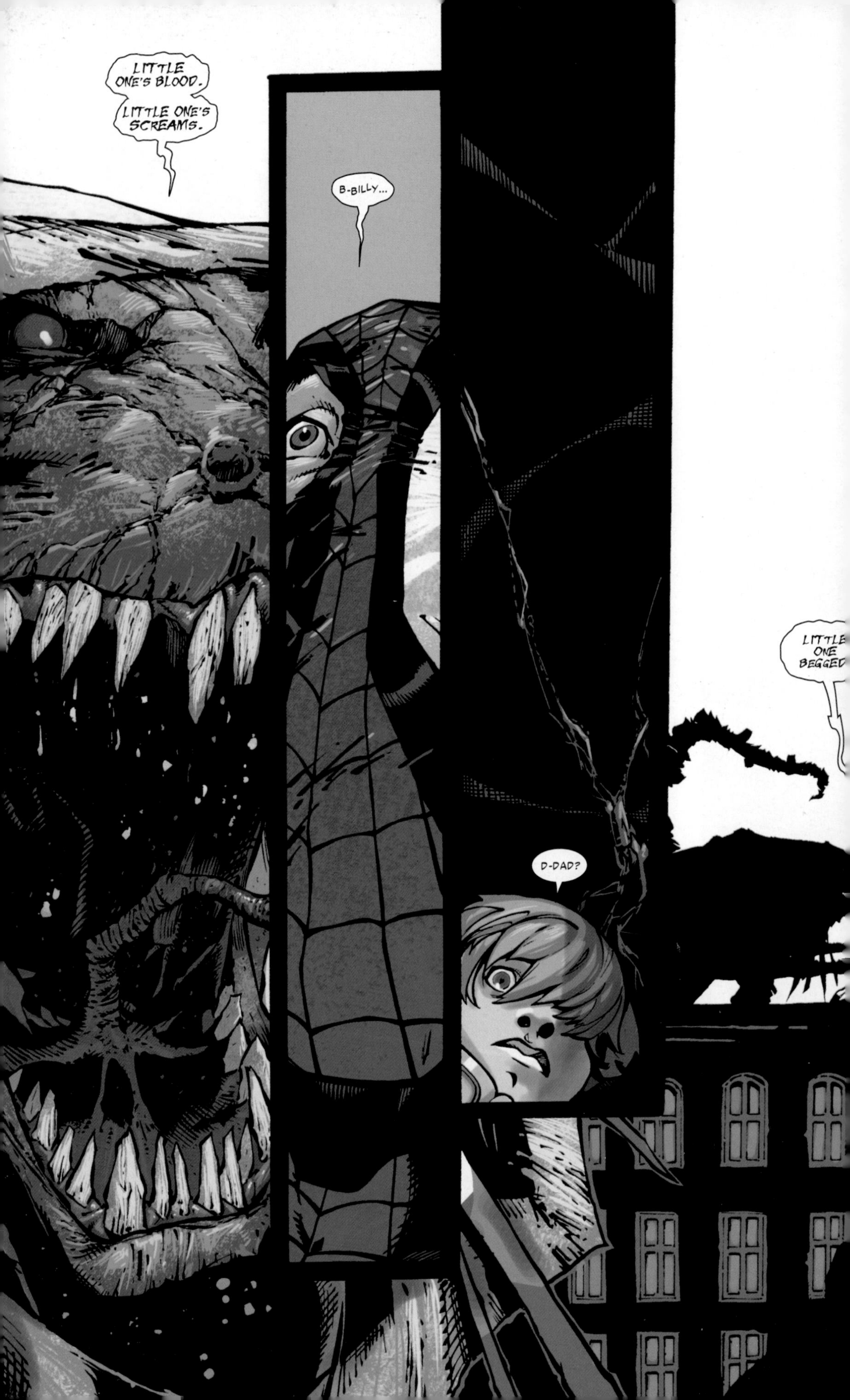
LITTLE ONE'S BLOOD.
LITTLE ONE'S SCREAMS.
B-BILLY...
LITTLE ONE BEGGED
D-DAD?

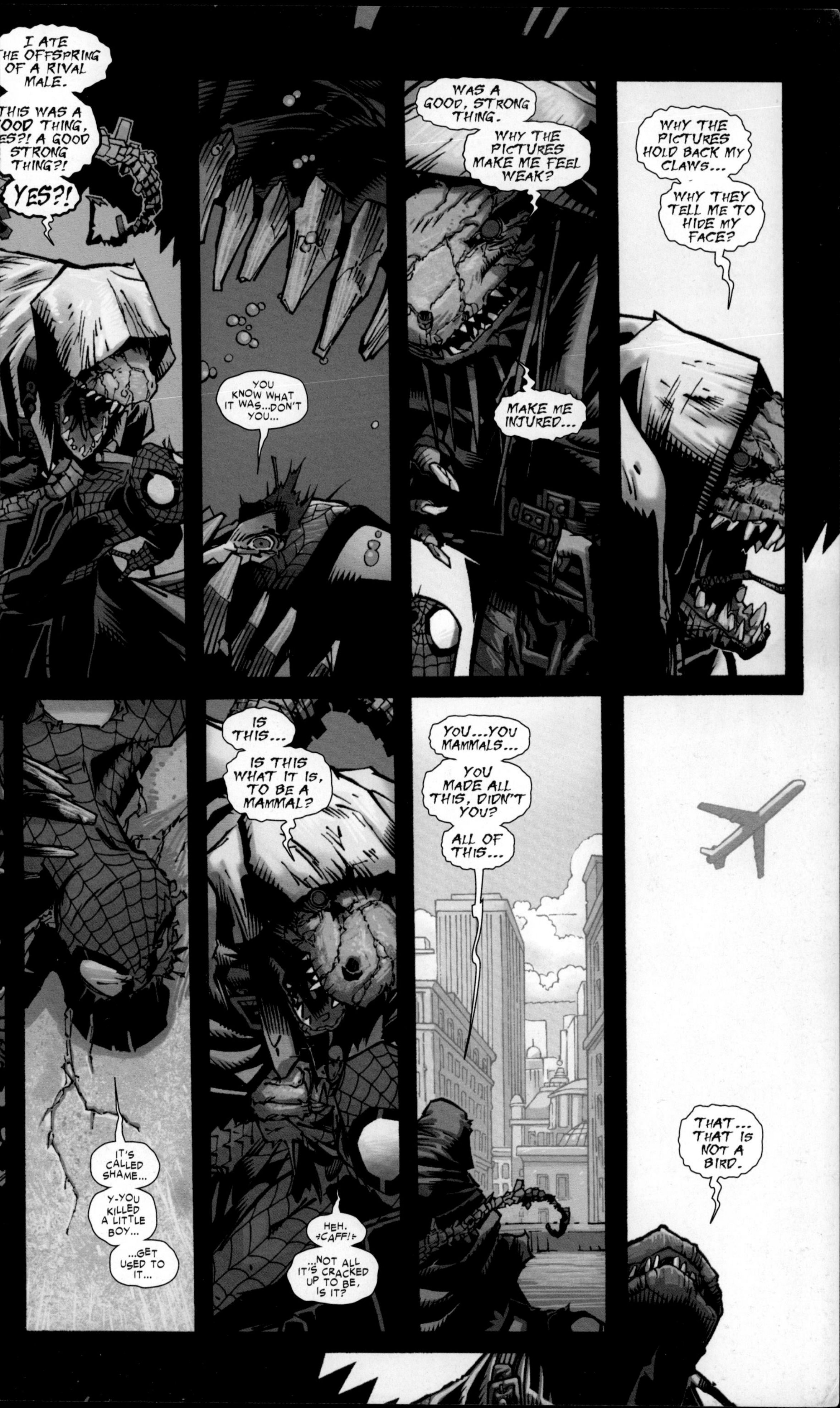

I ATE THE OFFSPRING OF A RIVAL MALE.
THIS WAS A GOOD THING, YES?! A GOOD STRONG THING?!
YES?!
YOU KNOW WHAT IT WAS...DON'T YOU...
WAS A GOOD, STRONG THING.
WHY THE PICTURES MAKE ME FEEL WEAK?
MAKE ME INJURED...
WHY THE PICTURES HOLD BACK MY CLAWS...
WHY THEY TELL ME TO HIDE MY FACE?
IT'S CALLED SHAME...
Y-YOU KILLED A LITTLE BOY...
...GET USED TO IT...
IS THIS...
IS THIS WHAT IT IS, TO BE A MAMMAL?
HEH. *CAFF!*
...NOT ALL IT'S CRACKED UP TO BE, IS IT?
YOU...YOU MAMMALS...
YOU MADE ALL THIS, DIDN'T YOU?
ALL OF THIS...
THAT... THAT IS NOT A BIRD.

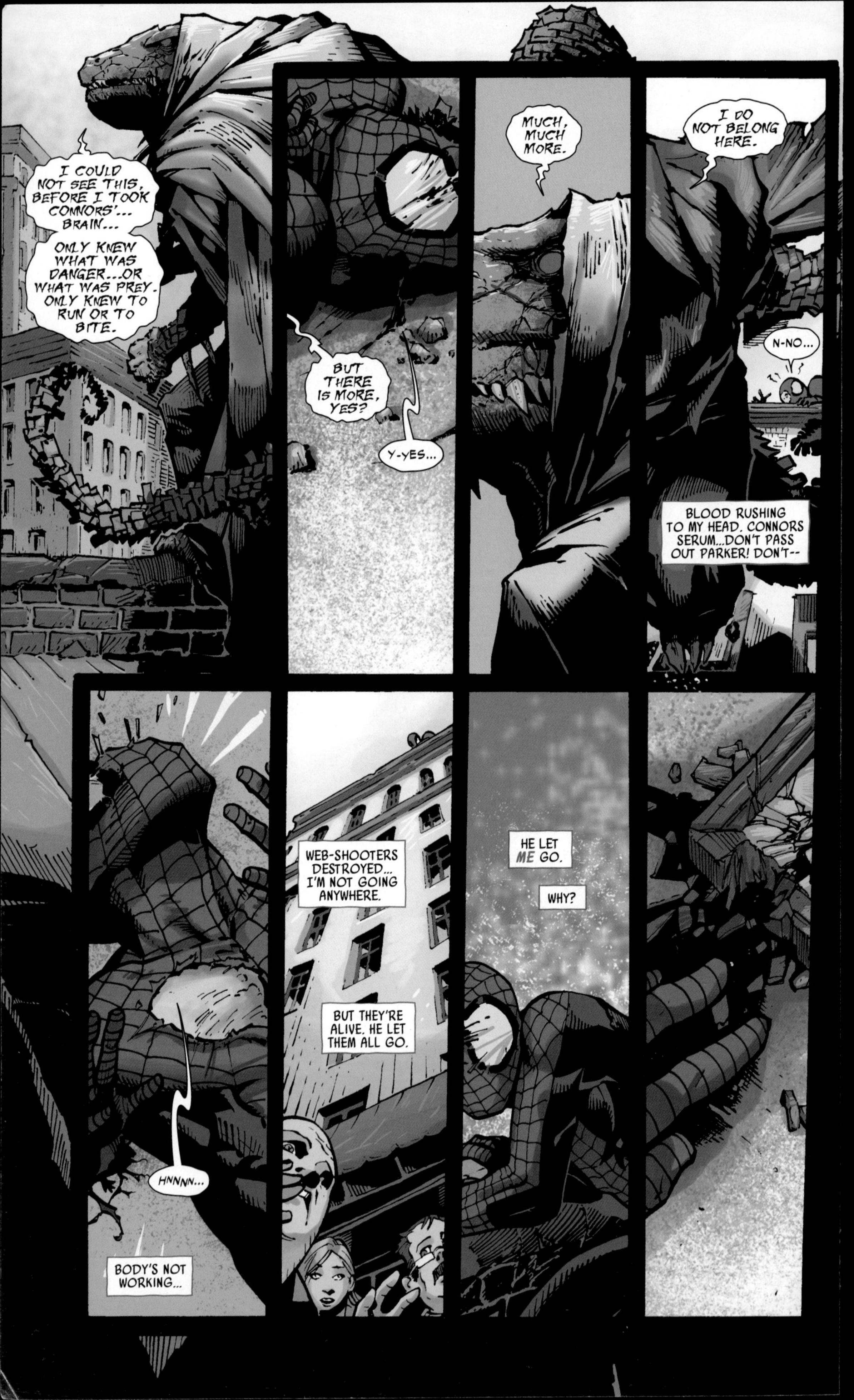
I COULD NOT SEE THIS, BEFORE I TOOK CONNORS'... BRAIN...
ONLY KNEW WHAT WAS DANGER...OR WHAT WAS PREY. ONLY KNEW TO RUN OR TO BITE.
BUT THERE IS MORE, YES?
Y-YES...
MUCH, MUCH MORE.
I DO NOT BELONG HERE.
N-NO...
BLOOD RUSHING TO MY HEAD. CONNORS SERUM...DON'T PASS OUT PARKER! DON'T--
HNNNN...
BODY'S NOT WORKING...
WEB-SHOOTERS DESTROYED... I'M NOT GOING ANYWHERE.
BUT THEY'RE ALIVE. HE LET THEM ALL GO.
HE LET ME GO.
WHY?

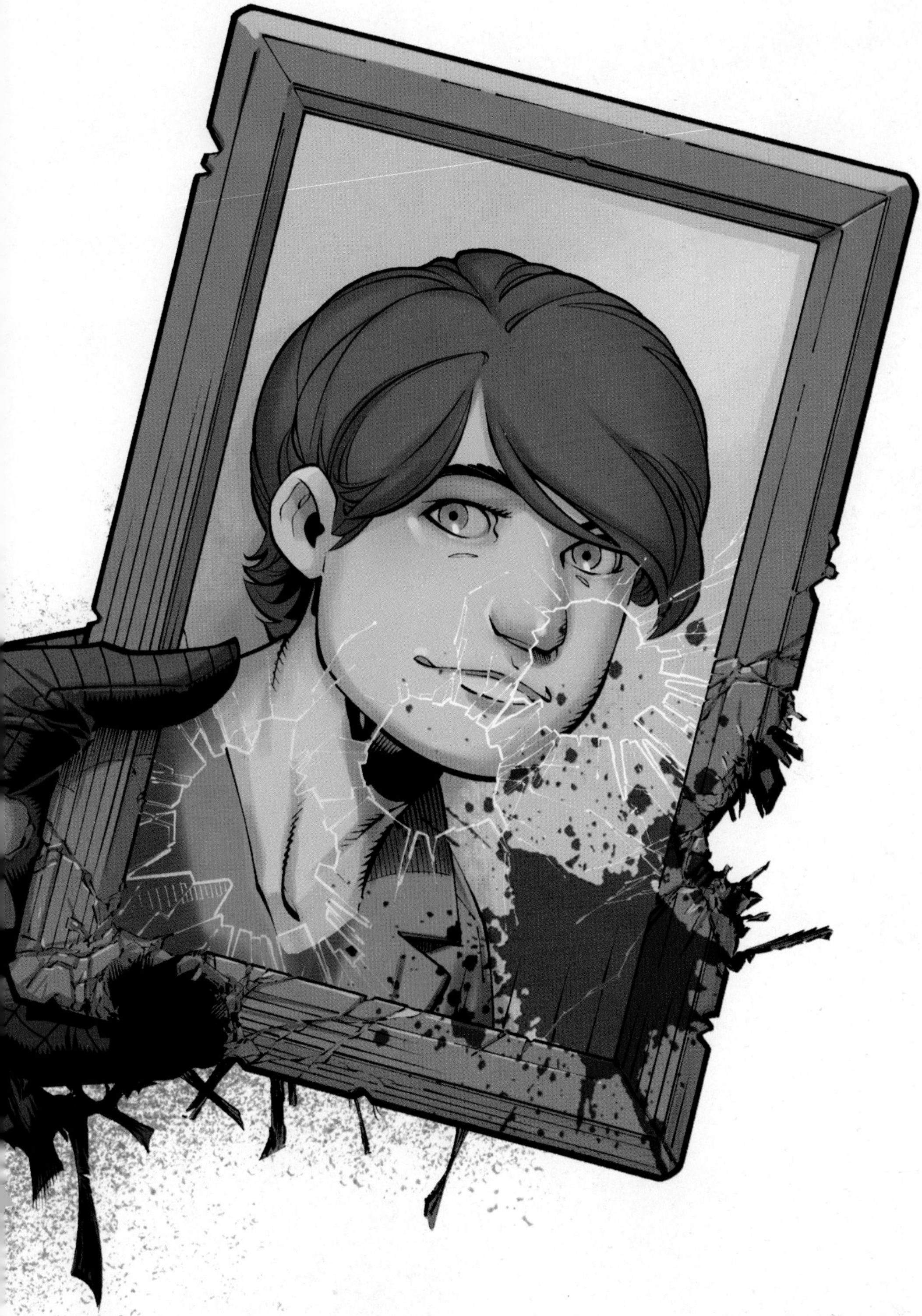

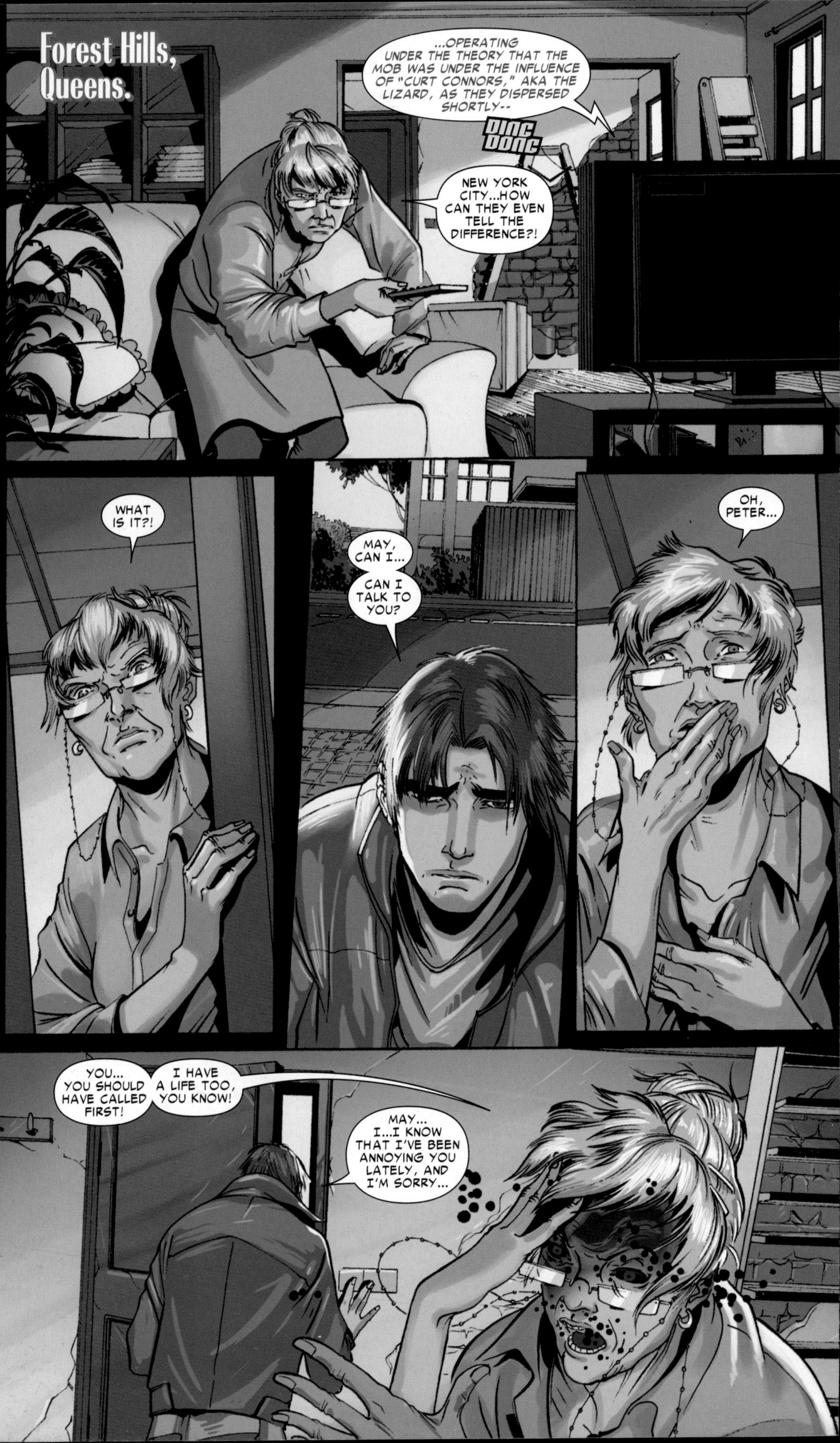
Forest Hills, Queens.
...OPERATING UNDER THE THEORY THAT THE MOB WAS UNDER THE INFLUENCE OF "CURT CONNORS," AKA THE LIZARD, AS THEY DISPERSED SHORTLY--
DING DONG
NEW YORK CITY...HOW CAN THEY EVEN TELL THE DIFFERENCE?!
WHAT IS IT?!
MAY, CAN I...
CAN I TALK TO YOU?
OH, PETER...
YOU... YOU SHOULD HAVE CALLED FIRST!
I HAVE A LIFE TOO, YOU KNOW!
MAY... I...I KNOW THAT I'VE BEEN ANNOYING YOU LATELY, AND I'M SORRY...

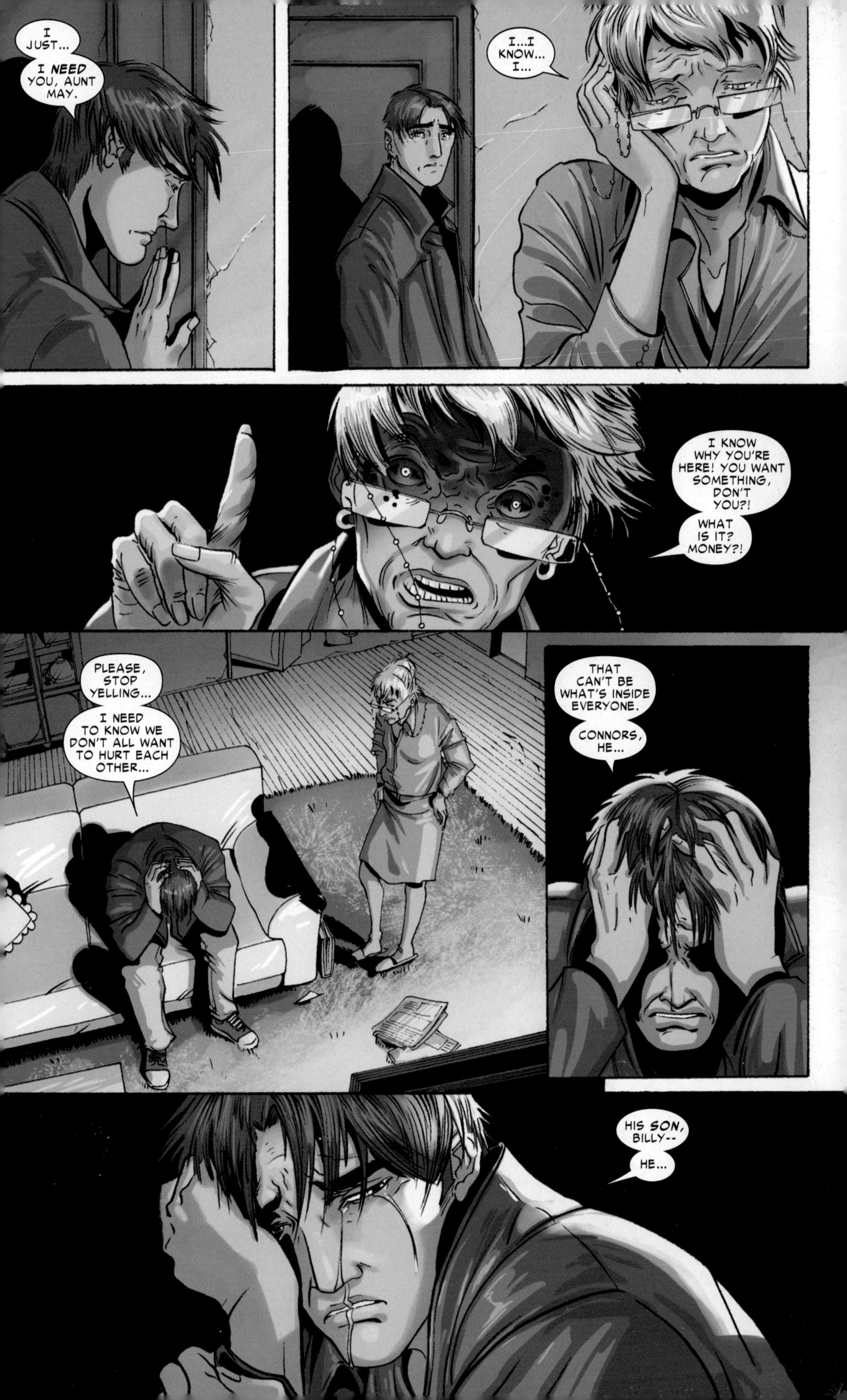
I JUST...
I NEED YOU, AUNT MAY.
I...I KNOW... I...
I KNOW WHY YOU'RE HERE! YOU WANT SOMETHING, DON'T YOU?!
WHAT IS IT? MONEY?!
PLEASE, STOP YELLING...
I NEED TO KNOW WE DON'T ALL WANT TO HURT EACH OTHER...
THAT CAN'T BE WHAT'S INSIDE EVERYONE.
CONNORS, HE...
HIS SON, BILLY--
HE...

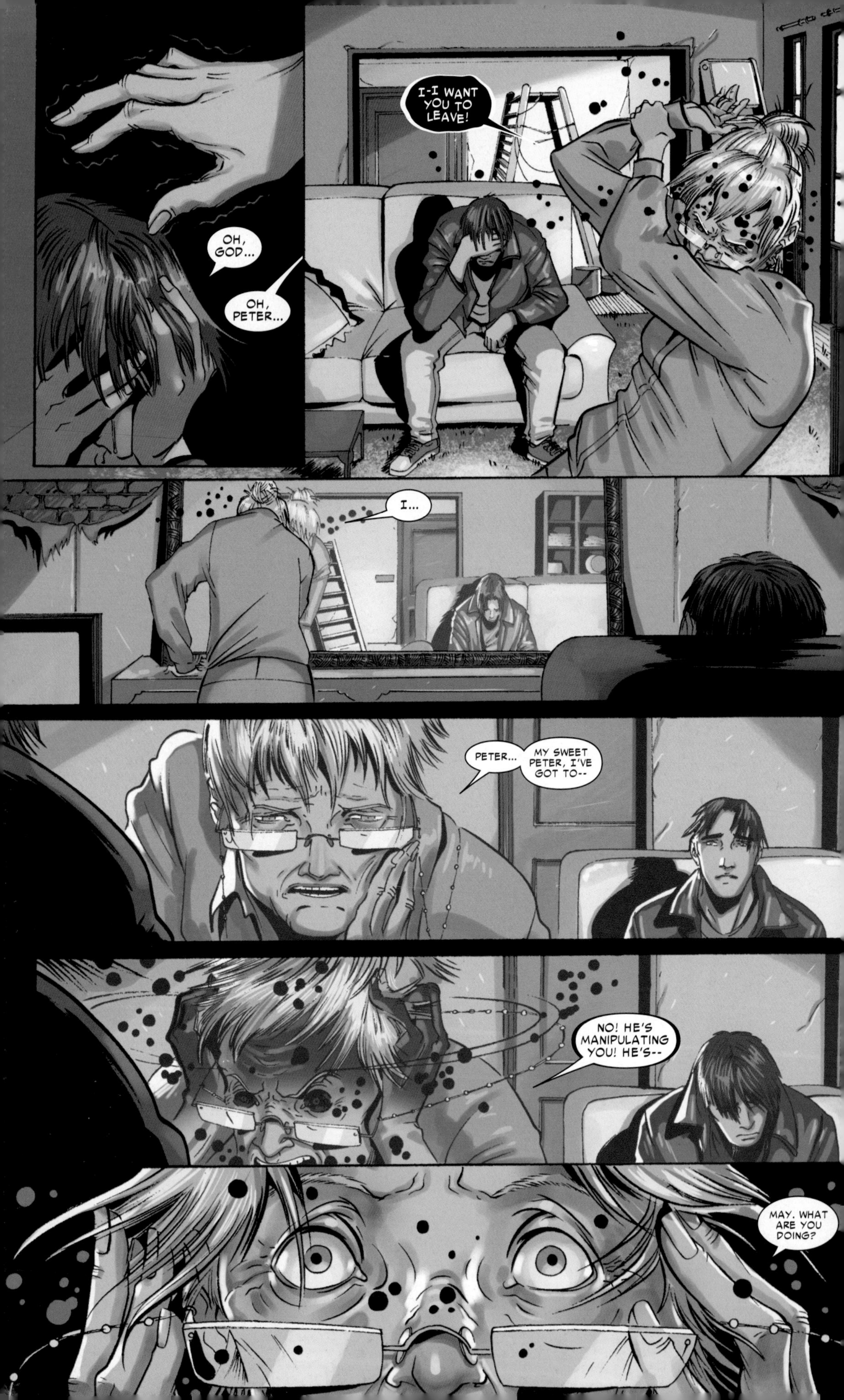
OH, GOD...
OH, PETER...
I-I WANT YOU TO LEAVE!
I...
PETER...
MY SWEET PETER, I'VE GOT TO--
NO! HE'S MANIPULATING YOU! HE'S--
MAY. WHAT ARE YOU DOING?

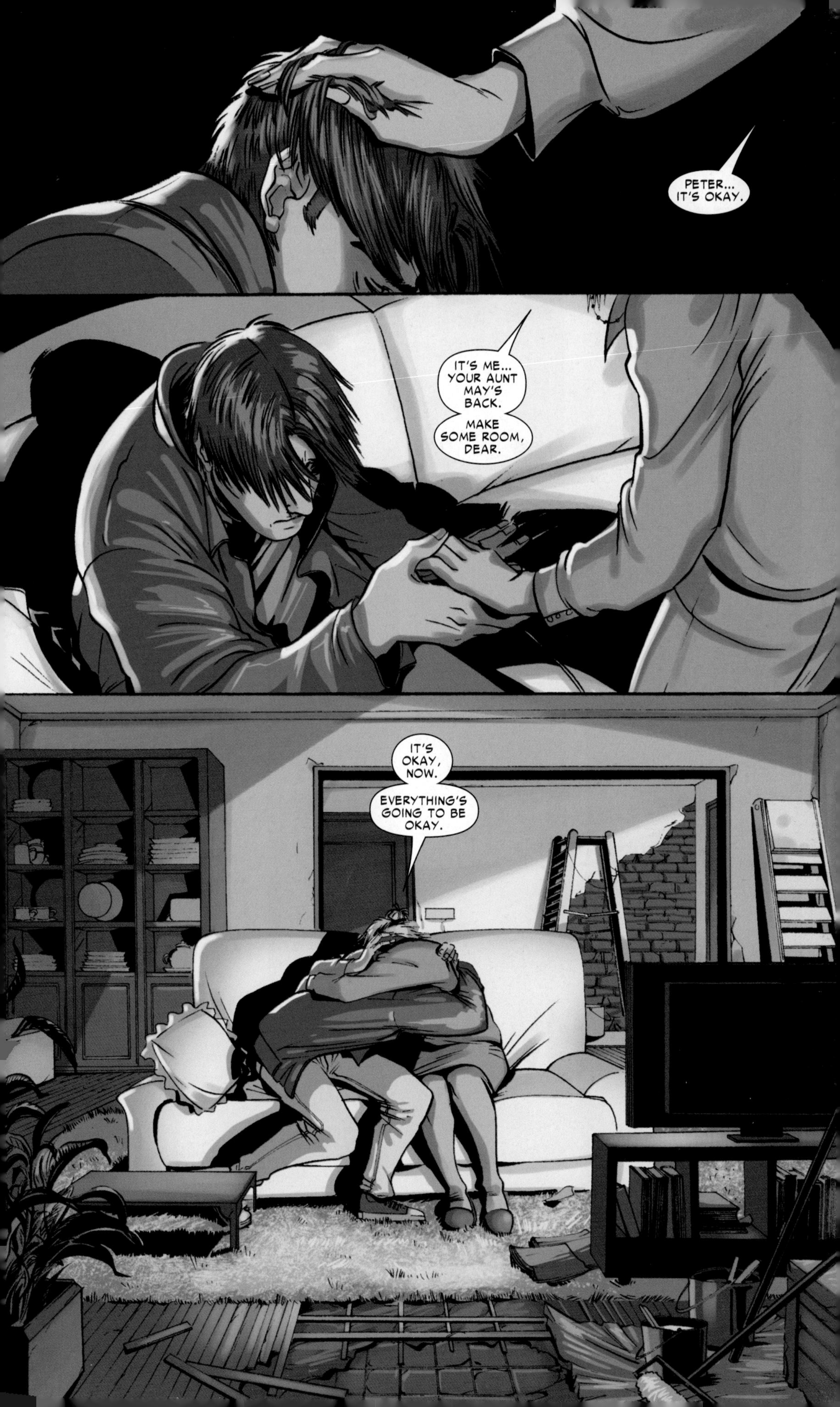
PETER... IT'S OKAY.
IT'S ME... YOUR AUNT MAY'S BACK.
MAKE SOME ROOM, DEAR.
IT'S OKAY, NOW.
EVERYTHING'S GOING TO BE OKAY.

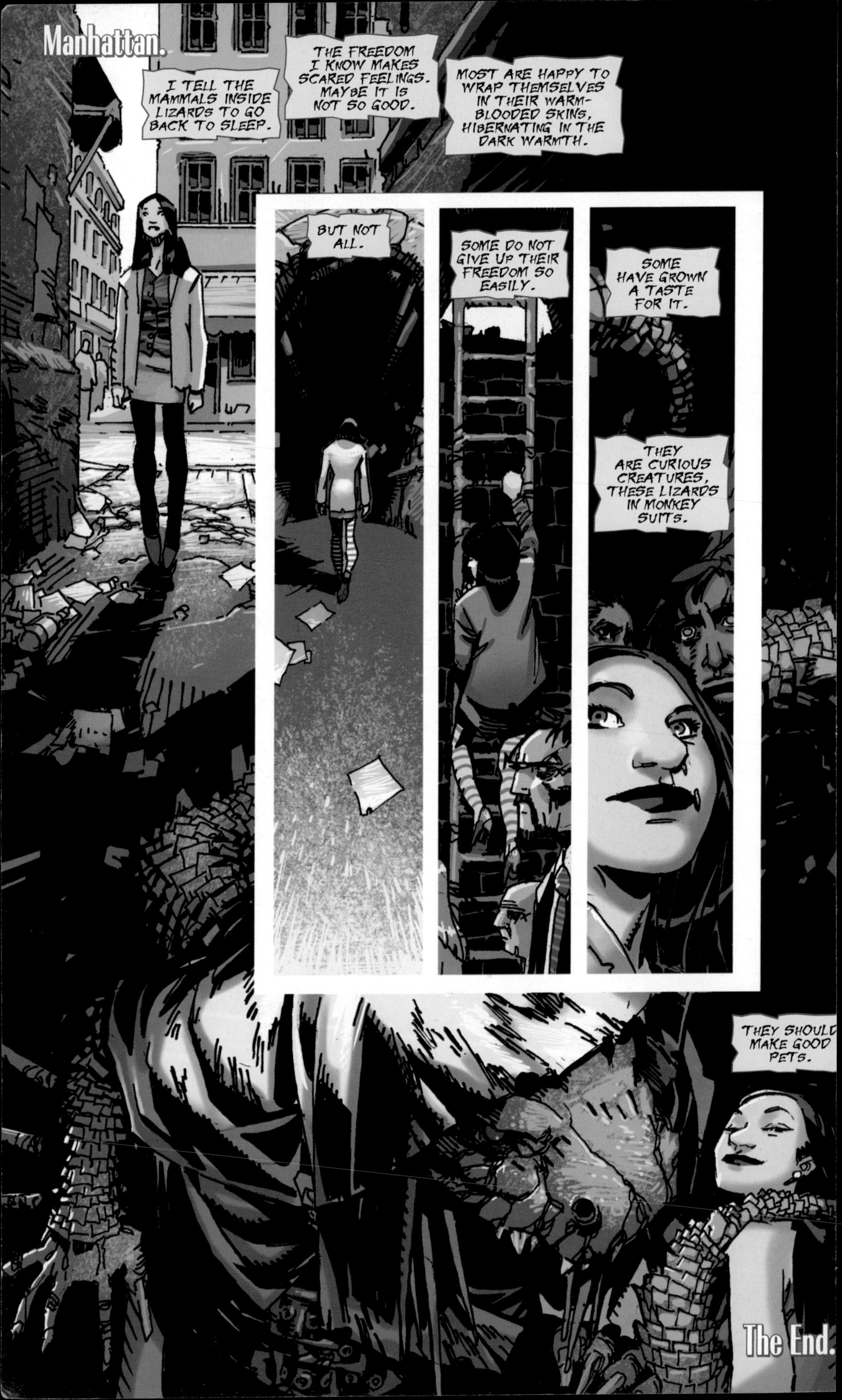

Manhattan.
I TELL THE MAMMALS INSIDE LIZARDS TO GO BACK TO SLEEP.
THE FREEDOM I KNOW MAKES SCARED FEELINGS. MAYBE IT IS NOT SO GOOD.
MOST ARE HAPPY TO WRAP THEMSELVES IN THEIR WARM-BLOODED SKINS, HIBERNATING IN THE DARK WARMTH.
BUT NOT ALL.
SOME DO NOT GIVE UP THEIR FREEDOM SO EASILY.
SOME HAVE GROWN A TASTE FOR IT.
THEY ARE CURIOUS CREATURES, THESE LIZARDS IN MONKEY SUITS.
THEY SHOULD MAKE GOOD PETS.
The End.

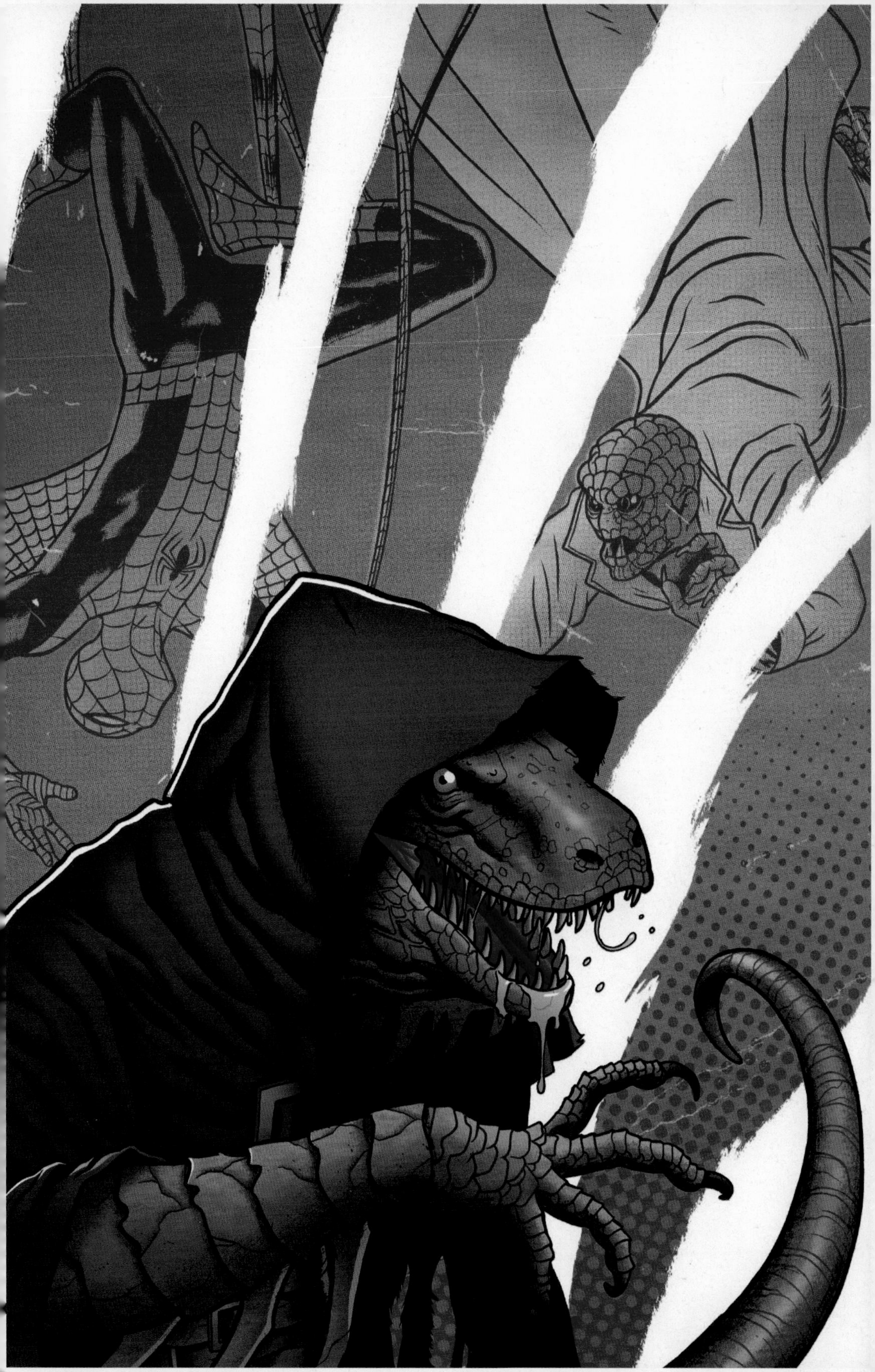

AMAZING SPIDER-MAN #630 VILLAIN VARIANT

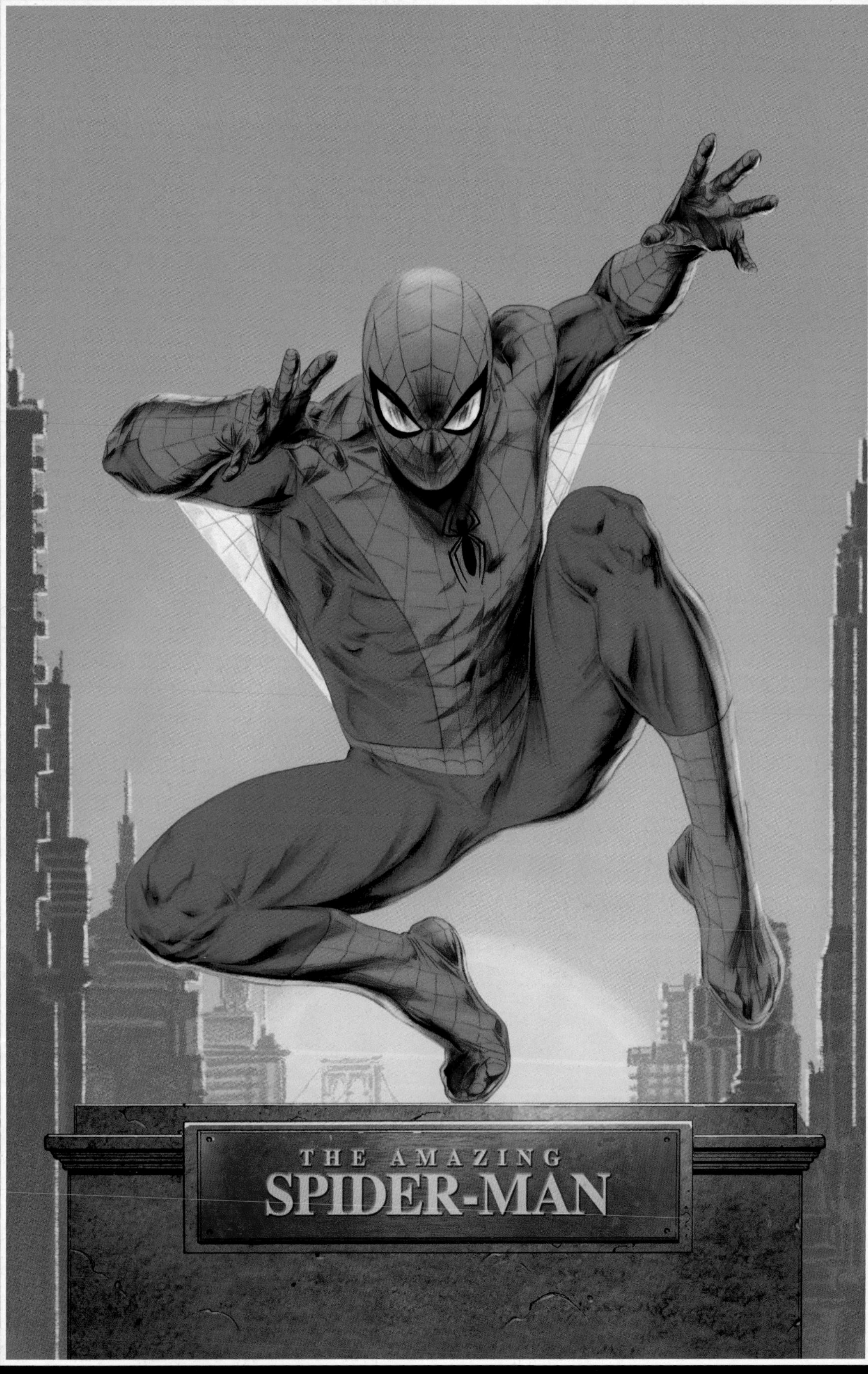
THE AMAZING
SPIDER-MAN

AMAZING SPIDER-MAN #631 HEROIC AGE VARIANT
COVER BY DOUG BRAITHWAITE

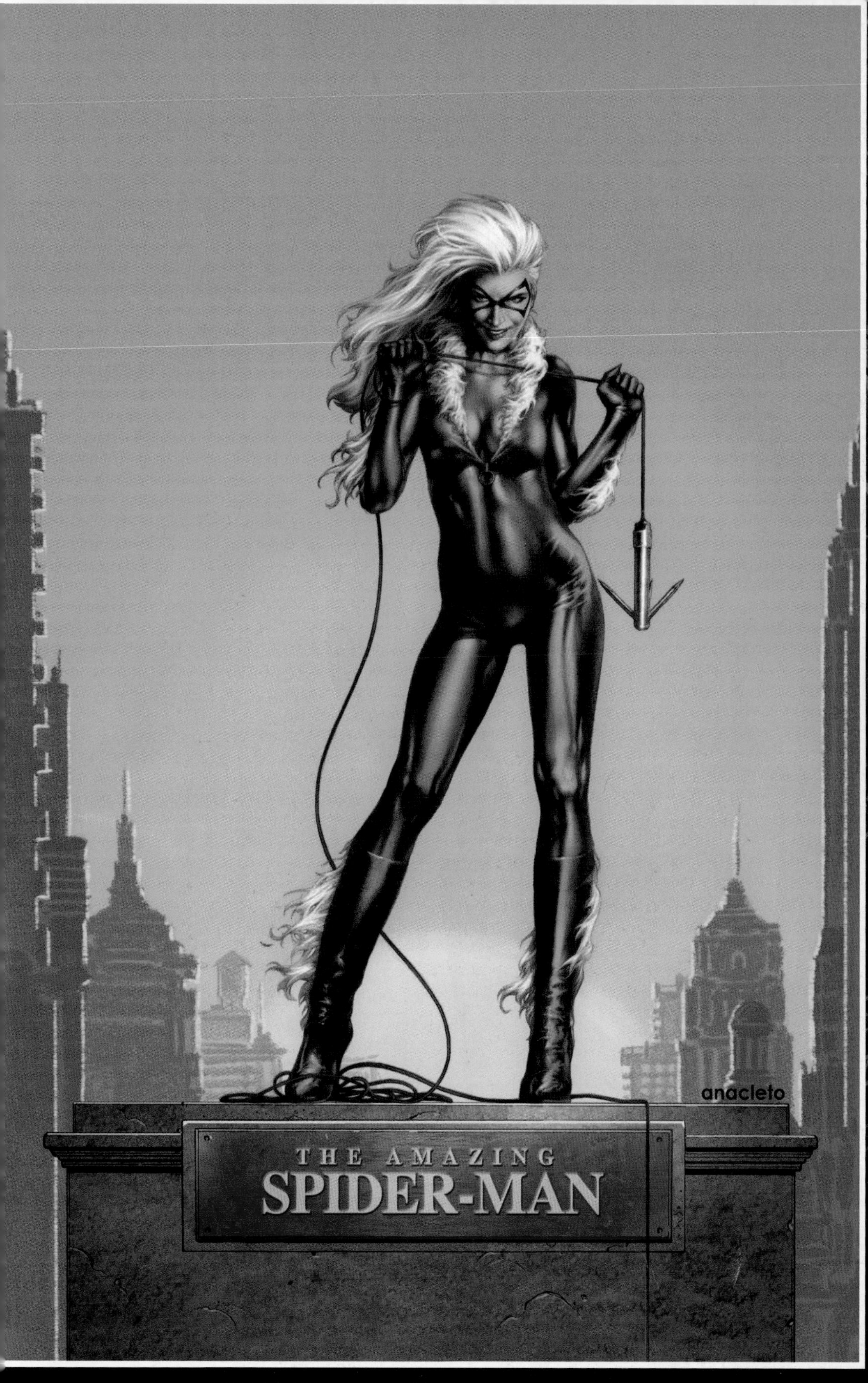
anacleto
THE AMAZING
SPIDER-MAN

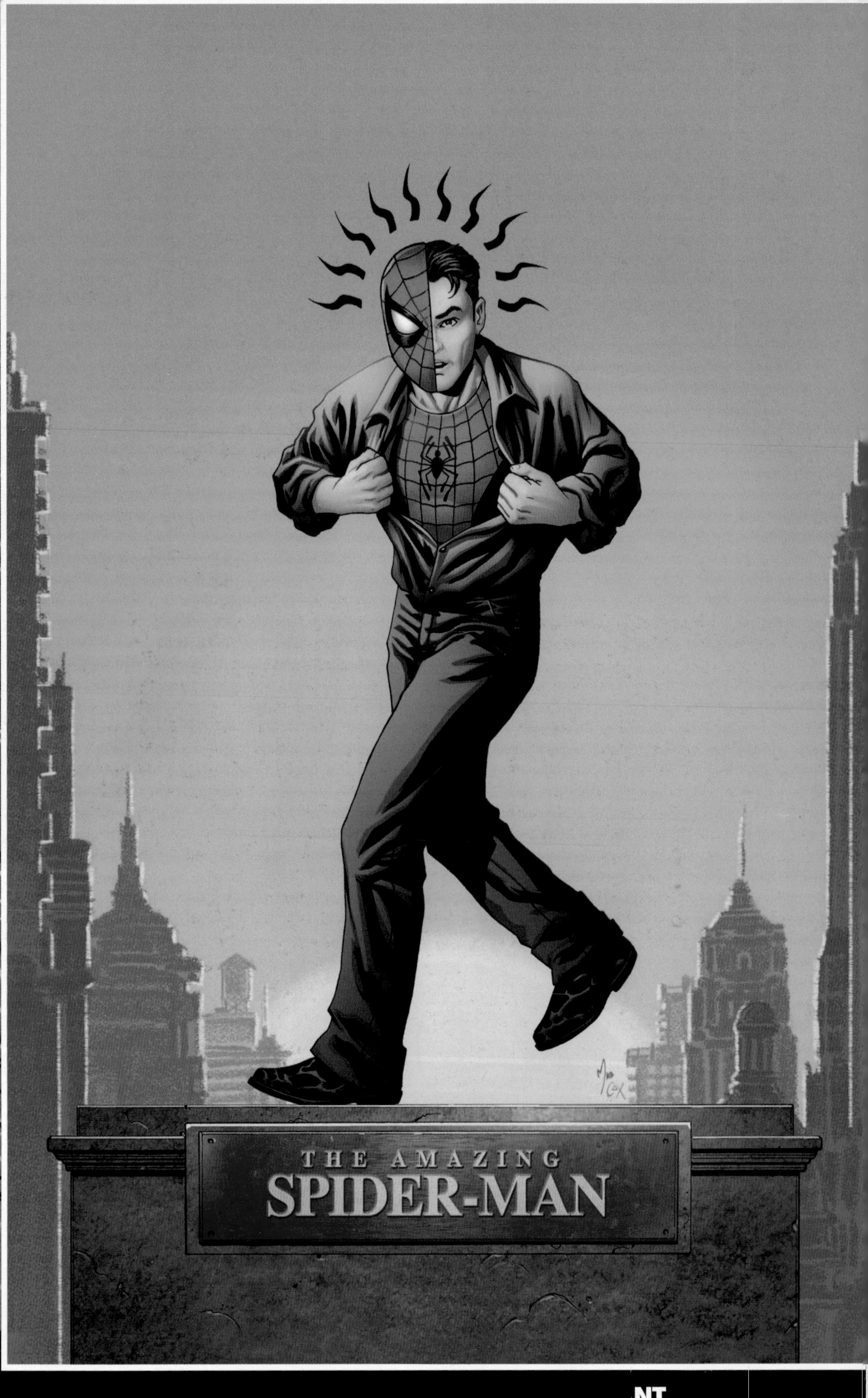
THE AMAZING
SPIDER-MAN

NT

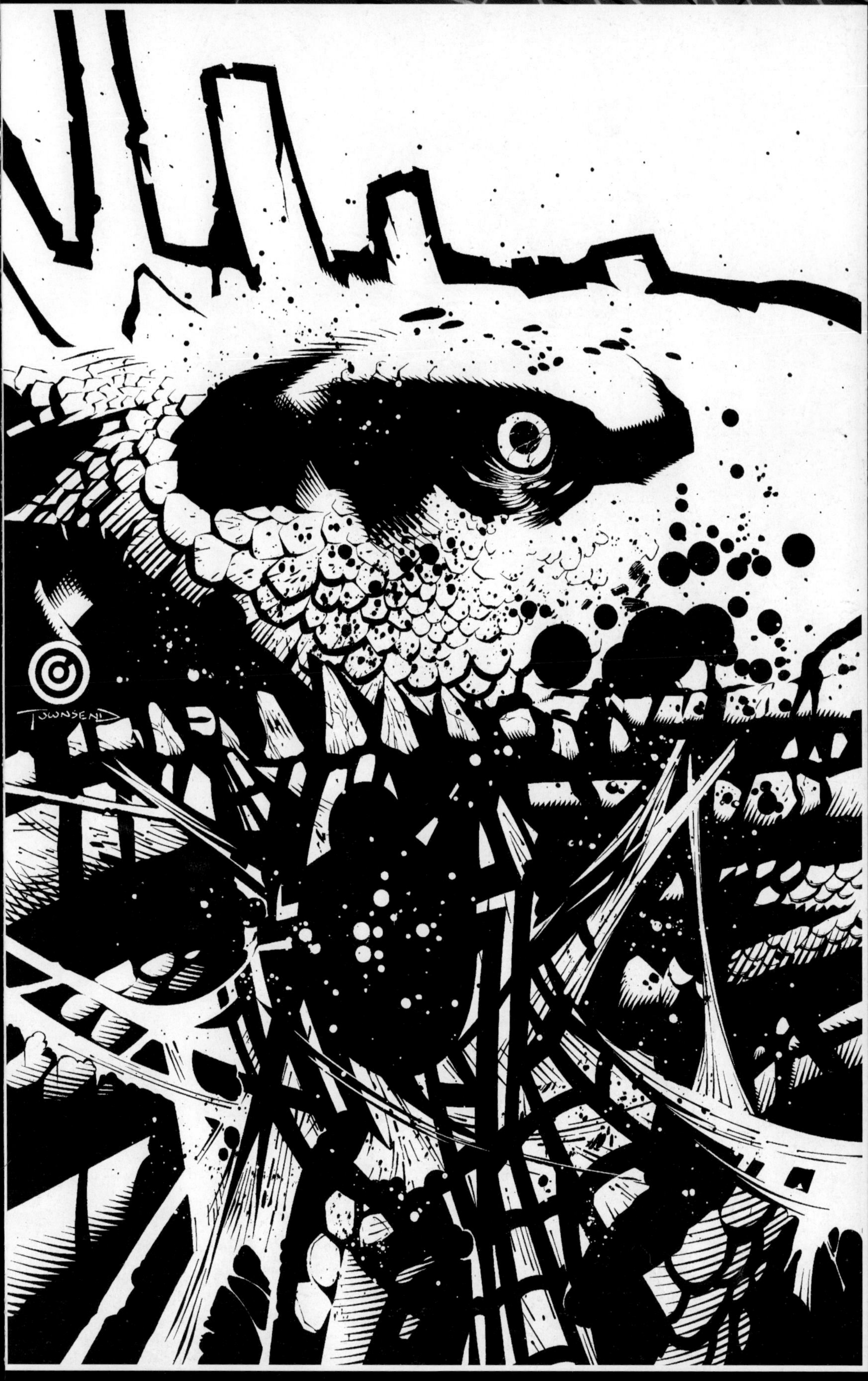
TOWNSEND

AMAZING SPIDER-MAN #630 COVER INKS
BY CHRIS BACHALO & TIM TOWNSEND

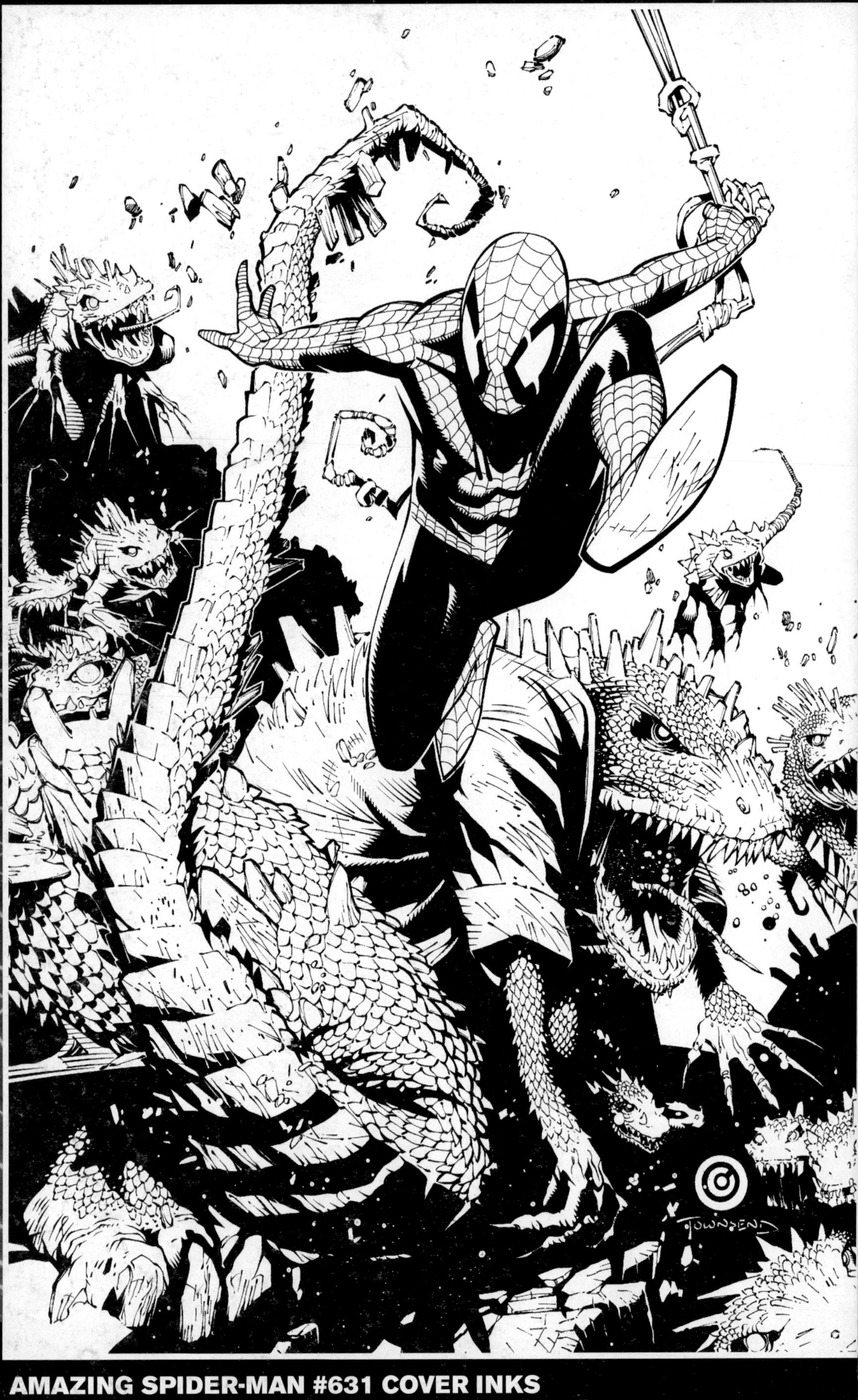
TOWNSEND

AMAZING SPIDER-MAN #631 COVER INKS
BY CHRIS BACHALO & TIM TOWNSEND